NOTHING BUT THE BEST

NOTHING BUT THE BEST

A Guide to Preaching
Powerful Sermons

Hyveth Williams

To order additional copies of this book, contact:
Xlibris
1-888-795-4274
www.Xlibris.com
Orders@Xlibris.com
771185

To the men and women who inspired,
challenged, and encouraged me on this
journey of faith and fortitude

CONTENTS

Part Four—Epilogue

ACKNOWLEDGMENTS

The idea for writing this book was impressed on my mind by Dr. Denis Fortin, former dean of the Seventh-day Adventist Theological Seminary. He took a risk when he hired me as the first female professor of preaching in our denomination whose responsibility is to teach a community of primarily men.

My beloved son, Steven, has been an inspiration. He surprised me with a powerful valedictorian speech, which I pray is a prelude to his preaching powerful sermons one day.

My dearest friend, Ella Taylor, and the seminarians who helped raise up and continue to contribute to the success of The Grace Place and its devoted members are the strong foundations on which this book is laid.

Dr. Stan Patterson and the incredible team of our Church Ministry Department have encouraged me, especially when I was flagging creatively.

Introduction: From Politics to Preaching

Lytton Strachey's description of the historian's task aptly pictures my journey: "He will row out over the great ocean of material, and lower down into it, here and there, a little bucket, which will bring up to the light of day some characteristic specimen, from those far depths to be examined with a careful curiosity."[1]

A Little Bucket of Characteristic Specimens

My professional journey has taken me from politics to preaching and is now much like "the historian's" dipping buckets in the vast ocean of homiletics, also known as the art of preaching.

I was serving as executive assistant to the mayor of Hartford, Connecticut, when I decided that the time had come to challenge my boss for the office I was already running in the background. After successfully organizing the last two of his campaigns and being a highly visible coordinator of a winning gubernatorial race, I unwisely decided to be a mayoral candidate instead of promoting one. Then

---

[1]   Quoted by Michael J. Quicke in *Preaching as Worship: An Integrative Approach to Formation in Your church*, (Grand Rapids, Baker Books, 2011), p. 13.

an unexpected divine intervention in the life and plans of this former atheist interrupted my foray into the personal side of a political campaign. The encounter led to an equally dramatic conversion and radical transformation from a profane, promiscuous lifestyle to being "determined," like the apostle Paul, "to know nothing among you except Jesus Christ, and Him crucified" (1 Cor. 2:2).[2]

The exciting and sometimes challenging task of dipping in the ocean of homiletics began decades ago when one of the pastors asked me—an untrained "Bible worker" in an evangelistic series of meetings during the summer of 1981—to speak at his church. Approximately sixty people attended, including many "seekers" from the neighborhood. In retrospect, from the perspective of an academician and professor of homiletics, my sermon was the worst I have ever heard or preached. But twenty-six people responded to my appeal to commit their lives to the Lord, and several asked to be prepared for baptism. It became clear to me then, as it is now, that the transformative result of preaching is not by might or power, but by the Holy Spirit, according to the profound prophesy recorded in Zachariah 4:6. I have also kept that sermon (handwritten on both sides of seventeen sheets of yellow legal pad paper) to remind me that preaching is not just about talent or verbal skills, but how God uses inadequate instruments to do a supernatural work (2 Cor. 4:7).

After my undergraduate studies in preaching, I reviewed that first sermon manuscript. It left me greatly humbled. I still retrieve it from its secret place and read it from time to time, especially when I am feeling too big for my preaching boots or overconfident about my ability based on the applause of others. I have come to the conclusion that only God's abundant grace could have caused the audience to make sense of the confusing "mishmash" of texts I read from that paper, head bobbing up and down like a duck drinking water. That humbling, yet exhilarating, experience left such a deep desire to learn how to preach that I was like a person bitten by an infectious bug.

---

[2]   See more details in my autobiography, *Will I Ever Learn?* (Hagerstown, Review & Herald Publishing, 1996).

But, like Mary (Luke 2:19), I kept it in my heart for a long time and thought of it every day until, one day, a visiting preacher at my local church (the late Dr. Bill Liversidge), who became a lifelong friend, called me out of the congregation and charged me with running from God. He announced that God was summoning me into the ministry of his Word, but I was afraid. He was right on both counts. I read into his audacious pronouncement a public remonstrance from God, so I went to Columbia Union College (now Washington Adventist University) in Takoma Park, Maryland, where I graduated with a bachelor's degree in theology.

At that small Christian center of learning, my homiletics professor, Dr. Kenneth Stout, had a profound influence on me. His friendship and encouragement shaped my choice to be a preacher, while a later introduction to *Koine* Greek left me wanting more. These and other theology courses not only fueled my passion for preaching, they propelled me on a lifelong quest to seek more knowledge in the discipline of homiletics.

After my undergraduate education as one of two females among about a dozen men, I was deeply disappointed, to the point of despair, when some of the men who had demonstrated the poorest preaching skills and lack of passion for the profession were hired as pastors, while the two women who stood at the top of our class got passed over. I couldn't seem to resist nursing both a grudge and an unrelenting anger toward God, from whom I felt a deep sense of abandonment as I worked in an office, like Moses when he tended sheep (Exod. 3:1).

At some point during that period, I responded to the urging of the Holy Spirit to apply for admission to the Seventh-day Adventist Theological Seminary (SDATS) located at Andrews University in Berrien Springs, Michigan. When I graduated, little did I dream that one day, I would return as the first female Professor of Homiletics and director of the homiletics program in our more than a century-and-a-half year-old denomination. Today, among many responsibilities, I coordinate our Doctor of Ministry preaching cohort and teach men and women from around our world church the incredible things I've learned about preaching powerful, transformative sermons.

During my days as a student at the seminary, one of six women among almost five hundred men, I was introduced to a variety of disciplines necessary for me to become a competent homiletician. I drank deeply and drained the dregs from those cups of knowledge as I learned to organize a sermon, exegete Scripture, and deliver expository messages. All I had learned was put to the test in my first parish as pastor of the Boston Temple in Boston, Massachusetts. But it was at Boston University School of Theology, in the Doctor of Ministry program, that I found myself further challenged and equipped with a variety of homiletical tools to dig deeply for gems in Scripture and consistently deliver transformative messages. There, I also discovered a wide field of sermonic methods and delivery styles presented in this volume.

When, as the first non-Episcopalian to be so honored, I received the prestigious fellowship from the College of Preachers at the National Cathedral in Washington, DC, that experience prepared me for a more inclusive ministry to people of all faiths. All these lessons became a firm foundation on which I have built my profession and from which I am writing, yet this effort is like using a thimble to drain the vast sea of resources available in this academic discipline and ecclesiastical profession.

Most of my professional life as a minister of the gospel has been spent in parish ministry. During those decades, I had several opportunities to teach and was able to serve as adjunct professor for the Loma Linda University Faculty of Religion and SDATS. Although it has now become a profession for which I have an ever-increasing passion, it was quite a challenging process to develop the various preaching curricula as I learned the language of pedagogy and settled exclusively into teaching the art of preaching. It is now several years since I received the invitation to go where no woman had gone before—to teach homiletics in our denomination's flagship seminary.

After developing and teaching several courses in this discipline, I was urged by our seminary dean to leave a legacy of the rich lessons I have learned through the years. I have had four books published with moderate success, but it took the strong pressing of several students and colleagues for me to develop the courage to pursue my dream of writing a book on preaching. To this effort, I invite your attention with a prayer that God will bless you for humoring one of his children in whom, I pray, he will be well pleased.

I am an adult orphan, a single parent of a now grown son, a grandmother, a great-grandmother, a sister, an aunt, a niece, and soul sister of a diverse host of witnesses who are born again—"not of the will of the flesh, nor the will of man, but of God" (John 1:13). By God's grace, I have had the privilege of living long enough to be all these and more. Being a mother, I am very well acquainted with the process of conceiving and giving birth. So when I say that writing this book is like being a mother, I know of what I speak. Being impregnated with the germ of an idea, living through the long period of gestation, and eventually birthing a manuscript, I now embark on the next phase with a lot of hope and prayer that it will grow up to be a successful book among a vast variety of such volumes. In fact, of my five such children, only one, born years ago, remains an infant, unwanted by publishers but loved and patiently cared for by me, its mother. Such a fate, I believe, will not be of this newborn, whose potential far outweighs the possibilities of all my other children.

A Transition from Politics to Preaching

Politics and preaching are not as far apart as some may surmise. Whereas politics depends on speeches to inform, preaching is the delivery of sermons to transform the lives of listeners. Both require speaking from a platform and demand authenticity, presence, articulation, elocution, great eye contact, and the discovery of one's natural voice (original tone quality, pattern or pitch, etc.) versus habitual voice (learned or influenced by cultural factors).

I have had the privilege of serving successfully in both professions. I have also endured censure, abusive language, and blame as a politician and certainly as a preacher, especially for being a female who dared to accept God's call to ministry. I am, however, convinced that my political experience prepared and molded me for a life of preaching the Gospel.

My journey from politics to preaching has been a dramatic, often amazing one as I meandered through decades of both private and public successes, challenges, failures, and follies. I have read numerous volumes on the subject of preaching and worship, as well as practiced and taught both subjects for several years in a variety of countries around the world. Yet, as I put pen to paper (rather fingers to keyboard, which doesn't alliterate as well as the former), I chide myself for waiting so long to produce a book on the subject I have come to regard as my sweet spot. To accomplish this goal, I intend to rely on the competencies I've learned and developed in this discipline during the past few decades. As you, my reader, pick up and open this book, questions may form in your mind. Questions such as those raised by a friend: Why should I read this book? What are the benefits? How will this one differ from the volumes already stacked on our shelves? Will it make a difference in my life or ministry? What will I gain, or, in other words, what's in it for me?

First, while these are great questions, I can only invite you to continue reading to determine whether or not I have fulfilled my intended purpose to present nothing but the best in this ever-changing field of study. Second, we are living in times when we all want to know "what's in it for me?" As a result, people select their churches like they do restaurants, books, and movies, based on such criteria as follows: "Who is the preacher? How many rating stars does this particular church have? What will it cost me, and how much time will it take?" Jesus himself recognized the "what's in it for me?" characteristic of those living in the last days of earth's history and provided a reward recorded in the last book of the Bible. There he said, through John the Revelator, in one of the seven beatitudes in Revelation, "Blessed [happy] is he [or she] who reads aloud the words of the prophecy, and blessed [happy] are those who hear and keep the things which are written in it; for the time is near" (Rev. 1:3, amplification mine).

In this volume, the reader will encounter not only the primary focus of many contemporary preaching books (i.e., "how to" preach to the meta-modern, emerging generations or deliver expository sermons) but also the "how can" expressed in the timeless words of the apostle Paul: "But how can people call for help if they don't know who to trust? And how can they know who to trust if they haven't heard of the One who can be trusted? And how can they hear if nobody tells them? And how is anyone going to tell them, unless someone is sent to do it?" (Rom. 20:14, 15, *The Message)*. I believe that this "how can" motif goes to the heart of the preacher's internal life and personal relationship with God. As a consequence, I intend to explore what the exterior manifestation of a preacher's life should be when he or she has completely surrendered to God and is faithful and trustworthy to the high calling of preaching.

An interesting response to the "how can" question was found in, of all places, *The Second Helvetic Confession:*[3] "The preaching of the Word of God *is the Word of God.* Wherefore when this Word of God is now preached in the church by preachers lawfully called, we believe that the very Word of God is proclaimed, and received by the faithful; and that neither any other Word of God is to be invented nor is to be expected from heaven: and that now the Word itself which is preached is to be regarded, not the minister that preaches; for even if he [or she] be evil and a sinner, nevertheless the Word of God remains still true and good" (emphasis mine).

I also discovered John Calvin's indelible opinion that "when a man has climbed up into the pulpit" (of course, this was in the days when only men preached and pulpits were positioned above the congregation), "it is that God may speak to us through the mouth of that man."[4]

---

3   http://www.ccel.org/creeds/helvetic.htm.

4   Quoted by T. H. L. Parker in *Calvin's Preaching,* p. 24.

My Philosophy of Preaching

My desire and goal is to inspire all proclaimers of God's Word to not just be good, but to be great preachers. This has been my philosophy of preaching since reading Jim Collins's powerful, inspiring, and relevant book written for businesses but applicable to all areas of life. Collins wrote that "good is the enemy of great. And that is one of the key reasons why we have so little that becomes great. We don't have great schools, principally because we have good schools. We don't have great government, principally because we have good government. Few people attain great lives, in large part because it is just so easy to settle for a good life. The vast majority of companies never become great, precisely because the vast majority become quite good—and that is their main problem."[5]

It is clear to me that our generation lacks great Christian preaching, principally because we have so many "good" preachers. There was a time when this was not the case. Back then, my denomination was known for a variety of powerful male preachers, such as E. E. Cleveland, Charles Bradford, C. D. Brooks, George Vandeman, and Morris Venden. At the same time, household names such as Peter Marshall, Dwight L. Moody, and Billy Graham (just to name a few) dominated the national pulpit. Today, one can literally count on one hand those who could be legitimately called "great" preachers. Perhaps that is because it takes more than personality and pulpit presence to be a great preacher, and many who are called either do not know how or are unwilling to make the necessary sacrifices to advance from "good" to "great" preaching in the twenty-first-century church. As a result, a dearth of great preaching has contributed to the troubling trend of low attendance at worship and paltry systematic giving in many denominations.

For instance, it was almost always guaranteed that churches would have a large attendance during the Easter season. But despite the giving away of supersize flat-screen televisions, expensive electronic

---

[5] *Good to Great: Why Some Companies Make the Leap . . . and Others Don't*, p. 1.

gadgets, and a variety of exclusive gifts to increase the lagging attendance at these services, the annual report continues to show the dismal truth: that nothing seems to attract the apathetic audience of our day. Furthermore, according to a 2014 report from the Religious News Service, "Americans are slowly pulling themselves out of a charitable slump—except when it comes to religious groups." While individuals gave a 3 percent increase in donations, "religious groups saw donations drop 1.6 percent from 2012 to 2013."[6] It is clear that people invest time and money where they feel inspired.

However, before we panic, throw up our hands in despair, or play the blame game, please note that this is not a new phenomenon in the Christian church. Oswald Chambers (1874–917), founder of a Bible college in London, England, and author of many inspiring articles and books, surmised that "the great passion in much of the preaching today," more than 150 years ago, was due to the preachers' zeal "to secure an audience."[7] Attitudes have apparently not changed much since then, for we generally measure the greatness of preachers by how many people they can attract to their meetings, how many books and DVDs they can sell, and how wide their reach or how high their media ratings rather than the content of their character, their commitment to Christ, and their faithful handling of the Word.

Chambers continued to say that "as workers for God, our object is never to secure an audience, but to secure that the gospel is presented to people." "Never presume to preach," he cautioned, "unless you are mastered by the motive born of the Holy Spirit. Instead, be like Paul, who said, 'For I am determined not to know anything among you except Jesus Christ and Him crucified [1 Cor. 2:2].'"[8] He added elsewhere that preachers should never have as their "ideal the desire to be an orator or a beautiful speaker; if you do, you will not be of the slightest use . . . An orator moves people to do what they

6   http://www.religionnews.com/2014/06/17/
     charitable-giving-religious-groups-philanthropy-improves-great-recession.

7   *Approved of God*, p. 34.

8   Ibid.

are indifferent about; a preacher of the Gospel has to move people to do what they are dead-set against doing, namely, giving up the right to themselves. The one calling of a New Testament preacher," he concluded, "is to uncover sin and reveal Jesus Christ as Savior. Consequently, the preacher cannot be poetical but must be surgical."[9]

Preachers today have both the privilege and challenge of proclaiming God's Word to a global, socially and culturally diverse generation. For example, those who show up to worship week after week, in any given congregation, now represent "every nation and tribe and tongue and people" (Rev. 14:6). Such diverse congregations include the following:

1. Baby boomers who are returning to churches as "visitors," and unless the preaching is outstanding enough to convince them to be "joiners," they will not commit themselves.
2. Generation X (commonly abbreviated as Gen X) moves freely in and out of various churches, regardless of denominational differences.
3. Generation Y, also known as millennials, who have eclipsed boomers in numbers but are few in our pews because social media has replaced "real" with "virtual" relationships they would otherwise seek and find in a church.
4. Generation Z, an increasingly popular nomenclature for the First World or Western generation, is also referred to as "the emerging generation." They are so called because they seem to be the most liberal of all the generations, and no one knows what they will ultimately become spiritually. These internet-savvy, technologically literate people, who have been shaped to multitask more than their predecessors, are generally disenchanted with organized religion. However, if and when they attend church, they prefer interactive sermons with short, pithy phrases they can text and tweet to their online followers.

---

[9] Ibid., pp. 22, 23.

To minister to such a diverse audience, our preachers must be great biblical, prophetic, and passionate proclaimers of the Word. Sermon delivery must be a balanced combination of homiletics (the method of preparation and application of Scripture) alongside rhetoric (the passionate, persuasive delivery of a sermon using language designed both to inform and transform audiences). Preachers must also exhibit and demonstrate more proficiency with the electronic devices and multimedia presentations on which today's generations have been weaned.

Haddon Robinson, a legendary homiletician and author of some of the most outstanding books in this discipline, reminds preachers that they are proclaiming God's Word to men and women who are "bewildered by seductive voices, nursing wounds life has inflicted upon them, anxious about matters that do not matter. Yet they come to listen for a clear word from God that speaks to their condition." Therefore, he suggests, in order to capture and hold the attention of such a diverse group, "we must preach to a world addressed by the TV commentator, the newspaper columnist, and the playwright. If we do not, we will have hearers who are orthodox in their heads but heretics in their conduct." However, he asserts, "while biblical ideas must be shaped by human experience, men and women must be called to conform to biblical truth." He also warns that "relevant sermons may become pulpit trifles unless they relate the current situation to the eternal Word of God."[10]

In his philosophy of ministry, the apostle Paul demonstrated a clear understanding of his target groups and the need to make appropriate adjustments in order to reach them as he preached. He declared that "to the Jews I became a Jew, to win the Jews . . . To those not having the law I became like one not having the law . . . to win those not having the law. To the weak I became weak, to win the weak. I became all things to all people so that by all possible means I might save some" (1 Cor. 9:20–23).

---

[10] *Biblical Preaching: The Development and Delivery of Expository Messages*, chapter 1.

Salient Elements of Great Preaching

While good preaching is the proclamation of the Word of God, great preaching must always strive for excellence with biblical and prophetic messages. The preacher must confidently open the inspired text, interpret, and expound Scripture with such authenticity, passion, authority, and sensitivity that God's Word comes alive so that his people find themselves persuaded to obey him. Therefore, twenty-first-century preaching must be prophetic, rooted in justice and mercy so as to move the church forward, as well as pastoral, rooted in charity and goodwill to all.

Great biblical preaching is also inadequate without ongoing exegesis of one's self, also known as self-evaluation or assessment. Here is a definition of self-assessment I have found helpful: "The evaluation or judgment of 'the worth' of one's performance and the identification of one's strengths and weaknesses with a view to improving one's learning outcomes."[11]

Some of the approaches I have used in this self-appraisal venture include (a) taking time to reflect on my spiritual life and to contemplate my career, professional direction, and accomplishments; (b) honestly considering my strengths and weaknesses (which can be dangerous if, like me, you have a streak of perfectionism that produces an overemphasis on personal weakness, which then leads to beating the breast in despair); (c) strategically thinking about where you would like to be five years from now; (d) brainstorming with the chair of our department during our annual report and assessment of my performance and review of student evaluations; and (e) recognizing my addiction to approval and the attachments it produces that cause me to cling to the opinions of others and despair when there's even a hint of disapproval.

While many companies ask employees to complete self-evaluations, I am not aware of leaders asking pastors and preachers

---

[11] Quoted in *Practical Assessment & Evaluation*, a peer-reviewed electronic journal, Vol. 11, Number 10, November 2006 - http://pareonline.net/getvn.asp?v=11&n=10.

to do likewise. Although some may scoff at such an idea, it has been invaluable in my personal advancement, spiritual development, and professional growth.

Great biblical preaching never neglects exegesis of the audience before and during the preaching moment. "If you plan to connect the message of the Scripture with your people in a meaningful and dynamic manner, you must know your people . . . You must never assume that all contemporary audiences are the same . . . You must spend time studying and reflecting on the spiritual, emotional, and educational situation of the specific audience you will preach to . . . What are the perspectives, presuppositions, issues, needs, concerns, and struggles of your people? What are their hopes, dreams, aspirations, fears, and challenges? . . . If you do not know . . . their needs, struggles, viewpoints, strengths, and weaknesses—you will struggle to preach effectively to them. Exegeting your audience, therefore, is a critical step if you are going to connect powerfully with them."[12]

Good preaching primarily focuses on the intellect, often to the exclusion of the emotion. On the other hand, great preaching includes both head and heart in the following approaches:

1. The listener's emotions—"The preaching of the Word should appeal to the intellect and impart knowledge, but it comprises much more than this. The heart of the preacher must reach the heart of the hearers . . . The object of preaching is not only to convey information or to convince the intellect. The words of the minister, to be effectual, must reach the hearts of the hearers."[13]
2. Performance that brings the sermon to life—It is noteworthy that homiletics does not define performance as "acting," something that can appear pretentious, cheap, and tawdry

---

[12] *Preaching God's Word: A Hands-on Approach to Preparing, Developing and Delivering the Sermon*, p. 85.

[13] Ellen G. White, *Testimonies to Ministers and Gospel Workers*, p. 62.

in the pulpit. According to theologian Paul Scott Wilson, "Preaching as performance normally focuses on the present moment [the now], on orality [enunciation and pronunciation] and aurality [the sense of hearing], memory, delivery, bodily enactment [posture and pulpit presence], and articulation of meaning in the 'now' before a congregation. *Performance*," he asserts, "is a more robust word than *delivery* and may be better able to account for both divine and human activity in preaching."[14]

3. Recognition of the various methods and styles of preaching— One must grow beyond expository preaching to include a variety of methods and styles, as well as the basic organization, outline, and progression of a sermon. I will address these in detail in a forthcoming chapter.

Cherishing Language and Words

When it comes to great preaching, we cannot overstate the significance of language and the importance of words. Great preachers prepare sermons in such a way that people will remember what was said not just for a few days but at least months, if not a lifetime. In addition, great preachers read widely, know how to develop characters in their story presentations, and describe events using living, lively, and creative words. Pastor Richard Farmer, in his classic lecture, suggests that such a combination will definitely "make the mummies dance."[15] He also reminds us that great preachers are students of rhetoric and wordsmiths who set people aflame by the sheer power of words. They take a good sermon and edit, edit, edit, until it becomes a great sermon, mindful that in the ancient Greek culture, people filled arenas and amphitheaters simply to hear the speeches and words of rhetoricians.

---

[14]   *Performance in Preaching: Bringing the Sermon to Life*, p. 37.

[15]   http://richardallenfarmer.com/product/making-the-mummies-dance.

I want to be such a great preacher, orator, and writer—don't you? Then fall in love with your language and treat its words well, for they are your servants; and when you send them out to do your bidding, you want them to execute it with precision and certainty. "Friends, we have the gift of words and we have The Person who is the Word! What a privilege to declare Him," said Richard Farmer.[16] Therefore, let us value the words into which God poured his truth so that they are never robbed of their richness or fail to fulfill their assignments.

The Content

Not everything that can be said about preaching is written in this volume. It is, however, what I consider to be a minestrone soup approach wherein the very best ideas, suggestions, and recommendations for great preaching are gathered in this one proverbial cup. It is for all who cherish a deep desire to preach, including those who may not have the privilege or opportunity of a seminary education.

Chapter 1. A Theology of Preaching. Addresses reasons plus the importance of a theology of preaching. These should be known by preachers and taught in seminaries to help preachers decide what significance should be given to research, sermon preparation, and delivery.

Chapter 2. Biblical Preaching. As in architecture, there's also a universal principle in preaching—it is called biblical preaching. It is a firm foundation on which sermonic methods and styles are to be built. This is expository in that it sets forth the meaning or purpose of a biblical pericope through which the preacher powerfully confronts or engages listeners with God's truth *entirely from Scripture.*

Chapter 3. Prophetic Preaching. Almost all who preach, teach, or write about prophetic preaching take their cues from Walter Brueggemann, who wrote, "The task of prophetic ministry is to nurture, nourish, and evoke a consciousness and a perception alternative to the consciousness and perception of the dominant

---

[16]   Ibid.

culture around us." Inspiring strategies for dismantling such a dominant consciousness of oppression—by way of the power of God and speaking truth to power—are the focus of this chapter.

Chapter 4. Preaching Definitions. In homiletics, the emphasis has been on expository preaching. This chapter provides helpful definitions of a variety of methods, forms, or types of preaching and delivery of sermons, such as topical, textual methods and narrative styles.

Chapter 5. Preaching: Problems and Solutions. A list of seven problems are presented, including the negative impact of poor preaching currently plaguing the Christian pulpit. Several solutions are presented, including the importance of proper preparation, self-exegesis, exegesis of Scripture, and the audience.

Chapter 6. Preaching the Literary Forms of the Bible. Many scholars, such as Thomas Long, consider the use of the Bible's literary forms as the most underdeveloped or neglected aspect of sermon preparation and biblical preaching. This chapter explores the dynamic rhetorical effects produced by a particular literary feature on a reader or preacher and how it is to be used in sermons.

Chapter 7. Preaching and Worship. With the proliferation of mass media communications and a renaissance in worship, preaching reached its zenith as the main portion of worship in the mid-twentieth century. During that worship resurgence, churches devoted more than half the time spent in worship to preaching. However, since the last decades of that century until now, there has been a tremendous paradigm shift in worship styles and content as music, drama, praise dancing, and video presentations usurped the centrality of preaching. This chapter presents recommendations to resolve the tension these have created in what some refer to as "warship."

Chapter 8. Women in the Word—A Spirit of Collaboration. While affirming women's divine call to proclaim the gospel alongside their brothers in ministry, this chapter does not focus on the pain encountered, suffered, and survived. It equips women to rise above adversity, rejection, or vilification to preach the Word with power by offering tips, advice, and even instructions to give nothing but the best.

Chapter 9. Preaching to the Contemporary Mind. The world and its people have changed—and so must our preaching! The cultural and philosophical shift from modernity to postmodernity requires it. The millennial generation who sees and understands the world differently from previous generations and who vote with their purses, feet, and diminishing presence in organized churches demands it. Recommendations to meet their spiritual developmental needs are provided.

Chapter 10. Preaching Beyond the Choir. Preachers are famous for preaching to the choir. This refers to the pointlessness of repeated attempts to convert those who are already convinced and who, by their consistent presence, demonstrate their faith in the doctrine and mission of the church. The use of social and public media is presented as a primary means of reaching two groups who are "beyond the choir"—children inside the church and nonbelievers outside.

Chapter 11. The Final Touch. The importance of illustrations is featured, along with exciting tips on the best use to engage an audience. Five specific types of illustrations are discussed and illustrated. These are the story, the word picture, the analogy, the list of examples, and the split story. These are followed by an appendix in which various types—such as prophetic, textual, and topical sermons—are illustrated.

Chapter 12. Sermons. The examples of the various styles of preaching discussed in the chapter regarding sermon definitions are provided in this final chapter.

Preacher, teacher, or lay leader—one day, the Great One, Jesus Christ our Lord, will ask you, "Did you do your best?" It is my hope that you will not be too quick or glib in your response but will be able to respond that, from this little volume, you learned and practiced never being comfortable with mediocrity. I pray that you will be able to answer Jesus confidently, saying, "Yes, Lord. According to my gifts and abilities, I gave nothing but the best!"

PART ONE—THEOLOGY

CHAPTER 1

A Theology of Preaching Review

For as the rain and the snow come down from heaven, and do not return there without watering the earth and making it bear and sprout, and furnishing seed to the sower and bread to the eater; so will My word be which goes forth from My mouth; it will not return to Me empty, without accomplishing what I desire, and without succeeding in the matter for which I sent it.[17]

My students repeatedly tell me that long after a semester ends, they can hear my voice in their heads cautioning them, as in our teaching moments. Some say they hear me declaring that one should quote others only when they better express the point. And when preaching, the quote should be short and pithy. And, since I practice what I teach, when it comes to homiletics, no one says this better than Fred Craddock: "We are all aware that in countless courts of opinion, the verdict on preaching has been rendered and the sentenced passed."[18] And we may add that nowadays, it's not very good. Part of the problem is that over time, preaching has been

---

[17]   Isaiah 55:10, 11.

[18]   As One Without Authority, p. 3.

excluded as mere "praxis," often observed or associated with a lesser discipline from theology. This exclusion has been primarily posited by systematic theologians. Several reasons for this exclusion have been noted by Richard Lischer:[19]

1. *A lack of substance* . . . "in which the preacher may present a charming and literate discourse, but because the speech does not emerge from and articulate the organizing principles of the church's life—its theology—because it does not offer the life of God in Christ, it suffers the same fate as the seed sown on rocky soil."

2. *The lack of coherence* because "many involved in theological education have puzzled at the low level of transference between the sophisticated skills acquired in the historical and exegetical fields and their simplistic execution in preaching and other ministry-related areas."

3. *Preaching's loss of authority.* "We have so thoroughly confused authority with an authoritarianism based on personal charisma, organizational genius, and persuasive public speaking, that responsible Christians hesitate to exercise the authority vested in preaching."

4. *The irrelevance of preaching.* "Many church members are bored or amused by the theological fads, the theologies *of* the death of God, secularity, play, hope, story, and the like, which replace each other faster than fashion styles or football coaches."

In response to this contrived dilemma, Lischer articulated what preaching does for theology, saying, "Preaching turns theology back to its center, which is the gospel, and insists upon a gospel-based budgeting of theology's resources." In other words, he asserts, "Preaching requisitions Christ from theology. It demands formulations that necessitate the cross. Preaching functions as a

---

[19] *A Theology of Preaching: The Dynamics of the Gospel,* pp.1–3.

corrective of theology. When theology moves toward synthesis with its dialogue partners of other disciplines, preaching recalls for it its character as *theo*-logy, reflection on God."[20]

Perhaps it should be noted, as did Lischer, that

> when theology loses interest in the Scripture, preaching continues with the Word—week in, week out. When theology becomes bogged down in words, the preached word continues to witness, in words, to an historical event. When theology looks with permission upon the vastness of the hermeneutical arch and the apparent impossibility of genuine understanding, preaching comforts it with a gospel that creates its own understandings and makes ready its own way. When theology produces unpreachable, that is, nonevangelical, words about God, preaching marks them REFUSED, and the church momentarily pauses, examines itself, and corrects its course.[21]

Lischer opines, "Preaching is the first and final expression of theology. It is first in the sense that the Christian movement was born in preaching. Certainly, the first preaching we encounter—and indeed the only preaching we will ever encounter—is theological. What is the nature of this original theology of the New Testament?" He then answers, "Preaching gives the clue. In preaching, theology recovers three elements it had at its origin: its kerygmatic impulse, its oral nature, and its character as worship."[22]

Like Lischer, when we speak of preaching, we are not addressing only "the academic discipline of homiletics, but preaching as the sum total of speakers, listeners, and settings throughout the church—that

---

[20]   Ibid, p. 9–10.

[21]   Ibid.

[22]   Ibid., p. 10.

is, preaching as the ceaseless activity of the church."[23] There's also an "element of theology's original nature that it recovers in preaching is its orality. The original proclamatory theology of the church was oral-aural [spoken and heard]. Our New Testament—both Epistle and Gospels—is a frozen record of oral discourse."[24]

However, before preaching can lecture theology about its exclusions and oral heritage, it must audaciously put its own house in order. This should begin with the admission that there exists no such thing as a perfect preacher or sermon. Even the best preacher can become better through attention to the impact of God's revelation on his or her life, and the best sermon can be improved by practicing more of the "how to" prepare a manuscript. But one of the greatest deterrents to learning "how to" be a great preacher is having preached a well-received sermon before understanding this fundamental principle: "how can" one "preach unless they are sent by God" (Rom. 10:15). Such premature applause often leads to what A. W. Tozer calls a "self-sin," such as self-confidence, which prevents some preachers from ever learning to become "great," because they have concluded that they were already "good," based on the response of a congregation to their first or previous sermons. So "what is needed today is not a new Gospel, but men and women who can restate the gospel of the Son of God in terms that will reach the very heart of our problems," wrote Oswald Chambers. He continued, "Today people are flinging the truth overboard as well as the terms. Why should we not become workers who need not be ashamed, rightly dividing the word of truth to our own people? The majority of orthodox ministers are hopelessly useless, and the unorthodox seem to be the only ones who are used. We need men and women who are saturated with the truth of God, who can restate the old truth in terms that appeal to our day."[25] Such qualities distinguish the humble learner, who prepares his or her own heart before stepping into the pulpit,

---

23   Ibid., p. 11.

24   Ibid.

25   *Approved Unto God*, p. 19.

from the puffed-up preacher who uses the pulpit for showmanship and self-promotion.

In fact, when it comes to preparing ourselves to preach, there are times when a process of personal deconstruction will help create the reconstruction of a new life in the Word. For just because we might "feel" the Spirit when preparing a sermon doesn't mean others will encounter him when we present it, unless there's a deeper relationship than just how we "feel" during the sermonic process.

The Wonder of God's Word

When preachers cultivate an intimate relationship with God, it transforms their preaching from "good to great."[26] However, just as "the modern scientist has lost God amid the wonders of his world," warned Oswald Chambers, "we Christians are in grave danger of losing God amid the wonder of His Word. We have almost forgotten that God is a Person and can be cultivated [relationally] as any person can."[27]

Such a loss can lead to an experience—a painful, profound reality described by St. John of the Cross as "the dark night of the soul." In this, the preacher can be invaded or driven by despair that shatters preconceived illusions and provokes deep questions about one's theology of preaching. I have had such a dry spell in my devotional life and ministry. It seriously affected my perception of and intimacy with God. It also impinged on my preaching and oftentimes led to "routine, perfunctory prayers and the ordinariness of life."[28] At such times, I buried myself in work, taking on more responsibilities, running to and fro to numb my heart and avoid what some describe

---

[26] Title of Jim Collins's classic book in which he makes an applicable observation that "good is the enemy of great . . . The vast majority of companies never become great, precisely because the vast majority become quite good—and that is their main problem," p. 1.

[27] *The Pursuit of God*, p. 2.

[28] Brennan Manning, *Souvenirs of Solitude*, p. 19.

as the difficult invasion of God's astringent grace that opens us to new realms of spiritual experience.

It wasn't until I read Brennan Manning's book in which are some troubling, yet thought-provoking, questions that awakened the dormant Spirit within me, that I dared to ask God the deeper questions about what he was up to in my life. In a chapter entitled "The Second Summons," Manning wrote: "Jesus Christ is the truth for me. His Word influences my judgment, affects the decisions I make and the ones I refuse to make. His truth has helped me determine what is central in life and what is secondary—what is marginal, fringe, peripheral. But is He real . . . Does rhetoric match reality?"[29] He followed this with a series of questions God prompted in him— questions that propelled me into days of reflection, contemplation, and eventually, transformation. I repeat them here in the hope that they will do the same for others regarding understanding of what it means to love and be loved by God and how this knowledge influences our personal relationship and trust in him as a preacher of his Word. Manning asked, as if speaking for God:

> When a tear-filled child comes up to you in the darkness of a thunderstorm and asks with tear-streaked face, "Are you still here? Will you stay with me until it is light? Are you disgusted with me because I'm little and afraid? Are you going to give me away?" And you are grieved and saddened over the child's lack of trust? Do you realize that you do the same thing to Me? Or don't you believe that I am at least as sensitive a father as you? Do you understand the word of my Son: "I do nothing by Myself? I do only what I see my Father doing" (John 8:28)? Who do you think first wept over Jerusalem when they refused to receive My Own Son? . . . Have you grappled with the core question of your faith, which is not "Is

---

[29]   Ibid., p. 20.

Jesus God-like?" but "Is God Jesus-like?" Do you comprehend that all the attitudes, values, qualities, and characteristics of My Son are Mine; that he who sees Jesus sees Me, His Father?"[30]

These poignant and potent questions haunted me, but they also confirmed the importance of including a theology of preaching in lectures or books on the art or act of preaching. Why, you may ask, is such a theology so important or necessary? Four reasons come to mind:

1. Preachers need a theology of preaching to help them decide what significance they should attach to research, sermon preparation, and delivery. This is addressed in the chapter on biblical preaching.

2. The methodology of "how to" preach—in which most preachers receive their training—seldom, if ever, answers the question or authority, or "How can or will they preach unless they are sent?" (Rom. 10:15). A very practical discussion on the importance of being human and holy takes this point into consideration.

3. A theology of preaching clarifies for the preacher what preaching does for theology and vice versa, so that sermons are not endless methodological rules and formulae or rhetorical gymnastics for showmanship in the pulpit (see part 2 on methodology).

4. As Richard Lischer noted, "Theology's exposition of the faith and its openness to the world corresponds with preaching's dual responsibility to the word and the world" as it functions "as mediator between exegesis and preaching."[31]

---

[30] Ibid., pp. 20, 21.

[31] *A Theology of Preaching*, p. 5.

A theology of preaching should also take into consideration the preacher's personal spiritual development. There are, however, "major issues within a theology of preaching, including the authority of the preacher, the relationship of the Bible to preaching, and the historical, social, and liturgical contexts of preaching."[32] Additionally, it is posited that "expectations of preaching range from proclaiming the Word of God to liberating the oppressed to providing pastoral counseling on a group scale. Although the range is broad, generally, expectations for preaching fall into two major groupings: those that expect preaching principally to play a role in the sanctification of the people of faith and those that expect it principally to play a role in the justification of human beings before God."[33]

David M. Greenhaw, from whose article on "Theology of Preaching" this is quoted, adds, "The office of the preacher is ideally preserved for those who are capable of careful and faithful interpretation of the traditions of the church. He or she is to have enough training and character to promote a fitting Christian style of life, to explicate the sources of the Christian faith and apply them meaningfully to the present setting."[34]

Since God calls pastors to these responsibilities—and because they are primarily trained to plan, prepare, and present worship—many seldom attend or participate in worship as congregants. Where, therefore, do pastors receive the personal spirituality, nurture, pastoral care, and redemptive work for their own lives and souls? For instance, outside of a weekly gathering for worship, some seminaries do not provide spiritual formation or discipleship experiences (not just courses) for seminarians. Additionally, when they graduate and are assigned a parish, members charged with assisting the pastor with spiritual care of the congregation seldom, if ever, include the pastor as a candidate for such concern. For example, in one of my large churches, I noticed that my elders regularly visited members to pray

---

[32] Ibid.

[33] *Concise Encyclopedia of Preaching*, pp. 477, 478.

[34] Ibid., p. 478.

with them in their homes, but I never received a phone call or visit because—as they explained when chided—they assumed that being the preacher/leader of the church, I "had it all together."

Church officers expect pastors to be holy, if not human; but without worshipping as one in need of grace, we tend to be either very human or holy, and both extremes are detrimental to our growth and that of our members. Such preachers tend to have a basic misunderstanding of the theology of preaching with moral and spiritual consequences, for they believe that as long as you have or embrace the words of truth, or can repeat fundamental beliefs stated as a code of truth, you "have the truth" and are living in the truth.

A. W. Tozer cautions us, saying one "can memorize all the texts of the Bible—and I believe in memorizing—but when you are through, you've got nothing but the body. There is the soul as well as the body. There is a divine inward illumination the Holy Ghost must give us or we don't know what truth means."[35]

What It Means to Be Human and Holy

Jesus deliberately worked diligently to correct this inadequate view that knowing the words of Scripture means one has him who is "the way, the truth and the life" (John 5:39 and 14:6). He was both human and holy and calls us to follow him. Scripture declares, "For we do not have a high priest who cannot sympathize with our weaknesses, but one who has been tempted in all things as we are" (human) and "yet without sin" (holy). We must strive for the ideal, although we will not be without sin in this current corrupt environment of a world spinning out of control. Additionally, being human, "Jesus did not die a death with dignity but a death endured, screaming to a God who did not answer. Jesus paid the price. He became utterly poor. In this total renunciation, Jesus professed what it means to be human. He endured our lot. He came to us where we really were and stood with us, struggling with his whole heart to

---

[35] Tozer, A. W. 2016. *God Still Speaks,* CrossReach Publications, p. 30.

have us say yes to our innate poverty," wrote Brennan Manning.[36] He continued, "The Christian who is really human is really poor," but it's not a poverty of material things but a poverty in spirit (Matt. 5:3) that drives one to total dependence on God. Such a preacher would, in these ancient words attributed to Ignatius Loyola, "work as if everything depended on God and pray as if everything depended on you."

"How does this poverty of spiritism [*sic*] reflect itself in day-to-day living?" Manning asked. Then he answered, "In conversation, the poor man always leaves the other person feeling, 'My life has been enriched by talking with you.' And it has. He is not all exhaust and no intake. He doesn't impose himself on another; he doesn't overwhelm him with his wealth of insights; he doesn't try to convert him by concussion with the sledgehammer blow of the Bible after another. He listens well because he realizes he is poor and has much to learn from others. His poverty enables him to enter the existential world of the other, even when he cannot identify with the world. Being poor, he knows how to receive and can express appreciation and gratitude for the slightest gift."[37]

To be holy is one of God's commands (Lev. 11:44). Because holiness is to the spiritual life what breathing is to the natural, it wasn't a principle that only Moses and the Israelites had to observe during the Exodus, for we find the same injunction repeated in Peter's first epistle addressed "to those who reside as aliens, scattered throughout" the world (1 Pet. 1:1, 15). Despite the biblical admonitions for holiness, a vast majority of those who claim Christianity as their faith have little or no concept of what it means "to be holy."

It may be surprising that a survey conducted by the Barna Research Group found the idea of holiness baffling to most church-attending Americans, both preachers and congregants. It concluded that they are and remain confused, if not daunted, by the concept. For instance, in the general population, "overall, three out of every

---

[36] *Souvenirs of Solitude*, p. 90.

[37] Ibid.

four adults (73%) believe that it is possible for someone to become holy, regardless of their past. Only half of the adult population (50%), however, says that they know someone they consider to be holy. And that's more than twice as many who consider themselves holy (21%)."[38] Regrettably, "the views of born-again Christians are not much different from the national averages. Among born-again adults, three-quarters (76%) say it is possible for a person to become holy, regardless of their past. Slightly more than half of the born-again group (55%) says they know someone who they would describe as holy. And roughly three out of ten born again (20%) say they are holy, which is marginally more than the national norm."[39]

If holiness is a gift from God to every born-again believer, how can we exercise it with confidence without feeling presumptuous? Perhaps the biggest challenge to practicing holiness is the "self." Jesus said, "If anyone wishes to come after Me, he [she] must deny [say no to, absolutely repudiate] self and take up his [her] cross and follow Me" (Mark 8:34, amplification mine).

A. W. Tozer describes it best, saying, "Self is the opaque veil that hides the Face of God from us. It can be removed only in spiritual experience, never by instruction. As well try to instruct leprosy out of our system. There must be a work of God in destruction before we are free. We must invite the cross to do its deadly work within us. We must bring our self-sins [he describes them as self-righteousness, self-pity, self-confidence, self-sufficiency, self-admiration, self-love, and a host of similar traits] to the cross for judgment. We must prepare ourselves for an ordeal of suffering in some measure, like that through which our Savior passed when He suffered under Pontius Pilate." Remember, Tozer cautions, "Self can live unrebuked at the very altar. It can watch the bleeding victim die and not be in the least affected by what it sees. It can fight for the faith of the Reformers and preach eloquently the creed of salvation by grace, and gain strength by its

---

[38]   https://www.barna.org/barna-update/article/5-barna-update/162-the-concept-of-holiness-baffles-most-americans.

[39]   Ibid.

efforts. To tell the truth, it seems actually to feed upon orthodoxy and is more at home in a Bible conference than in a tavern. Our very state of longing after God may afford it an excellent condition under which to thrive."[40] However, Tozer warned, "Let us beware of tinkering with our inner life in hope ourselves to rend the veil. God must do everything for us. Our part is to yield and trust. We must confess, forsake, repudiate the self-life, and then reckon it crucified."[41]

How are we to respond to our innate drive for "self" realization? In my studies, I have discovered both negative and positive approaches and herewith present one of each:

1. **Autosoterism**—a negative approach, the word of which is a combination of two Greek terms: *autos* ("self") and *soter* ("salvation"), the spiritual and eternal deliverance granted by God alone (Rev. 12:10), without human participation or intervention. It is very much unlike *sozo*, the temporal human and divine partnership of deliverance from sin. Instead, it is a naturalistic religious belief that we can save ourselves based on an individual's natural powers to accomplish everything God requires for salvation.

Autosoterism is, therefore, a most pernicious and false religious doctrine that proposes humans are capable of accomplishing what only God can do. It is almost always used synonymously with Pelagianism—a belief created by Pelagius, a fifth-century British monk who denied original sin and affirmed the ability of humans to save themselves without divine intervention. Jerome, one of the early Church Fathers, pronounced it the first organized system of self-salvation taught in the Christian Church. Though many have thoroughly rejected it as an unbiblical doctrine that appeals to human pride or desire for control, it continues to ring from evangelical nationalist pulpits and fundamental Christian circles in passionate

---

[40]   *The Pursuit of God,* p. 45.

[41]   Ibid., p. 47.

proclamations of what its contemporary adherents declare is the "whosoever will gospel." In such a humanistic claim, salvation is left purely to the human "will."

2. **Awareness coupled with the prayer of relinquishment**—a positive solution to the problem by waking up to the realities of life followed by surrender, not just renouncement, but relinquishing of all rights to one's "self" or possessions according to divine directives. It is a priority in the process of sanctification—the continual, daily growth in grace (2 Pet. 3:14–18).

When we speak of sanctification, it is a concept that defies nay concrete explanation, but the reality—the unhindered, continuously flowing reality—is that it is a transforming experience of a lifetime. Ellen White wrote:

> It is not the work of a moment, an hour, or a day. It is a continual growth in grace. We know not one day how strong will be our conflict the next. Satan lives, and is active, and every day we need to earnestly cry to God for help and strength to resist him. As long as Satan reigns, we shall have self to subdue, besetments to overcome, and there is no stopping place. There is no point to which we can come and say we have fully attained.[42]

As for awareness, the best explanation may be found in the writings of psychologist Anthony de Mello. He opines that most people are asleep even though they don't know it. "They're born asleep, they live asleep, they marry in their sleep, they breed children in their sleep, they die in their sleep without ever waking up." As a result, "they never understand the loveliness and the beauty of this

[42] Review & Herald, May 6,1862, quoted in The Seventh-day Adventist Bible Commentary, Vol. 7, p 947.

thing we call human existence,"[43] which can be experienced only by those who are awake and aware. My late grandmother used to charge us misbehaving children by saying "Watch yourself!" But this means one is to continuously watch or consistently observe what is happening within as well as around oneself because reality is not static; it is always flowing or moving. It is perpetually dynamic, as is life.

Richard J. Foster's formula for denying self is also illuminative. He recommends the following practice:

> We learn the Prayer of Relinquishment in the school of Gethsemane. Gaze in adoring wonder at the scene. The solitary figure etched against gnarled olive trees. The bloodlike sweat falling to the ground. The human longing: "Let this cup pass." The final relinquishment: "Not my will but yours be done" (Luke 22:39–46). We do well to meditate often on this unparalleled expression of relinquishment.[44]

He defines the prayer of relinquishment as a giving up of all rights to oneself to God:

> The Prayer of Relinquishment is a bona fide letting go, but it is a release with hope. We have no fatalist resignation. We are buoyed up by a confident trust in the character of God. Even when all we see are tangled threads on the backside of life's tapestry, we know that God is good and is out to do us good always. That gives us hope to believe we are the winners, regardless of what we are being called upon to relinquish. God is inviting us deeper in and higher

---

[43] Awareness, Penguin Random House, New York, 1990, p. 5.

[44] *Prayer: Finding The Heart's True Home*, p. 49.

---

up. There is training in righteousness, transforming power, new joys, deeper intimacy.[45]

How Being Human and Holy Affects the Preacher

First, the preacher should be as intense about worship as she or he is about preparing a sermon and preaching. Those who lack a balance between being human and holy tend to elevate preaching and separate it from worship in their personal practice. Such a one can become so disconnected from worship—the very context in which theology and preaching had their genesis—that worship becomes objectified as just another church program instead of a sacred moment in the presence of Almighty God. It is quite troubling to note, after decades of parish ministry and the last several years as a professor of homiletics, that many pastors generally seem uninterested in worship and, in some cases, are incapable of worshipping. Such preachers appear to respond to worship as a "gig" or performance in which they emerge from the seclusion of a "pastor's study" to make an appearance and preach after the disdained "preliminaries" have been completed.

To such preachers, "worship lies lower down the priority list behind preaching, leadership, pastoral care, and administration," Michael J. Quicke concluded. And he added, "Hubris plagues the act of preaching; rightly convinced of preaching's importance, preachers can wrongly become self-important. Investing all their effort in sermon-making, and claiming its importance for proclaiming the gospel (Rom. 10:9), they can sideline worship as a secondary matter."[46] If there is a chasm between preaching and worship in the mind or actions of some pastors, it may be due to what Jeff Crittenden suggested, saying, "Perhaps some preachers are growing weary of seemingly preaching into the wind, some listeners are tired

---

[45]   Ibid., p. 52.

[46]   *Preaching as Worship: An Integrative Approach to Formation in Your Church*, p. 28.

---

of preaching that says nothing to them, and perhaps the Holy Spirit is impatiently waiting to bless all."[47]

Furthermore, as Crittenden opines, because "the sermon carries a great deal of influence as the reading of Scripture," thus the sermon is "slowly becoming a blend of education, theological discernment, and inspiration for discipleship." While this trend can tempt preachers to think highly of themselves and usurp the role of God among his people, "the question emerges: are we preachers rising to this opportunity and responsibility?"[48]

What then is this opportunity? It is first to study to show oneself approved unto God (2 Tim. 2:15); and second, to plumb the depths of Scripture to bring out its beautiful gems of wisdom so as to transform worshippers. According to Crittenden (quoting Walter Brueggemann), the opportunity available to preachers is to capture the imagination of worshippers and reshape their experience of the world in such a way that justice, compassion, right relations, and hope abound.[49]

And what is the responsibility? To answer that, Crittenden referred to Augustine's statement that the preacher's responsibility is to educate, to delight, and to persuade. Further, according to Karl Bart, the preacher should have the newspaper in one hand and the Bible in the other, in order to function legitimately as a human and holy ambassador of Christ.

Second, the preacher should show that he or she is human by preaching hope and grace, with loving understanding, to people coping with life's many transitions. When I graduated from seminary, I could exegete Greek and Hebrew and give a discourse on eschatology, soteriology, and ontology. I could write a second letter to the Romans and decipher Augustine's *De Doctrina Christiana*, but I had no idea how to preach sermons related to such life challenges as death and dying, marriage and divorce, to name just a few. Upon entering my

---

[47]   Ibid., p. 41.

[48]   *Three Goals for Preaching in Our Context,* p. 40.

[49]   Ibid.

first parish as solo pastor, I literally had to create substance, on-the-go, in many of these practical facets of ministry.

Insensitivity and lack of understanding of a community's suffering can cause havoc in a congregation. For instance, when I was a pastoral intern in a large congregation on the East Coast, a famous guest speaker left our church in shambles. He was unaware that a beloved young teacher had passed away the day before he spoke, from an aggressive brain tumor that took her life within weeks of diagnosis. She left behind her devastated husband and three little children. Oblivious to our grief, and having not undertaken a smidgen of exegesis of his audience, he stood in the pulpit like an ayatollah and remonstrated us for not adhering to our denomination's health message. He declared that because we failed to give up meat, sugar, and other unhealthy habits, some were dying of cancer and other tragic terminal diseases. Stunned by his insensitive remarks, some boldly stood up and left as he barked, "You are leaving because I'm stepping on your toes and you can't take it!" Not only was this sermon the topic of conversations for a long time, it took equally as much time for some members to get over it.

"Preaching through transitions," Crittenden observed, "demands that the preachers be carefully tuned into the context of the community they are serving."[50] This can only be accomplished when preachers are actively human and holy. Times of grief and loss are some of the most challenging and dreaded responsibilities of pastoral ministry. The pastor should use such difficult times to (a) honor the memory of the loved one with authentic vignettes of his or her life; (b) comfort the bereaved in their loss with a homily or short sermon, not with long evangelistic sermons to capture the minds of people who would not otherwise attend their church; and (c) avoid controversial theological discourses. Instead, point to the biblical promises of Jesus Christ that death will one day be overcome (1 Cor. 15:26), because mourners remember very little of what preachers may say, but they will always recall the care demonstrated, the well-chosen phrases of

---

[50]   Ibid.

comfort, and the time spent with the bereaved family. Thomas G. Long suggests that "the main purpose of a funeral sermon is not to soothe the brokenhearted or to provide explanations but, instead, to confront head-on the lies proclaimed by the other preacher at the funeral: Death."[51] While visitation and homilies are important tools for comforting a bereaved family, counseling and compassionate conversation can bring a lot of relief to those going through a divorce or are facing the realities of death and dying.

Although weddings are happier occasions, they require as much sensitivity and preparation as funerals. According to Charles L. Rice, "The celebration and blessing of a marriage presents the preacher with a unique opportunity. The ambiguity of the marriage ceremony, in which secular and sacred elements combine, challenges the preacher's imagination, pastoral skills, and powers of communication."[52] Weddings are also great opportunities for pastors who "bring good news" to demonstrate that they are both human and holy. Rather than attempting to reinvent the wheel, here's a link to an article on "How to Write Wedding Sermons" by Shea Drake.[53]

As Crittenden noted, it is also important "to honor the tradition" of the community being served. "Perhaps," he continues, "the preacher might offer familiar words of assurance, courage, and hope as many in our congregation navigate the 'golden years' with all its trials and tribulations. What we need now, more than ever, is preaching that helps hearers make transitions from what was toward to what is emerging, including in their personal lives."[54]

Finally, the benefits preachers can derive from the proper understanding of and interaction between the disciplines of preaching and theology are too great to communicate in this short review. From a cursory survey, it is clear that a theology of preaching encompasses authority the preacher brings to this sacred task, the content of

---

[51]   *The New Interpreter's Handbook of Preaching*, pp. 385, 386.

[52]   Ibid., p. 426.

[53]   http://www.ehow.com/how_5424865_write-wedding-sermons.html.

[54]   *Three Goals for Preaching in Our Context*, pp. 41, 42.

preaching as well as the exegesis and interpretation of scripture that exposes one's perspective and character of preaching. All these are addressed with joyful boldness and desperate urgency in forthcoming chapters.

CHAPTER 2

Biblical Preaching

Biblical preaching encourages the listeners to have open bibles, to turn to Scripture passages, to make notes in their margins, and to take notes as needed (2 Tim. 2:15) . . . [It] trusts in the sufficiency and power of the Word of God . . . gets no pleasure out of scolding, insulting, or tearing someone down . . . connects truth to practice . . . is bold and authoritative.[55]

Ravi Zacharias, a powerful preacher, prolific author, and outstanding Christian apologist, once told about a visit to Ohio State University to present a series of lectures. On the way to the lecture hall, he and his driver passed what was then the "new" Wexner Art Center. The driver proudly pointed to the building, saying, "This is a new art building for the university. It is a fascinating building designed in the postmodernist view of reality." His interest piqued, Zacharias asked the driver to stop for a brief tour of the building. Here's how he described the so-called "fascinating" structure: "The building has no pattern. Staircases go nowhere. Pillars support nothing. The

---

[55]   www.relevantBible.

architect designed the building to reflect the postmodernist view of life, so it went nowhere. It was mindless and senseless."

The driver, however, was apparently so enthralled by the creative design that he continued to regale Zacharias with more flowery descriptions until the apologist turned to the man and asked, "Did they do the same with the foundation?" The man laughed and retorted, "Absolutely not! You can't do that with a foundation! Don't you know, there are construction codes that can't be violated?"[56]

Architects, engineers, and building officials all agree that—regardless of the upper structure of a building, whether it's simple or complex—its foundation must follow accepted principles of structural design preserved in an international code. In other words, all buildings (ancient, modern, or postmodern) must have a foundation able to withstand unexpected earthquakes, floods, storms, and other destructive forces.

As in architecture, there's also a universal principle in preaching—it is called biblical preaching. It should be the introduction for a firm foundation on which one builds all sermonic methods and styles. This foundation is expository in that it sets forth the meaning or purpose of a biblical pericope through which the preacher powerfully confronts or engages listeners with God's truth *entirely from Scripture*. It guards the messenger against false teaching because listeners hold him or her accountable to God's Word. Furthermore, it focuses the preacher's attention so that they can address many issues in life that would otherwise be neglected or avoided. Making the sermon an effective inspiration for, or initiator of, Bible study and spiritual conversations, it brings about changes in people's lives and opens Scripture to them as they hear and interact with the preached Word.

Biblical preaching forces the preacher to grow and mature as a believer as the Holy Spirit uses the Word to search his or her heart as well as to transform the listener's life and eternal destiny (Rom.

---

[56] Modified from sermon illustration found at http://www.sermoncentral. com/illustrations/sermon-illustration-sermon-central-staff-stories-foundation-79625.asp.

1:11, 12). Not merely talk about God, it is God himself speaking through the message and personality of the preacher to confront and transform men and women. Such preaching does not use Scripture only as a quote or prop to support a pep talk from the pulpit. Nor is it sermons in which the preacher subjects Scripture to his or her thoughts. Rather, the preacher permits Scripture to impact him or her before offering listeners the best from the Word of God.

To improve proclamation of the gospel so that it is consistently transformative, the Christian church must produce a new generation of great preachers who, having learned the firm foundation of preaching, then practice what they preach. Such preaching must proclaim the biblical story of Jesus that is becoming the greatest story never told to this generation. True biblical preaching must encompass the first book, or Old Testament; the second book, or New Testament; and the book of nature (Rom. 1:20), sometimes referred to as the third testament. Biblical preaching must be profoundly prophetic (a topic discussed in the next chapter) and consistently great. It is the responsibility of homiletic authors and teachers to clearly define and present the art of biblical preaching so that it can bring about the desired revival in Christianity.

What Is Biblical Preaching?

Sometimes it is better to first define a thing by stating what it is not. Biblical preaching is definitely not giving a few off-the-cuff thoughts or remarks on the spur of the moment. It is not a display of oratorical skills or intellectual abilities liberally sprinkled with human opinions and offhanded references to Scripture so that the audience can applaud, whether or not they hear and understand the message. Nor is it lecturing, as in a classroom or at a midweek Bible study; for though such teachers delve into details, biblical preaching illustrates, interprets, and gets to the point of the felt or observed needs of the audience for which the Bible provides unlimited resources.

True biblical preaching is a passionately delivered, structured summation of God's message which, as it exalts him, draws the listener into a dialogue of the mind and heart with him. Only such preaching will ever save anyone (Mark 16:15–16; 1 Cor. 1:17–21). It makes known God's truth and power (Joel 2:27–28; Heb. 4:12–13) and builds up his church (1 Cor. 14:4).

Principles of Powerful Biblical Preaching

Any type or style of preaching must adhere to three basic principles: hermeneutics, exegesis, and authority. But they are absolutely essential for powerful biblical preaching.

1. Hermeneutics

The term *hermeneutics* comes from Hermes, the Olympian messenger or god of speech in Greek mythology. Also known as *heilsgeschichte*—German from *heils* (salvation) and *geschichte* (history)—it is defined as "an interpretation of history emphasizing God's saving acts and viewing Jesus Christ as central in redemption."[57] Many use the word *hermeneutics* interchangeably with *exegesis*, although more than subtle differences exist between them. For instance, hermeneutics is a wider discipline that includes written, verbal, and nonverbal communication, while exegesis focuses primarily on examining and understanding the text under scrutiny. In essence, hermeneutics is the study of the methodological principles of interpreting the Bible. It informs the particular ways in which a biblical preacher/teacher interprets the ancient texts of Scripture to explain what the author or speaker intended to get across. Richard Lischer identifies three methods of hermeneutics popular among preachers today,[58] but they are not recommended for great biblical preaching.

First is the "flat" reading of Scripture that approaches every text in a verse-by-verse fashion on the unspoken assumption that the content of each verse is as important as that of every other verse in the text.

---

[57] *Merriam-Webster Dictionary.*

[58] *The End of Words: The Language of Reconciliation in a Culture of Violence*, pp. 63–66.

Consequently, it tends to miss the theological and emotional curve or direction of the passage. It approaches the text the way broadcasters read their cue cards. "The flat reading appeals to many preachers who—finding themselves stuck for something to say or unwilling to do the hard, synthetic work of the theological imagination—fall back on verse-by-verse explanation as the 'most faithful' method of biblical interpretation," explained Lischer. The sermon it produces lends itself to teaching a variety of lessons in serial form, but at the expense of the transforming power of the entire text.

Second, the "convenient" reading of Scripture has no difficulty finding useful ideas in the text as the interpreter reads and rereads the text until a usable notion pops out. The only problem is the ideas don't arise from the text's center in the gospel. For example, the convenient reader concludes that if Jesus wept over his friend Lazarus, perhaps it's okay for us to show our emotions more freely. If Jesus turned over the moneychangers' tables, perhaps we too ought to express anger about injustice. Since the Master could call lowly tax collectors and prostitutes into the kingdom, surely we too can recognize the potential of unlikely people. Although such are agreeable assumptions, "in so doing," Lischer wrote, "he or she may be lured away from the overriding purpose of Scripture, which is to save people from sin, form them for community, and equip them for lives of discipleship in the world."

Third, the "ironic" reading of Scripture makes much of God's greatness and the Bible's importance, but often at the expense of God's saving grace. This approach focuses on the distance between him and humanity, but it does little to bridge the gap. Thus, humanity appears doomed to live in ironic discrepancy, which Lischer opines is the gulf between its own pretensions and God's majesty. As a result, the preacher who reads from this perspective consistently demonstrates the inferiority of everything human compared to the divine; and while that is true enough, she or he never gets around to presenting God's identification with humanity in Jesus Christ (Heb. 4:15).

Craig G. Bartholomew articulates the doctrine of the Trinity[59] as the best hermeneutical method for Christians. He asks, "How then does the doctrine of the Trinity shape a biblical hermeneutic?" His answer makes it clear under the following eight banners that a trinitarian hermeneutic

1. approaches the Bible as authoritative Scripture.
2. approaches the Bible as a whole as Scripture.
3. views ecclesial reception of Scripture as primary.
4. exalts and humbles academic interpretation.
5. will attend to the discrete witness of the Testaments.
6. rightly discerns the goal of reading the Bible.
7. does not close down but opens up interpretation of the Bible.
8. takes God's address for all of life seriously.

In my studies, I have discovered a variety of methods of hermeneutics that dominate the discipline of biblical studies and preaching. They are all different and useful, but none is being presented as better than the others, and at least one is considered not useful to a more conservative preacher or teacher. I have summarized a few prominent ones under the following titles.

Analysis is the method primarily favored by men. Studies have indicated that males tend to stand outside the text and scrutinize or carefully analyze its content to discover meaning before making application. For example, in the story of the Syrophoenician woman, an analytical perspective may overlook the subtle nuance in a word that Jesus employed when he said, "It is not good to take the children's bread and throw it to the dogs" (Matt. 15:26). The Greek term for "dog" is *kuon* (a mature animal), one the Jews used to describe Gentiles, because of their ceremonial impurities and a manner of worship that sometimes sounded like snarling dogs as they jumped about, groaning and cutting themselves. However, the term Jesus used and which Matthew recorded is *ta kuneria*, the word for a

---

59   Introducing Biblical Hermeneutics: A Comprehensive Framework for Hearing God in Scripture, pp. 8–15.

diminutive dog or "pretty little pup," which turns out to be a subtle term of endearment.

Women seem to step into the world of the text and thereby prefer the *experiential* hermeneutic. In doing so, we imagine the sound, smell, and taste, as well as the unspoken nuances, before finding meaning and application. One example is the story of the prodigal son in Luke 15, from which a female preacher delivered a narrative sermon focusing on the perspective of the mother, who is seldom, if ever, included. Of course, one might say that is exegeting the text. But remember, Jesus began the story with "A man had two sons"— ergo, there had to be a mother somewhere. Perhaps Jesus deliberately left out the part of the mother so that the preacher would never forget a mother's contributions, whether she be overprotective like Sarah or deceitful as Rebekah.

Fundamentalists, who lean largely on the understanding of their community's beliefs more than careful exegesis of Scripture, practice a *traditional* hermeneutic. For instance, they will insist on preaching that a cock crowed because Jesus said to Peter, "Truly I say to you, that this very night before a rooster [cock] crows twice, you yourself will deny Me three times" (Mark 14:30). However, research reveals a Jewish prohibition against the rearing of fowls (hens and cocks) in Jerusalem and forbade their presence during Passover.[60] However, the Romans divided the night into four watches (6:00–9:00 p.m. evening; 9:00–12:00 midnight; 12:00–3:00 a.m. cockcrow; and 3:00–6:00 a.m. morning). At the beginning of a watch, one blast of a trumpet notified soldiers of the time to change guards, except the cockcrow watch, when two blasts came from the Castle Antonia battlements to arouse soldiers and the sleeping city. The Romans called the signals the *gallicinium*, or "cock-crow,"[61] perhaps to irritate the Jews, who turned the impact of its negative connotations by using it themselves as the *alektora phoneo* (the sound of a cock).

---

[60] *The Interpreter's Dictionary of the Bible*, vol. 1, p. 656.

[61] *Barclay's Commentary on Matthew*, pp. 346, 347.

Feminist and womanist theologians, in vociferous protest against patriarchy in Scripture, promote the hermeneutic of *suspicion*. Conservative segments of Christianity generally reject it. However, one can find in it useful insights for a fresh look at Scriptures, such as their suggestion regarding the authority of naming found in Genesis. They propose that the fulfillment of one of the first divine proto-evangelism prophecies ("Yet your desire will be for your husband, and he will rule over you," Gen. 3:16) was fulfilled when Adam named Eve (verse 20). They propose that ancient Jews believed that one names that which is under one's control. Prior to that, God gave the first couple permission to name everything, except each other.

Finally, the hermeneutic of *anticipation* carefully examines all categories and selects the best scholarship and biblical collaboration from each to bring fresh meaning to the Word of God. For example, most speakers generally present the story of Martha and Mary (Luke 10:38–42) as a salvific issue that regards Martha as caring more about cooking, while Mary focused on salvation as taught by Jesus. But that could not be any further from the truth. Rather, the brief narrative shows how Jesus used humor to break a potentially disruptive tension between two sisters. For, contrary to what has been preached and taught to lead some women who have the gift of hospitality to say "I'm just a Martha," the account is a really funny exchange between Jesus and Martha (who is later presented as a powerful theologian in John 11:18–27).

Picture this. Martha is preparing several dishes to impress Jesus and his unexpected entourage when she notices that her sister isn't at her side helping her to sharpen knives and sling dishpans. In frustration, mingled with a lot of anger, she bursts into the room where Jesus is sitting with Mary at his feet and demands that he order her sister to help her. Here's Jesus's response: "Tsk, tsk! Martha, Martha, you are worried [anxious and stressed out] and bothered [troubled and agitated] about so many things [or dishes, as the Greek word suggests]; but only one thing [dish—perhaps pointing to himself with a broad smile and a wink] is necessary, for Mary has chosen the good part [or portion of the dish, meaning himself], which shall not be taken away from her."

2. Exegesis

This second principle of powerful biblical preaching (also referred to as *formgeschichte*, because it seeks to reconstruct the history of the transmission of the materials), *exegesis* means "to lead out." It is the science—or art, as some would argue—of interpretation, explanation, or exposition of a word or text to determine the exact meaning of a particular passage of Scripture. It is definitely not *eisegesis*, the reading of meaning "into" a text to create or support one's own interpretation. Exegesis is not interpretation, because it explores the etymology and linguistic meaning of words in the original language to discover the text's significance or relevance. Interpretation, on the other hand, is the outcome of thoughts inspired by the Holy Spirit while reflecting on and contemplating the meaning of a passage of Scripture before seeking affirmation in commentaries and lexicons.

Once exercised almost exclusively in the study of theology, exegesis is, in the age of the internet, no longer the sole domain of theologians. Anyone using Google, Wikipedia, or other search engines for information and definitions, whether driven by scandal or interest in the origin or history of a text of Scripture, is doing exegesis. To recall the process of exegesis, one can follow these four "Cs":

a) **Context**—Who speaks to whom, where, what was said and heard (e.g., see remarks on Matthew 15:21–28 above).

b) **Content**—What is the purpose? Is it to inform, entertain, call to action, or persuade? (e.g., if Jesus loved Lazarus and his sisters as much as reported in the text, why did he stay "two days longer in the place where he was" instead of rushing to the side of his beloved friend? [John 11:1–7])[62]

---

[62] The official religious leaders, called Sadducees, didn't believe in the resurrection, the number one theological controversy, and taught that not even God could raise a person after three days. "Jesus permitted Lazarus to fall under the dominion of death . . . to demonstrate His divinity and to give irrefutable evidence that He was indeed the resurrection and the life . . . [and] to give crowning evidence to the disbelieving Jews that He was the Messiah, the Savior of the world" (*SDA Bible Commentary*, vol. 5, p. 1012).

c) **Communication**—Where did it take place, and was it private or public information? (e.g., the conversation between Nicodemus and Jesus was a very private one, yet John was able to report it, because Jesus apparently repeated it to his disciples. It appears that the retelling of this event ended at John 11:15, but when the disciples, like Nicodemus, couldn't understand the new birth of which Jesus spoke, his explanation to them was verses 16–21).

d) **Conclusion**—What does the content of the pericope mean to and for us today? This is where the preacher finally makes a contemporary, contextual application of the text to inspire the minds and transform the hearts of the audience.

Scriptures of all religions were written in the context of a particular culture and system of belief. However, as time passes, worldviews and the meaning of words change—so exegesis is not only important, it is necessary to understand the ancient writings of the Bible. The following four-part formula for exegeting a passage, excerpted from an article (now lost) by Andover Newton Seminary, has been very helpful in my own preaching and teaching homiletics:

a) **Common sense**—Start with the commonsense meaning of the text, that is, reading it as one would a newspaper.

b) **Critical sense**—Check out the insights discovered by others who have studied the passage's background and original language.

c) **Canonical sense**—Compare the findings with the rest of the biblical author's writings and the context of the particular text for consistency.

d) **Contextual sense**—What does the passage mean in terms of personal and contemporary cultures?

It is important to note that some traditional interpretations of Scripture do not necessarily have their basis in biblical exegesis. For example, the dominant view that Mary Magdalene was a prostitute (Luke 8:1–3) did not originate from exegesis of the pericope. Although Scripture tells us that Jesus cast out seven devils out of her (some of which could be lying, stealing, cheating, etc.), the Bible does not mention her as having a reputation as a "fallen woman." Pope Gregory reportedly identified her as such in one of his sixth-century sermons.[63] Unfortunately, the Christian church has adopted the unproven characterization of Mary Magdalene as subsequent preachers and teachers of her story have passed it on. One reason given for her designation as a prostitute derives from the fact that she came from the commercial town of Magdala, where disenfranchised and desperate women plied such a trade. Another is that Luke reported "seven demons had gone out of her." Because some consider them to be sexually immoral habits, therefore, she was apparently a fallen woman. But as we all know, not all demons induce or produce sexual immorality.

Great preachers not only conduct careful exegesis of the text, they also exegete the situation in which they preach, the audience or congregation, and most important, themselves and their denomination. Yet *exegesis of oneself* is the least taught subject in the discipline of homiletics. Volumes stress the importance, quality, and process of exegeting the text, the situation, and audience—but seldom, if ever, do they address exegeting oneself.

The great nineteenth-century preacher Phillips Brooks defined *preaching* as "truth through personality," adding that "the truth must come through the person, not merely over his [her] understanding and out through his [her] pen. It must come through his [her] character, affections, his whole intellectual and moral being. It must come genuinely through" her.[64] Whatever else preachers bring into the pulpit, "they always take themselves. It is always appropriate,

---

63 http://www.biblicalarchaeology.org/daily/people-cultures-in-the-bible/people-in-the-bible/was-mary-magdalene-wife-of-jesus-was-mary-magdalene-a-prostitute/.

64 Lectures on Preaching: Delivered Before the Divinity School of Yale College in January and February 1877.

---

therefore, for a preacher to engage not only in an exegesis of the text or the situation, but also of the self," wrote Stephen Farris.[65] He further noted that "an examination of one's character would be a wise precaution for preachers, lest our hearers say to us, 'Practice what you preach!' In principle, however, this is no different from the self-examination that is required in the spiritual life of any Christian (or, for that matter, any spiritually sensitive person)."[66] While the personal exegesis of the characteristics and tendencies that impinge most directly on his or her preaching is important, it should also include a review of sermons preached over an extended period of time, as well as timely evaluation by the congregation that he or she serves. This will reveal strong tendencies toward certain kinds of denunciations or pronunciations that the preacher needs to outgrow.

Like a person, a denomination has a dynamic life in which doctrines develop, are debated, and changed. Thus, the *exegesis of one's denomination* or tradition is also important. "The reception of a sermon is filtered through a complex web of personal and institutional history or narrative . . . Although a particular sermon may be useful in a considerable range of churches, especially of the same denomination or theological tradition, in extreme cases, even the intelligibility and certainly the relevance of the sermon may be at stake."[67] A great preacher will never neglect the exegesis of his or her denomination to ensure that the message and philosophy reflect its doctrines or, when necessary, is preaching truth to power.

In the last decade or more, the *exegeting of one's audience* has risen to parallel exegeting the text. Generally, most preachers give little, if any, attention or time to considering the context of the lives of the people to whom they deliver a sermon. But in exegeting the audience, preachers and teachers realize that faithful expository biblical presentation of the Word is inadequate apart from an ongoing understanding of their audience. For instance, if you are a preacher or teacher of the Word,

---

[65] *The New Interpreter's Handbook of Preaching*, p. 267.

[66] Ibid., p. 268.

[67] Ibid., p. 266.

ask yourself, "How often does the lives of my congregation enter my mind as I prepare to speak to them?" Do you think about what may be going through their minds as you present the Word of God? Perhaps the following tips might help in effectively developing your own style or manner of exegeting your audience.

First, exegete the audience before delivering the message. This is also known as exegeting the situation. If the recipients are not your regular congregation, ask the person who invited you such questions as the following:

a) How diverse is the audience in age, culture, and gender?
b) What are some of their main theological concerns or confusion?
c) How do they view preaching—as the main part or as worship itself?
d) What are the audience's needs?
e) What problems or struggles are they facing?

Such a conversation will also produce many additional questions.

Second, exegete the audience during delivery of the message. A sense of the congregation's history is important for effective long-term ministry. The speaker should be familiar with the context of the lives and the experience of the congregation in his or her parish. However, you will most likely encounter the following types of attendees at any given worship event:

a) Some are *seasoned believers* with deep theological understanding and who long for the "meat" of God's Word.
b) Others are *new to the Christian faith* and are wrestling through the more elementary principles of faith and practice.
c) Still others are *weak, wounded, hurting, and afflicted* Christians.
d) A number will have been *poorly taught* and received bad doctrines, but don't necessarily want or need correction.
e) And finally, some will have been *poorly treated* or are *wayward* Christians.

If all else fails, "preach to the suffering and you will never lack a congregation, for there's a broken heart in every pew," declared Joseph Parker, a great American preacher of the twentieth century.

3. Authority

Today's preachers are perhaps least aware of the significance of this third principle (authority) in preaching. The word *authority* comes from *exousia*, a Greek term that originally meant permission, to which has been added "that which is lawful, legal, the right to exercise power and strength with which one is endued."

It appears in the following passages: "But as many as received Him, to them He gave the *right [authority]* to become children of God, even to those who believe in His name" (John 1:12, emphasis mine). "Now the salvation, and the power, and the kingdom of our God and the *authority* of His Christ have come, for the accuser of our brethren has been thrown down, he who accuses them before God day and night" (Rev. 12:10, emphases mine).

Power without such authority will eventually become oppressive, but when it springs out of authority, it is always redemptive. In essence, any discussion of the Christian preacher's authority must begin with its negation, because it seeks not its own. Only Jesus had the right to publicly claim such authority and did so (Matt. 28:18). He amazed his listeners and baffled detractors with his authority (Matt. 7:29). Then he gave this authority to his disciples, both then and now (Luke 9:1; 10:19).

"Usually, when we speak of someone in authority," Thomas Long proposed, "we are referring to the possession of a certain kind of recognized and legitimate power, but Christian preachers (and the Hebrew prophets before them) have often insisted that they do not have such power, at least in the conventional forms. Jeremiah shirked the mantle of the 'prophet,' protesting that he was 'only a boy' (Jer. 1:6), and Isaiah cowered in the temple before the smoke-shrouded mystery, exclaiming that he was lost . . . 'a man of unclean lips' (Isa. 6:5). Amos protested that he was neither a prophet nor the son of a prophet, but a mere 'herdsman, and a dresser of sycamore trees' who had been plucked out of the pasture and thrust, without much to say in the matter, into the task of prophecy (Amos 7:15)."[68] In the words of an old-time African American preacher, such authority cannot be bought or caught, learned or earned—it is a divine gift (cf. Matt. 28:18; Mark 11:27–33; Luke 9:1–2; John 1:12). Listeners can hear it in the presentations of Christ's messengers and ambassadors, because there's a holy boldness in preachers empowered by the Holy Spirit to speak from and with the heart of the Lion of Judah.

Ten Basic Steps to Preaching with Authority

Almost every book on preaching worthy of your attention will include practical steps to preaching with authority. Here are my ten steps that will guide you in the preparation and delivery of effective sermons.

Step One

(a) **Prayer and Bible Study.** We cannot emphasize enough the importance of personal, extended time spent in prayer and silent meditation prior to studying a passage of the Bible for preaching or teaching. While reading books, articles, plus careful exegesis and consultation of commentaries will yield good sermons, starting with consistent prayer will produce great sermons. Oswald Chambers wrote that preachers must take time before God and find the highest ideal for a message, adding that we should never mind if we don't reach the ideal, but should keep working at it and never say fail because by prayer, work, and steady application, we will acquire power to do with ease what at first seemed difficult. He wrote, "The time a Christian gives to prayer and communion with God is not meant for his natural life, but meant to nourish the life of the Son of God in him. God engineers the circumstances of his saints in

---

[68] *The New Interpreters Handbook of Preaching*, p. 440.

order that the Spirit may use them as the praying house of the Son of God."[69]

(b) Preparation. Almost all preachers worth their salt[70] will attest to the fact that ten to twenty hours of preparation time will not only strengthen the content of a twenty-minute message but will produce a great sermon that leaves an indelible impression on the minds of hearers. However, it is important to remember that the most important preparation is not the sermon, but the preacher. And, by the way, if the preacher is not personally affected or influenced, even transformed, by the message, she or he should not preach it until this occurs. Otherwise, it will be like a tasty dish served too soon. Leave it to simmer until it's really done, and then dish it out to—in the words of another African American preacher—to "comfort the afflicted and afflict the comfortable."

(c) Proclamation or Delivery. Begin with an illustration that grabs the audience's attention. Speak clearly and articulate each point so that, no matter how diverse those listening, all can understand what is preached. Then end with an appeal based on ethical, social, spiritual, and other motivations that call the congregation to decision and action for Christ's sake.

After prayer and during preparation, start with an idea that you want to communicate. If there's no thought to develop, you don't have a sermon. Stringing a series of Scripture texts together does not a sermon make, especially when it comes to the following sermonic processes:

1. **Modification**—Sermons that ask and answer the questions of why, how, when, and where.

---

[69] Biblical Ethics, p. 46.

[70] Ancient Romans paid soldiers with salt that was valued as gold is today. If they failed to carry out their duties, others would say they were not worth their salt, and the opposite if they did—expressions still in circulation.

2. **Classification**—Sermons that allow answers to what and who, while discovering the nature, meaning, and identity of the subject.

3. **Investigation**—A sermonic process also called life situational preaching, it involves the examination of a problem to find an appropriate application from the context of the passage being preached.

Step Two: Select the Pericope or Preaching Portion of Scripture. It is vital to decide on the exact truth that the chosen passage is capable of addressing. For instance, if my pericope is 1 Corinthians 13:4–8, one of the truths it contains is "love." If the sermonic idea comes from outside sources such as magazines, books, life experiences, always test the concept or thought with Scripture. Remember, you must use Scripture itself, because (a) the Bible is the original and authoritative source of the gospel and (b) the Bible offers a wide range of moral, religious, and social truths relevant for, and applicable to, all generations.

However, texts can also be misused if they are (a) mistranslated (cf. John 20:17 KJV versus NASB or NIV), (b) only used as a launching pad for sermons or to prop up topical sermons, and (c) not used in their original, natural meaning.

A Few Dos and Don'ts About Texts[71]

Don't be clever. Never choose a text. Instead, let it choose you. When a text does exactly that, the Holy Spirit will impress you with its inner meaning for the moment or context and then will cause you to labor to reveal its meaning to your congregation.

Do be careful. Nothing discovered by anyone else will be of authentic use to you until you rediscover it for yourself. Never take an explanation of a text until and unless you see it that way for yourself.

---

[71] *Approved unto God*, p. 41.

Don't be controversial. Never select disputed texts for the sake of argument. The spirit that does so is boldness born of arrogance, not the fearlessness bred by grace. Never denounce anything that you know little or nothing about (1 Tim. 6:3–6).

Do be consecrated. Never forget who you are, what you've been, and what you may be by God's grace.

Don't be conceited. Conceit means that your own point of view is right, and you don't care what others think or say. That's being "wise in your own estimation" (Rom. 11:5).

Do be concentrated. Strenuous mental effort to interpret the Word of God may wear one out physically, but when one allows the Word to speak, it recreates and renews one spiritually. Great preachers focus on what the Word has to say, not on what they think it says.

Step Three: Determine the Subject of the Sermon. The subject is the broad, general truth to be discussed. It is "an organized and systematized body of ideas. It may consist of one idea or a combination of several."[72] A subject can be one word or a simple phrase. The purpose of the subject is to define and limit the discussion for the preacher, as well as to focus the attention of the hearer. For example, since, in step 2 above, I identified "love" as the truth in my pericope (1 Cor. 13: 4–8), it would be too broad, so I narrowed it to "God's love."

Step Four

a) **Determine the Topic.** The topic is a particular phrase of the broad subject you want to discuss. For example, "God's Love" is too broad for one sermon, so you must narrow it down to something more manageable that, when you preach it, the congregation can grasp the applications and meaning for themselves. Therefore, in this case, the topic should be "God's Transforming Love."

---

[72] *Classification in the 1970s: A Second Look* (rev. ed.), pp. 51–80.

b) **Determine the Title.** The title of the sermon is a label primarily intended to arouse curiosity and attract attention. It sometimes comes to mind before you select the Scripture, but more often develops after you have prepared the sermon. It can also be the same as the topic.

Step Five: Determine the Theme. Sometimes called the thesis or proposition, the theme is the sermon's gist or central point stated in one precise sentence. For example, since my topic is "God's Transforming Love," my theme would be "God's transforming love changes the behavior of sinners." The theme should (a) be clearly formulated before the body of the sermon, (b) appear in the introduction, (c) guide the structural development of the sermon, and (d) be echoed, though not necessarily stated, in every point.

Step Six: Construct a Transitional Sentence (TS). The TS serves as a bridge from the theme to the main division of the sermon. A kind of punctuation, it both unifies and separates the opening illustration from the main discussion. It always includes (a) the theme or proposition wherein the sermon is reduced to one sentence and (b) an interrogative or interrogative substitute that asks and answers four questions:

i. Why?—Interrogative substitute is "because of" (e.g., "God's transforming love changes the behavior of sinners *because of* principles in 1 Cor. 13:4–8")
ii. How?—Interrogative substitute is "by" plus words ending in "ing" (e.g., "God's transforming love changes the behavior of sinners *by adhering* to the *principles* in 1 Cor. 13:4–8")
iii. When and Where?—Interrogative substitute is "in which" or "at which" (e.g., "God's transforming love changes the behavior of sinners according to *provisions* in 1 Cor. 13:4–8, in which we find our lessons for today")

The TS also includes a *key word* that (a) is usually a noun in the plural, such as "principles, provisions, methods, reasons," etc.; (b) characterizes the main points of the sermon; and (c) appears in the TS, but never in the theme or proposition. While you will use only one key word in each sermon, not having one that fits all main points is a major error. Remember, people come to church frustrated, tired, stressed, and even angry. They need a bridge to help them cross from the daily routines of life to hearing God's Word.

Step Seven: Organize Your Main Points. This requires an outline, or plan, that organizes what you want to say in an orderly, logical manner. The outline also enables the preacher to keep different parts of the sermon balanced and assures its proper progressions. Besides enabling listeners to understand what is being said and where the preacher is headed, it also provides them with a needed emotional rhythm or cadence and aids them in remembering what is or was being said.

Outline Content

As in the discipline of writing books, so it is in the act of preparing sermons. An outline is absolutely necessary. The following is not the brief outline one tucks into one's Bible for outline preaching, but is what one prepares before writing the verbatim manuscript of a sermon:

1. Introduction: This lets the congregation know what the message is about and includes a *short story* or *illustration* that illuminates or throws light on the subject to help listeners interpret what they hear in terms of what they already know. Illustrations can be humorous (although the preacher should not try to be a comedian) or a personal experience that helps the audience to remember the message. Never use an illustration that attracts attention to itself or veers away from the main truth. Avoid putting yourself at the center of many illustrations, especially as the "good" person, or any that require too much explanation. Next you will present *the theme* and *the interrogative substitute* that completes the TS.

2. Main Discussion/Body: The largest part of the sermon, it develops the points, ideas, and applications. The ideal is to avoid points (i.e., triplets such as: Point one, the power of God; two, the presence of God; three, the person of God), especially in inductive sermons. But if you must use points, such as in deductive sermons, divide your main points into two to five, but no more than seven points. Remember, three points are the ideal, because the number lends itself to the long-term memory. Do everything to avoid sub-points.

3. The Conclusion and Appeal: Here is the portion of the sermon in which the preacher drives home the message with a summary underscored by a short story, a personal testimony, a verse from the pericope (avoid introducing a new text at this stage since there is no time or place for further exposition), a poem, or a song that leads into the appeal.

4. Characteristics of a Good Outline: (a) It has unity and centers around a central truth or theme; (b) it has movement that carries the truth forward one step further to the climax, but without repetition of preceding points; (c) it has a climax that gathers strength as it moves along, employing both reason and emotion and bringing listeners to the point of decision and action; (d) it has proportion, appropriating proper weight or emphasis to each point or application; and (e) if points are used, they should treat the subject adequately and not feature many sub-points.

Step Eight: Flesh Out Your Main Discussion. The labor-intensive part of sermon preparation involves reading the pericope in a variety of versions of Scripture and researching commentaries, lexicons, and dictionaries, as well as exegeting the text, searching for appropriate illustrations, and taking notes. In addition, the preacher must decide the type of sermon or style of delivery (see the chapter on sermon definitions) that he or she will use for the specific pericope.

Step Nine

a) The Preparation—Remember, with step 8, this takes about twenty hours of preparation (done over a period of months or weeks, not on the last day) for a thirty-minute sermon. The time has now come to write a full verbatim manuscript, so choose active and interactive words that will invoke pictures in the minds of the audience and edit, edit, edit until short sentences and vivid language characterize the message. Remember, just as it takes time to be holy, so also it does to prepare and deliver a great transformational sermon that embodies imagination, uses appropriate metaphors, and delivers with a timely appeal.

b) The Delivery—This is the highlight of all the work put into the process of preparing a sermon. The preacher should, like a professional singer, warm up his or her voice before delivering a sermon.[73] Speak clearly and articulate each point. Let the message determine and drive your physical movements so as to avoid pacing, flailing hands, nervously touching one's face, or grabbing the pulpit like a drowning person to a lifeline. If you are preaching from a manuscript, make sure that you learn the introduction so that you can immediately establish and maintain eye contact with the audience before focusing on the script. Since preachers, like comedians, make their living from words, watch the latter, but avoid those who use profanity and violent words. Learn from them proper timing, projection of one's voice, and the power of a word well-delivered.

Step Ten: The Conclusion and Appeal. The concluding summary of the sermon contains a call for a specific decision. The goal of an appeal is to (a) communicate the revelation of God/the gospel and relate it to the needs of the people; (b) urge believers to continue being reconciled to God and help sinners accept Christ as their personal Savior; (c) allow the Holy Spirit to use ambassadors of Christ in an alien world (1 Cor. 5:20) to stir the mind, emotions, and will of

---

[73] Check out the outstanding video in *Performance in Preaching: Bringing the Sermon to Life* by Schmidt and Childers.

every hearer of the truths of Scripture to become complete in Christ. Remember, not all appeals should require standing, hands raised, or coming to the altar. If you are a guest speaker, be mindful to defer to the resident pastor, because when people respond to an appeal, especially when invited to the altar, you should connect them with the person or persons who will be there after the sermon to minister to the obvious emotional expressions of their decision.

While many creative ways exist to end a sermon, I have found the following six most beneficial:

1. **End with a story**—Use one that sums up key points of your message or connects with the introductory illustration. Your personal experience is generally the best, but avoid the land mine of self-exaltation.
2. **End with an action**—Think of a symbolic action (something to touch, tear, or write on) that would reinforce the key ideas and applications of the message.
3. **End with a celebration**—It should be a crescendo of hope that gives a vision of God's presence and power over sin to empower the worshipper to face the struggles and trials of life with confidence in Christ.
4. **End with prayer**—However, avoid using prayer to add to the sermon, to correct its content, to preach a new sermon, or to chastise the congregation.
5. **End with a poem or song**—Avoid anything that will involve the addition of forgotten points or in any way delay the preacher from "landing the plane." And sing only if you can carry a tune!
6. **End with Scripture**—It should be one already included in the sermon. Do not introduce a new text at the end of the sermon.

The aim of all great preaching is to create what Walter Brueggemann refers to as a "moment in consciousness" during which

God enters into a dialogue with his people, using the preacher as a conduit in the process. It seeks to meet the felt, perceived, and real spiritual needs of the audience through the ministry of the Word. Such preaching will inform, persuade, and inspire the congregation to commit to Christ, to dedicate themselves to service to others, and to eliminate hindrances to knowing, believing in, and acting on Scripture (James 1:22; Rev. 1:3).

Great preachers do not speak over the heads of their audience, but they provide appropriate incentives, rewards, and motivations for their listeners to want to do God's entire will. Such preachers also use an appropriate balance of knowledge, emotions, passion, and challenges to motivate and keep the audience engaged; and they are never afraid or reluctant to speak prophetically as in speaking truth to power.

CHAPTER 3

Prophetic Preaching

When I mention to friends and acquaintances that I am writing a book on prophetic preaching, the first question I am usually asked is "What do you mean by that term?" If truth be told, that is a highly reasonable question because "prophetic" is currently used in church circles in ways that can be confusing and even conflicting.[74]

Prophetic preaching is a form of proclamation distinct from preaching biblical prophecy. To summarize the complexity of this definition, I must turn to other experts in the field. An overview of their dominant definitions will contribute to a more thorough explanation of this inspiring way of proclaiming the gospel, also known as speaking truth to power or challenging the status quo.

First and foremost is Walter Brueggemann, William Marcellus McPheeters Professor Emeritus of Old Testament at Columbia Theological Seminary. Almost all who preach, teach, or write about prophetic preaching take their cues from Brueggemann. "The task of prophetic ministry," he said, "is to nurture, nourish, and evoke a consciousness and a perception alternative to the consciousness

---

[74]   *Prophetic Preaching: A Pastoral Approach,* p. 3.

and perception of the dominant culture around us."[75] He defines "alternative consciousness" as the dismantling of the dominant consciousness of oppression through the power of God, who is allowed to be who he will be, as Moses did with Pharaoh in Egypt. On the other hand, "royal consciousness" consists of the entrenched political, economic, social, or religious powers that are largely "uninterested in the freedom of God." Royal consciousness occurs when a king or government sets up temples or places where they "confine" God, although he may be made accessible to or scheduled to meet those who seek him. Solomon, he claims, "was able to counter completely the counterculture of Moses when he countered: (1) the economics of equality with the economics of affluence, (2) the politics of justice with the politics of oppression, and (3) the religion of God's freedom with the religion of God's accessibility."[76]

In order for a message to be deemed prophetic, Brueggemann suggests it must be composed of two aspects. The first is *radical criticism*, which he defines as the message in which "the assured and alleged power of the dominant culture is now shown to be fraudulent." He also underscored the fact that "criticism is not carping and denouncing. It is asserting that false claims to authority and power cannot keep their promises, which they could not in the face of the free God. It is only a matter of time until they are dead on the seashore"[77] like the Egyptians at the Red Sea. The problem is, however, that "the Solomonic regime [and all future regimens of royal consciousness] was able to silence criticism" in two ways. "One is the way of heavy-handed prohibition that is backed by forceful sanctions (1 Kings 11:10)," and the second is that "the prophet is ignored" as the "royal" or ruling regime "develop[s] a natural immunity and remain[s] totally impervious to criticism."[78]

---

[75] Ibid.

[76] Ibid., p. 30.

[77] Ibid.

[78] Ibid., p. 31.

The second, which Brueggemann calls *energizing*, "is closely linked to hope." It rejuvenates the community to fresh forms of faithfulness and vitality in its ongoing relationship with God.

> We are energized not by that which we already possess, but by that which is promised and about to be given . . . Egypt was without energy precisely because it did not believe anything was promised and about to be given. Egypt, like every imperial and eternal now, believed everything was already given, contained and possessed. If there is any point at which most of us are manifestly co-opted, it is in this way. We do not believe that there will be newness but only that there will be merely moving of the pieces into new patterns. It is precisely the prophet who speaks against such managed data and who can energize toward futures that give genuinely new and not derived.[79]

He also suggests the prophet must speak metaphorically about hope, but concretely about the real newness that comes to redefine our situation, adding that there are "three energizing dimensions":

1. "Energy comes from the embrace of the inscrutable darkness. That darkness, which is frightening in its authority, appears here in the hardness of heart."
2. "In Exodus 11:7 there is a wondrous statement of a new reality that surely must energize when God declared, 'But against any of the people of Israel, either man or beast, not a dog shall growl, that you may know that the LORD makes a distinction between the Egyptians and Israel.'"
3. "The great songs of Song of the Sea (Exod. 15:1–18) and Song of Miriam (Exod. 15:21) are the most eloquent, liberating, and liberated songs in Israel. The last energizing reality is a

---

[79] Ibid.

doxology in which the singers focus on this free one and in the act of the song appropriate the freedom of God as their own freedom."[80]

To Brueggemann's two components of prophetic preaching (radical criticism and energizing, also described in African American preaching as protest and praise), I have created and added the concept of "Divine Directive," because a prophetic preacher is not free to challenge a status quo or address issues that may have their origin in his or her own angst, lack of early childhood developmental needs, or spurious complaints that he or she is too cowardly to speak about to power. Rather, the message must be the result of a divine directive with a "thus says the Lord," as it was with the prophets of old (Obad. 1:1).

Philip Wogaman, former pastor to the Clintons during their White House years, refers to prophetic preaching as "prophetic witness." He wrote that "to be prophetic is not necessarily to be adversarial, or even controversial. The word in its Greek form refers to one who speaks on behalf of another. In Hebrew tradition, a prophet is one who speaks for God."[81]

Dawn Ottoni-Wilhelm, Alvin F. Brightbill Professor of Preaching and Worship, Bethany Theological Seminary, stated that "prophetic preaching proclaims God's Word from within the Christian tradition against all that threatens God's reconciling intention for humanity and for all that creates and sustains a vital and necessary ministry of compassion to neighbors near and far." She adds that "because it is not exclusively either moral exhortation or predictions regarding future events, prophetic preaching envisions past, present, and future concerns within the context of the reign of God realized in Jesus Christ and empowered by the Holy spirit."[82]

---

[80] Ibid., pp. 14–16.

[81] *Speaking the Truth in Love: Prophetic Preaching to a Broken World*, p. 3.

[82] Quoted in *Anabaptist Preaching: A Conversation Between Pulpit, Pew, and Bible*, p. 77.

Marvin McMickle, President and Professor of Church Leadership, Colgate Rochester Crozer Divinity School, whom I have the good fortune of calling friend, affirms Brueggemann's definition of "royal consciousness," saying it "represents 'the deeply entrenched forces—political, economic, social, or religious—of Israel.'" Then he adds emphatically, "They are the status quo, and they only offer to people a vision of the future that allows them to remain in power and requires that masses of people remain marginalized in society. The work of the prophet," therefore, "is to combat that single vision and show that God can and will bring about a future different from that envisioned by the ruling elite."[83]

McMickle and his colleagues are not suggesting that a prophetic preacher is combative and is always in conflict with society, though at one time this was the general consensus about prophetic preaching. In fact, according to Stephen D. Long, "The assumption held by many preachers [was] that to preach prophetically is to side for justice against charity, to be prophetic against pastoral" preaching.[84]

The general homiletical consensus is that pastoral preaching is distinct from prophetic preaching. For instance, prophetic preaching is a divine directive that creatively speaks on behalf of others about the injustices and inadequacies of the present and the unfulfilled possibilities of the future, while pastoral preaching focuses on the nurture and indoctrination of a congregation. Prophetic preaching can definitely play some pastoral roles, such as speaking for the oppressed, articulating their pain, and giving voice to their concerns. However, providing a vision of a better world and confronting evil powers that would thwart it is part of the mission of both prophetic and pastoral preaching.

To correct the misunderstanding, "the following notions provide an alternative to negative assumptions about prophetic preaching: (1) the prophetic preacher stands under the community of faith; he or she is not set over and against it. (2) To be prophetic is not in

---

[83] *Where Have All the Prophets Gone?* p. 11.

[84] *Concise Encyclopedia of Preaching*, p. 388.

opposition to being pastoral. Prophetic preaching is the most pastoral of activities [because it focuses on the small and large concerns of the community]. (3) Prophetic preaching is never discontinuous with the past, but finds resources internal to the tradition of the community of faith to call that community to its true identity."[85]

John S. McClure, Charles G. Finney Professor of Preaching and Worship, Vanderbilt Divinity School, defined prophetic preaching as "an imaginative reappropriation of traditional narratives and symbols for the purpose of critiquing a dangerous and unjust present situation and providing an alternative vision of God's future."[86]

Leonora Tisdale, Clement-Muehl Professor of Homiletics, Yale Divinity School, whose book on the subject was my very first introduction to this wonderful method of proclamation, provides "seven hallmarks of prophetic preaching." These are "(1) Rooted in the biblical witness: both in the testimony of the Hebrew prophets of old and in the words and deeds of the prophet Jesus of Nazareth. (2) Prophetic preaching is countercultural and challenges the status quo. (3) Prophetic preaching is concerned with the evils and shortcomings of the present social order and is often more focused on corporate and public issues than on individual and personal concerns. (4) Prophetic preaching requires the preacher to name both what is not of God in the world (criticizing) and the new reality God will bring to pass in the future (energizing). (5) Prophetic preaching offers hope of a new day to come and the promise of liberation to God's oppressed people. (6) Prophetic preaching invites courage in its hearers and empowers them to work to change the social order. (7) Prophetic proclamation requires of the preacher a heart that breaks with the things that break God's heart; a passion for justice in the world; the imagination, conviction, and courage to speak words from God; humility and honesty in the preaching moment; and a strong reliance on the presence and power of the Holy Spirit."[87]

---

[85] *Concise Encyclopedia of Preaching*, p. 388.

[86] *Preaching Words: 144 Key Terms in Homiletics*, p. 117.

[87] *Prophetic Preaching: A Pastoral Approach*, p. 10.

According to these definitions, prophetic preaching is a homiletical genre in which divine authority is exercised in the mode, if not exact manner, of Old Testament prophets to (a) critically question the status quo; (b) speak truth to power; (c) offer biblical/theological insights into current situations; (d) challenge listeners to repent; and (e) exercise God's righteousness as well as his justice. It is the one method and style designed to immediately shift the focus of a community of faith from what may or may not be affecting their lives to what will ultimately do so. Prophetic messages also redirect the attention of listeners from that which is happening in their immediate existence to the wider society.

In *Where Have All the Prophets Gone?*,[88] McMickle reminds us that it points out the false gods of comfort, luxury, fame, and fortune; and it encourages worshippers away from a lack of concern as a brother's or sister's keeper. It seeks to lead believers to escape religious or social evils, such as narcissistic pleasures and materialism, that vie for and even usurp the role, place, and power of God in the lives of his people. Furthermore, it calls true believers to actively pursue justice and righteousness for every member of society, no matter what the personal cost. Prophetic preaching never allows the community of faith to believe that mere participation in the rituals of its religious life can ever be adequate substitutes for that form of ministry designed to uplift "the least of these" (Matt. 25:40).

Under divine directive, unction, and instruction, prophetic preaching must condemn those who exploit the poor, as did such Old Testament prophets as Amos and Micah. They condemned Israel for being focused on sacrificing animals and observing feasts and religious days while ignoring the economic exploitation and subsequent cries of the poor. For instance, God commanded the Israelites to hold sacred assemblies, observe the seventh-day Sabbath, and offer sacrifices (Exod. 12:16; Num. 10:2; 1 Chron. 23:31). However, the time came when, repulsed by the lawlessness of his people, God declared through his prophet, "Stop bringing Me your

---

[88]　See chapter 5, "When Prophetic Preaching Gives Way to Praise."

meaningless gifts; the incense of your offerings disgusts Me! As for your celebrations of the new moon and the Sabbath and your special days for fasting—they are all sinful and false. I want no more of your pious meetings" (Isa. 1:13, *New Living Translation*).

I was attracted to and remain passionate about prophetic preaching. Like Walter Brueggemann, "I am drawn to prophetic witness, in the first instance, because I believe that the prophets of God—both in ancient times and today—have been harbingers of hope, naming reality as it is and placing before us a vision of the new future God will bring to pass."[89] But where are the prophets to challenge the Christian Church today, to reclaim its God-given role of speaking truth to power while calling God's people "to do justice, and to love kindness, and to walk humbly with your God" (Mic. 6:8)?

In the words of Marvin McMickle, they are "off in other directions: Gone in search of mega churches, everyone . . . Gone in search of faith-based funding . . . Gone in search of personal comfort . . . Gone in search of political correctness . . . Gone into a ministry that places praise over speaking truth to power . . . when will they ever learn?"[90] He adds that they are also "gone" to emphasize just two "justice issues, abortion and same-sex marriage, while the poor we still have with us; while two million people are packed into overcrowded prisons." Furthermore, he asserted, those who should be sounding the alarm by way of prophetic preaching have strayed into ministries that place praise over speaking truth to powers. Such pastors, he reported, have either become "patriot pastors," who worship with upstretched hands in praise, but do not also become

---

[89]   Ibid.

[90]   *Where Have All the Prophets Gone?* p.8.

outstretched hands to lift a fallen brother or sister.[91] That, he says indignantly, is an abomination to God.

McMickle also opined that, while conservative evangelicals focus on their two-pronged agenda, chief executive officers are looting companies too big to fail, not caring that they are leaving workers and retirees in financial ruin. As important as the current two-pronged agenda may be, prophetic preachers must broaden their message to include the abuse of insider trading by politicians as well as the exploitation and fleecing of the poor by the prosperity gospel that has weaseled its way into the Christian pulpit.

Prophetic preaching in the twenty-first century must answer three important questions:

1. By what authority is the speaker preaching? Not only will the congregants know if someone is faking a divine directive, the devils will also recognize it. Therefore, a prophetic preacher must avoid being like the seven sons of Sceva. Remember, "God was performing extraordinary miracles by the hands of Paul . . . but also some of the Jewish exorcists, who went from place to place, attempted to name over those who had the evil spirits the name of the Lord Jesus . . . Seven sons of Sceva, a Jewish chief priest, were doing this. *And the evil spirit answered and said to them, 'I recognize Jesus, and I know about Paul, but who are you?'*" (Acts 19:11–15, emphasis mine). A prophetic preacher must be like Jeremiah (Jer. 1:9, 10), confident of his or her divine directive to speak truth to power and to present reality with authority, regardless of the personal repercussions.

2. What exactly is the content of the prophetic message? Is it dealing with trivial or difficult issues? Does it only address the recurring evil of racism and the continued existence

---

91 McMickle says patriot pastors are those whose allegiance is to a political party instead of God. A few years ago, one such pastor in North Carolina disfellowshipped nine members of his church, because they didn't obey him and vote for George Bush.

of segregation? Does it "lack substance," or is it "what Spurgeon called 'treacle' and H. H. Farmer, 'French lacquer preaching'"?[92] Does it have internal consistency and logic? "If the preacher has mastered Freshman Composition, the message may possess internal coherence, but externally, the sermon does not look to the rock from which it was hewn. It coheres to nothing."[93] Should one focus only on the evil acts of the royal consciousness regimes but fail to point the listener to the awesome redemptive power of the God who makes the crooked places straight (Isa. 45:2), that sermon may tickle the ears (2 Tim. 4:3, 4), but it will not bring about the salvific, energizing purposes of prophetic preaching. "The preacher may present a charming and literate discourse, but, because the speech does not emerge from or rearticulate the organizing principles of the church's life—its theology—because it does not offer the life of God in Christ, it suffers the same fate as the seed sown on the rocky soil. But in this case, its rootlessness derives from the preacher's rather than the hearer's lack of depth."[94]

3. Can prophetic preaching accomplish the challenge of preaching ethics? To do this, one must consistently filter observations and answer questions, such as the following, through theological/biblical perspectives: (a) Where have the people gone wrong? (b) What role did the leaders play in their error? (c) How have they turned away from God? (d) Where have they strayed from covenant living? (e) What can they do to restore a fractured relationship with the God who created and called them?

It is further evident that in our twenty-first-century Christian community, with its proliferation of denominations and

---

[92] *A Theology of Preaching: The Dynamics of the Gospel*, pp. 1, 2.

[93] Ibid.

[94] Ibid.

nondenominational venues of worship, there exist more false than true prophetic preachers. Such false prophets bring a whitewashed word that is compromising, superficial, and verbose. Prolific author and preacher Barbara Brown Taylor observes that they promise a smooth road that goes around the wilderness rather than one that leads people through it with its rough places and crooked paths. At one time or another, she wrote, "Everyone who passes through the wilderness of disillusionment passes through these places where the wild beasts of wrath and resignation stalk their prey."[95]

We must be aware that false prophets abound, because we have many cowards in the pulpit who use flowery language and threats to manipulate silent saints in the pews of churches that have disintegrated into groups of people, cliques that no longer yearn for a prophetic word. In such congregations, it seems as if the prediction of the apostle Paul is being fulfilled where he declared, "For the time will come when they will not endure sound doctrine; but wanting to have their ears tickled, they will accumulate for themselves teachers in accordance to their own desires, and will turn away their ears from the truth and will turn aside to myths" (2 Tim. 4:3–4). However, regardless of the situation, environment, audience, or intimidation of the "royal regime," a true prophetic preacher, like the ancient counterparts, will not mince words. She or he will boldly call the people out of their idolatries and false hopes, because the goal is redemption and the purpose is restoration in Christ. They preach about a God who is known by them, can be known by all, and who can be trusted in all things.

Strategies for Speaking Prophetically

As long as the struggle between good and evil rages on, ministers of the gospel will be divinely directed to preach prophetically, but no one can do so every week. Not only is it emotionally and physically

---

[95] *The Preaching Life*, p. 9.

draining, but those uncomfortable with its pronouncements will resist it, as in the Old Testament.[96]

Although the following will not eliminate such reactions, here are some helpful strategies for those who dare to follow the divine directives to speak truth to powers or challenge the status quo:

1. Preach truth in love, as did the apostle Paul (1 Cor. 13:2).
2. Preach the Word with power and passion, even if you know it's going to cost you dearly, as it did Stephen (Acts 7:1–53).
3. Allow God to speak through you, as he did through Peter (Acts 4:8–12).
4. Recognize that disappointment with your pulpit performance, and squirming in agony after a sermon is part of the process. It is the Elijah syndrome (1 Kings 19:1–4).
5. Avoid thinking that a prophetic message must always challenge an institutional status quo. It can be personalized to address the wretched excesses of materialism or immorality in a person, congregation, denomination, or society.
6. Remember, prophetic preaching emphasizes the importance of God's law and is energized by the good news of his amazing, abundant grace.
7. While prophetic preaching must produce change, we must not forget that such change requires patience because it is often slow and imperceptible in people.

Prophetic preaching is distinctive from preaching prophecy, although prophecy can be preached prophetically. The apostle Paul subtly underscored the difference in his instruction to the church (1 Cor. 14:20–32). Many scholars, such as Gerhard Friedrich, have noticed this distinction. Friedrich, when describing prophetic preaching or the act of forthtelling, noted that

---

[96] See my interview in https://www.ministrymagazine.org/archive/2011/07/prophetic-preaching.

primitive Christian prophecy is the inspired speech of charismatic preachers through whom God's plan of salvation for the world and the community and His will for life of individual Christians are made known . . . The prophet speaks out on contemporary issues . . . He does not say only what God intends to do; he also proclaims what God would have done by men . . . The prophet admonishes the indolent and weary and consoles and encourages those under assault . . . Through his preaching, he brings to light the secret of wickedness of men, 1 Corinthians 14:25. Since he speaks with a sense of God-given authority, he gives authoritative instructions, though he is not above criticism.[97]

On the other hand, those who have and exercise the gift of prophecy are foretellers, like Old Testament prophets whose primary element in prophecy is prediction or revelation of the future. Again, Friedrich explains the distinction, saying,

All prophecy rests on revelation. 1 Corinthians 14:30. The prophet does not declare what he has taken from tradition or what he has thought up himself. He declares what has been revealed to him. The *apokalupsis* of 1 Corinthians 14:26 is the revelation which is imparted to the prophet and which is to become prophetic proclamation in the congregation . . . Thus prophecy is very closely related to revelation 1 Corinthians 14:6, 30; Ephesians 3:5; 1 Peter 1:10–12. God is the subject in revelation, but only indirectly the subject in prophecy.[98]

---

[97] *Theological Dictionary of the New Testament*, vol. V1, p. 848.

[98] Ibid., p. 853.

While it is a biblical requirement that the predictions of those who have and exercise the gift of prophecy must be fulfilled to authenticate and validate this charisma (Deut. 18:21, 22), no such prerequisite exists for those who preach prophetically. In an article entitled "Speaking Truth in Love: Strategies for Prophetic Preaching,"[99] Leonora Tubbs Tisdale provides "seven strategies [five of which are mentioned below] that we preachers might employ to occasion a genuine hearing of God's prophetic gospel, so that people can decide for it or against it." They are as follows:

1. **The Importance of Trust and Speaking Prophetic Truth in Love.** Tisdale quotes Philip Wogaman (author of *Speaking Truth in Love*), saying, "If the whole point of the prophetic word is God's love, how on earth can that message be heard if it is not expressed in a context of love? . . . We cannot preach about love unlovingly; it is a self-contradiction." She also adds, "If prophetic preaching is born out of thinly disguised anger at a congregation, out of frustration with a congregation, or out of a desire to appear loving so that the message will be heard and accepted, people will know it. We can't fake love in the pulpit."

2. **Starting with the Familiar and the Comfortable, and Moving Toward the Unfamiliar.** "By starting with the familiar and comfortable, and then pressing toward the unfamiliar and the uncomfortable," Tisdale suggested, "we can allow people the time and the space to have their horizons stretched from inside out. And in the process, we can also establish points of identification with them that strengthen the bonds between pastor and people—even while prophetic words are being spoken."

3. **Using a Congregation's Own History as a Bridge for Forging the Way to a New Prophetic Vision for Its**

---

[99]   reflections.yale.edu/article/future-propheticvoice/
speaking-truth-love-strategies-prophetic-preaching.

Future. Tisdale relates how "one of the stories I tell in my book *Preaching as Local Theology and Folk Art* is about Tom Hay, a seminary classmate of mine who was at one time the pastor of a small church in a very conservative community in eastern North Carolina that was seriously divided by race. One week—during which the Gospel lectionary text was focused on the story of the Syrophonecian woman and how (as some commentators suggest) she pressed Jesus to expand the community of his ministry to include even her, a Gentile—Tom decided to use his sermon to address the issue of race."

4. **Standing with the Congregation Under the Word of God, Rather Than Opposite the Congregation Armed with the Word of God.** "Walter Brueggemann draws what has proved for me a very helpful and insightful analogy between preaching and family systems theory," Tisdale notes. "He says that in most church situations of biblical interpretation, three voices are operative: that of the biblical text, of the pastor, and of the congregation. Yet all too often, pastors team up with texts to 'triangle' against their congregations in preaching, leaving the congregation 'a hostile, resistant outsider.' How much better, contends Brueggemann, if the pastor stands with the congregation against the text, letting the radical Word of God offend both."

5. **Articulating the Opposing Viewpoint in a Sermon in a Manner that Is Fair, Accurate, and Believable.** According to Tisdale, "If we are going to tackle the position of someone who disagrees with us in a sermon, it is often very important that we state their position as fairly and as accurately as we can. Otherwise, we can easily raise the ire and the defenses of people who feel that we've diminished or misrepresented their points of view in our preaching."

Again, Tisdale said, "For many preachers . . . prophetic preaching is the most difficult kind of preaching we do," adding that some equate it "with head-on, confrontational preaching."[100] The bottom line is that prophetic preachers must be more than gunslingers (vigilantes or persons who act aggressively). While it is the responsibility of such preachers to "afflict the comfortable and comfort the afflicted,"[101] they must always leave the congregation with hope in the redemptive power and tenderness of God, as exhibited in the story of the father's love for his sons in Luke 15:11–32.

[100] Ibid.

[101] An expression widely used in sermons though coined in 1902 to describe the role of newspapers in society, http://www.dictionaryofchristianese.com

PART TWO—METHODOLOGY

CHAPTER 4

Preaching: Problems and Solutions

Suddenly, contemporary Christianity sales pitches don't seem adequate anymore . . . Our attempt to reduce this gospel to a shrink-wrapped presentation that persuades someone to say or pray the right things back to us no longer seems appropriate . . . We have taken the infinitely glorious Son of God, who endured the infinitely terrible wrath of God and who now reigns as the infinitely worthy Lord of all, and we have reduced him to a poor, puny Savior who is just begging for us to accept him.[102]

The profession or practice of preaching is a biblical mandate. In his final commission to his disciples, Jesus told them to "go into all the world and *preach* the gospel to all creation" (Mark 16:15, emphasis mine). Under the inspiration of the Holy Spirit, the apostle Paul wrote, "Preach the word; be ready in season and out of season, reprove, rebuke, exhort, with great patience and instruction" (2 Tim. 4:2). No other skill in the vast spectrum of communication allows one human being the power to influence the thoughts and transform the lives of listeners as does preaching. Politics is a close second, but

---

[102] David Platt, *Radical: Taking Back Your Faith from the American Dream*, p. 36.

its speeches tend to inform more than transform lives. However, modern preaching is not without problems for, as humans, we have all sinned and fallen short of the glory of God (Rom. 3:23). Year after year, men and women saved by grace through faith in Jesus Christ, from the power and penalty of sin, must preach to congregations who live in and under its presence and terror. Additionally, "every week, preachers stand before men and women who approach life through the lens of their occupations—either they are searching for employment, actively engaged in their work, or are retired from a career in the marketplace. Week after week, they hear sermons preached. Yet for many preachers and listeners, the pulpit seems to be a great distance from the factory, the retail store, the corporate desk, and even the unemployment office."[103] The sad result and reality is that nowadays, "preachers and listeners struggle to connect their worlds."[104]

I have personally observed many reasons for this situation and offer the following short list of seven problems, as well as potential solutions. First, the problems:

1. Poor preaching, resulting from lack of proper preparation, exegesis, Scripture, the audience, and one's self.
2. The tendency toward either the one extreme of entertaining congregations or the other of moral denouncements that lack the love and compassion of Christ for the human condition (Heb. 4:15).
3. The surrender to mediocrity by preachers whose sermons eventually numb parishioners to the value of excellence in preaching.

---

[103] Scott. Gibson, *Preaching Today: 6 Problems of Preaching on Faith and Work*, http://www.preachingtoday.com/skills/2014/august/6-problems-of-preaching-on-faith-and-work.html.

[104] Ibid.

4. Failure to consistently use language and articulation that really connects with and inspires the audience to act on what is heard.

5. Infrequent use of biblical hermeneutics to interpret Scripture, while allowing personal interpretations and human opinions to dominate sermons.

6. Failure to use tried, true, and tested foundations for sermon preparation or to focus on one single theme or big idea in one sermon at a time.

7. Failure to "land the plane" or end the sermon with an appeal so that "finally" actually means the conclusion.

This troubling condition of Christian preaching may well stem from the fact that preachers today have little or no awareness of its origin. A brief history of preaching reveals that it began in the Old Testament with God himself, when he spoke to the Israelites (Exod. 20:1–19). The Hebrew word *qara* (to proclaim, to call or read aloud) captures the essential definition of preaching or proclamation and is used when God said to Moses, "I Myself will make all My goodness pass before you, and will *proclaim* the name of the Lord before you" (verse 19). The message was so powerful the people implored Moses, saying, "Speak to us yourself and we will listen; but let not God speak to us, or we will die'" (verses 18–19).

In the New Testament, preaching was identified as discourses (extemporaneous speeches of a missionary type) presented by Jesus, Peter, Paul, Stephen, and others. In the third century, the homily (a brief oration or shorter version of a sermon) replaced the discourses as a way to avoid the lengthy, colorful liturgies bishops introduced to celebrate religious festivals and commemorate saints.

Origen, the great thinker of the Greek Church, is said to be the father of the sermon as a structured theological exposition and application of a specific text. The sermon emerged to refocus the worshippers' attention away from saints and religious festivals back to God. The intent was that, through the message, listeners would be drawn into a dialogue of the mind and heart with God and inspired to search and study Scripture (2 Tim. 2:15). Thus, early preachers urged, a sermon should embody a fluidity of movement that embraces relationships, expresses vulnerability, and enhances the creative powers divinely used to touch rebellious human hearts and point them to Jesus Christ, who alone can save (Acts 4:12).

Here are a few solutions to the various maladies cited above:

(1) It is evident that God uses many different ways to communicate with or speak to people (Heb. 1:1, 2), such as personal witness, tracts, Bible reading, dreams, and visions. However, his primary instrument today is preaching (Rom. 10:11–15) as an integral part of worship. As a result, each week, people gather with the expectation that, through the medium of preaching, God will empower and transform them. Thus rhetoric—effective persuasive speaking or writing using language designed to have a transformational effect on audiences—is an important pillar in the foundation of sermonic preparation and delivery. There are three principles, also known as the Aristotelian styles of rhetoric, woven throughout the fabric of homiletics.[105] They are as follows:

a. Ethos (Greek for "character") refers to the credibility and trustworthiness of the speaker/author. Often it is conveyed through tone, style, and the manner in which the speaker addresses or refers to differing views and opinions. Ethical appeals convince a listener by the winsome character and demeanor of the one issuing them, because listeners tend to believe people who are likeable and appear worthy of respect.

b. Pathos (Greek for "suffering" or "experience") is often referred to as emotional persuasion by appealing to the listener's/reader's emotions, because language and word choices affect our emotional responses. A better equivalent meaning is an appeal to the audience's sympathies and imaginations through a narrative or story that can

---

[105] For more details, see A. Resner, *Preacher and Cross: Person and Message in Theology and Rhetoric* (1999).

turn the abstraction of logic into something concrete. Joseph Parker, a late nineteenth-century preacher and author from England, is reported to have counseled preachers saying, "Preach to the suffering and you will never lack a congregation, for there's a broken heart in every pew."

c. *Logos* (Greek for "word") indicates the internal consistency of the message when it comes to the clarity and effectiveness of its supporting evidence. One accomplishes logical persuasion through the use of reasoning (both deductive and inductive) involving facts or statistics employed to support a point or position. Scripture describes Jesus as "the word" (*logos*) that "became flesh and dwelt among us . . . full of grace and truth" (John 1:14). The amazing part of preaching is that, through the spoken word, we as preachers have the privilege of proclaiming Jesus "the Word." Preachers also have the privilege of becoming the Word, "enfleshed," for their parishioners because the greatest sermon they will ever experience is a life lived consistently, compassionately for Jesus Christ.

During the beginning of preaching, these rhetorical principles attracted masses of people who sat for hours as someone expounded the Word of God. If and when they are omitted from preaching, proclamation sounds watered down, boring, and uninspiring, like lukewarm dribble. Proponents of such poor preaching run the risk of being spat out of God's mouth (Rev. 3:16) if they persist in the poverty of inspiration dogging today's pulpits. Despite such a dire warning expressed in the absence or avoidance of congregants from worship, a dearth of great preaching continues in many Christian churches.

(2) At the top of any list of reasons for poor preaching are (a) the lack of rhetorical competency and (b) the need to recover the original kerygmatic power of the gospel. For instance, Richard Lischer quotes Martin Luther as saying of the apostles that "before they wrote, they first of all preached to the people by word of mouth and converted them, and

this was their real apostolic and New Testament Work."[106] We must preach so that the Word comes alive to awaken or resurrect the living dead. As Richard Farmer suggested, our sermons should and must be so spiritually potent that they will "make the mummies dance."[107]

(3) Preachers must move beyond just being aware of the missing generations in today's churches to taking radical action, such as understanding the language of, and relating to, the diverse congregations so as to win back their allegiance to Christ and his church.

While larger congregations—such as mega churches with two thousand or more attendees on an average weekend—boast the best preachers and appear to be always thriving, smaller churches, which make up the majority of worship centers, are woefully declining, especially when it comes to the participation of millennial and emergent generations. Scholars estimate millennials (a title coined in 1988 as they entered kindergarten, anticipating their high school graduation in 2000) to be more than 100 million strong, eclipsing the size of baby boomers (1943–1960).

The emerging generation, also known as Generation Z, is in their teens and is so called because, even more than their millennial predecessors, they are deeply steeped in and influenced by the postmodern philosophy that rejects the truth and authority of Scripture as Christians define them. They have received the title "emerging" because no one knows what or how they will determine right from wrong in their consistently shifting worldview.[108] The result is that we have overlapping generations who have lost the ability to discern right from wrong because they have rejected the truth about the person, character, and nature of God espoused by

[106] *A Theology of Preaching*, p. 13.

[107] http://www.richardallenfarmer.com/product/making-the-mummies-dance.

[108] See *Emergent Christianity* by Phyllis Tickle.

"organized" religious groups, especially Protestants, all of whose authority they reject.

The various scandals that have rocked several denominations during the past few decades, as preachers failed to practice the strict morality they preached, may have led many to reject organized religion. Or perhaps their rejection has resulted from the fact that some in these generations test preachers by the amount of people they can attract at any given event, their reality television programs, or the volumes of music, books, and other articles they are able to advertise and trade in a culture where Jesus seems to sell more than he saves. To add to the problem is the pervasive absence of older generations who are able to attend Christian worship services yet seldom, if ever, do.

Where do absentee young people go for their spiritual development? The internet and social media suggest they show up at mega churches such as Hillsong in New York or Los Angeles, where the music is free and as good as that presented by professional artists in the music or entertainment industry. They gather in masses at large arenas to hear rhetoric in spiritual poems promoted by outlets like P4CM (Passion 4 Christ Movement) and other such organizations. To many who profess Christianity, Christians are "fake" because they do not practice what they preach and teach yet have the audacity to declare that all other religions are false.

"Americans today are more devoted to seeking spiritual enlightenment than at any previous time during the twentieth century. Yet at this moment of optimum opportunity, Christianity is having less impact on people's perspectives and behaviors than ever. Why is that?" asks Christian sociologist George Barna, who has done some of the best research on trends among Christians in America. His response: "Because a growing majority of people have dismissed the Christian faith as weak, outdated, and irrelevant." But he adds, "Interestingly, the stumbling block for the church is not its theology but its failure to apply what it believes in compelling ways . . . its failure to practice those truths."[109] In essence, to these generations,

---

[109] *The Second Coming of the Church*, chapter 2.

worship events in "organized" churches no longer offer inspirational, relational, practical preaching, especially in smaller congregations, principally because some preachers are overscheduled, overworked, underpaid, and have settled for the mediocrity of "good" rather than the excellence of "great" preaching. For more opinion on this matter, see also "The Death of Christianity in the US" by Miguel De La Torre, Baptist News Global, baptistnews.com. Therein he asserts, alongside many other strong sentiments, that, "Christianity has died in the hands of Evangelicals. Evangelicalism ceased being a religious faith tradition following Jesus' teachings concerning justice for the betterment of humanity when it made a Faustian bargain for the sake of political influence. The beauty of the gospel message — of love, of peace and of fraternity — has been murdered by the ambitions of Trumpish flimflammers who have sold their souls for expediency."

At the same time, technology, the internet, mass media, and social media—which provide instant information, in and at hand—have significantly and permanently changed the way we receive and process things, yet the church continues to use antiquated resources and insists on preaching from and praying in King James English. This condition is a major contributor to the troubling trend of low attendance at worship and the resulting paltry financial support of the work of the church by these contemporaneous generations.

Another contributing factor may be that the various missing generations embrace a postmodern philosophy and culture that rejects the possibility of objective knowledge and absolute truth. The result is that they are skeptical of truth as discovered in the Bible and proclaimed by traditional Christianity. Church growth statistics confirm this situation. They propose that 80 percent of young people who become Christians today do so not because Christianity is true, but because it happens to be the best thing to come along at a particular moment. If not ultimately taken into the depths of God's Word through Bible studies and powerful relational preaching, as soon as something appears that today's youth perceive is better, they drop out of the church. Consistently great preaching is therefore important, necessary, and significant in God's plan of salvation for this generation because Christianity, more than any other world religion, is a religion of the Word through which the human family is offered the gift of salvation.

(4) Twenty-first-century preachers must become familiar with a variety of preaching definitions, especially these three words in *Koine* Greek that underscore the meaning of preaching: (a) *euangelizo* denotes any message intended to cheer the hearer, to bring, declare, or show good news and glad tidings (cf. Acts 13:32; Rom. 10:15; Heb. 4:2); (b) *kerusso* means "to herald" (1 Tim. 3:16; 2 Tim. 4:2), "to publish, preach or proclaim" good news (Luke 4:18), while (3) *kerugma* describes the substance of what is preached as distinct from the act of preaching itself.

The common denominator in these words is the strong emphasis on the importance of proclamation. "The work of the apostolic preacher," opined Professor Edmund Clowney when explaining the significance of these words, "is described in contrast to jovial flippancy, high-flown speculation, sentimental gush, moralistic nagging, and a dozen other abuses of the pulpit. Nor can it be applied readily to such sermon substitutes as book reviews, interpretative dancing, feature movies, or baptized vaudeville."[110]

In his book *The End of Words: The Language of Reconciliation in a Culture of Violence*, Richard Lischer describes preaching as an open and public instruction in faith and behavior whose purpose is the forming of mature men and women. He writes that it derives from both reason and from "the authorities" we believe to be found in the Old and New Testament Scriptures. He also describes preaching as "a vocation of agony," adding that "Paul portrays the ministry of the word as a continuous action of being put to death and being renewed every day, as if pastoral care consists of thousands of mini-funerals and mini-Easters, moments of truth when this cancer or that divorce,

---

[110] *Preaching and Biblical Theology*, p. 20.

this breakthrough or that triumph, puts the crucified and risen Lord right there with us on the razor's edge of ministry."[111]

The problem nowadays is that preaching, once an art, has few masters or mistresses of it. Everyone is doing his or her own thing! Chuck Swindoll, profound biblical preacher and teacher, said—and I concur—that many preachers are simply talking in someone else's sleep. Some are unaware that, while speech is to inform (head knowledge), preaching is intended to transform (heart conviction) both the speaker and hearer. Consequently, we hear a lot of noise in the pulpit where preachers are pounding the desk to imitate passion and pushing emotional buttons with little or no convicting content to transform. As a result, congregations endure what Swindoll described (using Texas cattle as a metaphor) as "longhorn sermons" with "a point here, a point there, and a lot of bull in between." Tony Evans, prolific author and preacher, says a mist in the pulpit will inevitably produce a fog in the pew.

(5) One of the most profound solutions to the problems facing preaching is a greater realization of the importance of words in the art of communication. Preachers must recognize that preaching is a profession that uses words to paint pictures of the Word in the minds of hearers. Preaching is the form of verbal communication that mediates some structural understanding of the Word of God into the worshipper's mind. At the same time, it engages the heart so that the soul becomes aware of God's presence and his sanctifying power to transform the listener. Ellen G. White, prolific author and founder of the Seventh-day Adventist Church (also listed among the one hundred influential Americans by the Smithsonian Institute),[112] wrote that "the object of preaching is not only to convey information or to convince

---

[111] The End of Words, p. 272.

[112] http://www.adventistreview.org/church-news/
ellen-g.-white-named-among-100-most-significant-americans.

the intellect. The preaching of the Word should appeal to the intellect and should impart knowledge, but it should do more than this. The words of the minister, to be effectual, must reach the hearts of the hearers."[113]

Thus, preaching is a profession to which men and women are divinely called but ought to be academically trained in order to accomplish such a noble professional goal. Yet it is, perhaps, one of the few professions that allow untrained practitioners, without professional credentials, to perform the work of its trained professionals. Therefore, I recommend that anyone taking on the task of preaching should at least be self-educated by reading widely. If, however, as a Christian author asserts, the average American encounters approximately six thousand messages per day, why should one of them called "gospel" stand out? The answer lies in the words chosen to convey the message, because when it comes to great preaching, the significance of language and the use of appropriate, timely, descriptive words cannot be overstated.

Ellen White further wrote that "*God is offended* when His representatives descend to the use of cheap, trifling words. The cause of truth is dishonored" (emphasis mine).[114] Harold Best, former dean of Wheaton College, in a classic book on worship, said, "I believe there is a form of profanity that goes beyond our everyday definitions . . . It is taking language itself in vain, which is second only to taking the Lord's name in vain. Empty speech is vain repetition; exaggerated speech is vain repetition. Imprecise and sloppily crafted speech is vain repetition."[115] He asks, "To what extent do we Christians pledge ourselves to forsake verbal worldliness—taking language in vain—and discipline ourselves so thoroughly as to be able to go into . . . every societal setting to articulate, eloquently and precisely, what it means to explore the full counsel of God and articulate this to

---

[113] Testimonies to Ministers and Gospel Workers, p. 62.

[114] Ellen G. White, Evangelism, p. 210.

[115] *Unceasing Worship: Biblical Perspectives on Worship and the Arts*, p. 193.

a culture that has lost itself in meaninglessness?" Then he adds, "With what quality of thought and speech do we craft and deliver our public prayers, our sermons, teachings, and public witness? To what degree has the 'old tradition' of the fullness of prose . . . been forsaken in preaching, teaching, mentoring, and praying?" Finally, he underscores his response with these powerful, profound words: *"I cannot insist enough on the strategic importance of a speech-rich church to a speech-degraded culture"*[116] (emphasis mine).

(6) Be aware of the seven fatal flaws preachers should avoid in preaching. We, the messengers of God and heralds of the Word and divine will, have clay feet like the rest of humanity. But while we have many foibles and faults, we can avoid some of those flaws when we are authentic and possess an insatiable passion for preaching God's Word with his authority (Luke 9:1, 2). Here are seven of the many flaws we need to avoid in preaching:

a) *Proof-texting*, also known as taking a verse out of context or limiting a verse to only one meaning. It can run the spectrum from amusing to extreme irreverence, but it always fails to interpret and apply the Word of God properly. For example, in the report of a conversation between Jesus and his disciples on the road to Emmaus, Dr. Luke, the author of the Gospel that bears his name, wrote that "two of them were going that very day to a village named Emmaus, which was about seven miles from Jerusalem" (Luke 24:13). Almost every preacher, even those who declare their commitment to "progressive light," continues to say that the two disciples were men. Since we know that one was a man named Cleopas (verse 18), therefore, they claim, the other unnamed individual must also be male. However, the Gospels repeatedly note that Cleopas was married to Mary (the aunt of Jesus), who stood by the cross of Jesus

---

[116]   Ibid., pp. 193, 194.

with Mary, his mother (John 19:25; cf. Mark 15:40). Isn't it more feasible that Cleopas was on his way home with his wife, Mary?

If that raises your hackles, because you have been taught or have preached otherwise, note this statement: "There is no excuse for anyone in taking the position that there is no more truth to be revealed and that all our expositions of Scripture are without error. The fact that certain doctrines have been held as truth for many years by our people is not proof that our ideas are infallible. Age will not make error into truth, and truth can afford to be fair. No doctrine will lose anything by close investigation."[117]

To avoid the problem of proof-texting, we need to realize that good biblical preaching requires more than looking up and lacing together a string of isolated verses. An anonymous professor of preaching once said (and I agree) that "many applicational elephants dangle from interpretative threads."

b) *Being too literal* or making figures of speech too literal. It is, metaphorically, the result of putting furniture in rooms that didn't exist when the author lived or forcing contemporary lifestyle and objects into illustrations. To avoid this, remember that biblical authors communicated in a variety of ways, as we do, through metaphors, similes, symbols, and a variety of genres such as parables, epistles, proverbs, psalms, and prophecies. When reading the Bible, learn to identify the type of language and literature the writer is using in order to avoid a wooden literalism. If this concept is new to you, please see the upcoming chapter on "Preaching the Literary Forms of the Bible."

c) *Ignoring the Bible's culture and background.* In our postmodern age where many reject or deny the authority of Scripture, bizarre interpretations become accepted because people believe they have a right or responsibility to decide for themselves what a passage of Scripture means. One result is that some preachers ignore the Bible's culture and background as they decide what is truth for themselves. Others continue to depend on traditional interpretations rather than

---

[117] Ellen G. White, *Review & Herald*, Dec. 20, 1892.

exploring the results of excellent scholarship that throw new light on the background and cultural world of the Bible.

A good example is in the angel's message to Laodicea (Rev. 3:15–16). The background is that Laodicea was one of three sister cities, including Colossae with its cold springs (about ten miles east) and Hierapolis with its hot springs, much prized for their healing properties (about six miles north of Laodicea.) The water in Laodicea flowed through aqueducts from Colossae and Hierapolis, and by the time it reached the city, it was lukewarm and polluted by calcium carbonate. It is easy to lose the force and focus of the imagery used by Jesus about the function and utility of hot, cold, and lukewarm water without this background. For instance, hot water heals, cold water refreshes, but lukewarm water is useless for either purpose and can only serve as an emetic. Therefore, Jesus wants believers to be either hot with healing properties or cold and refreshing—but not tepid and barren, a condition that will cause him to vomit them out.

d) *Relying on faulty translations and unchecked traditions.* For instance, consider the belief that Joseph was an old man when he married Mary.[118] We have no biblical evidence to support such an assertion. In fact, the *McCintock and Strong Encyclopedia* observes that in Judaism, boys could marry and make religious vows, with parental permission, at the tender age of 14 and without it at 21. During the first century AD, it was a rabbinic requirement that boys must be married by the time they were between 18 and 21. Note the tone of consternation on the part of the mother and siblings of Jesus when he began his ministry at 30 while still single (Mark 3:31–35). It appears that the Roman Catholic Church's tradition seeks to substantiate and preserve their doctrine that Mary remained a virgin after the birth of Jesus by depicting Joseph as an old man.

e) *Reading our own ideas into Scripture.* To avoid this if we do not know or have access to the original language, we should read Scripture in a variety of versions, with particular attention to the

---

[118] According to the *Catholic Encyclopedia*, Mary was about 12 and Joseph approximately 90 years old when they married.

---

different words, grammar, and sentence structure of the same passage. This is especially important for Westerners, who often read and interpret Scripture as if it reflects a Greco-Roman thought and perspective. In our day of multiple search engines and the availability of interlinear bibles in Hebrew and Greek, as well as a proliferation of Bible software, we have no excuse for emphasizing our own interpretations without proper exegesis of Scripture.

f) *Thinking that any one denomination has all the facts or truth about Scripture.* More reliable Bible dictionaries, commentaries, and other resources exist today than at any other time in history. Remember, Bible study is both a spiritual and mental exercise. For example, Scripture instructs believers to "be diligent to present yourself approved to God as a workman who does not need to be ashamed, accurately handling the word of truth" (2 Tim. 2:15). Notice two points: (1) Study, think, and reflect for oneself, and (2) it is God who grants understanding (cf. Ps. 119:18) to all who ask, seek, and knock (Matt. 7:7).

g) *Failing to apply what we have learned.* Scripture promises a blessing for all "who read and those who hear the words of the prophecy, and *heed [keep themselves true to]* the things which are written in it [*heeding them and laying them to heart*]" (Rev. 1:3 Amplified Bible, emphasis mine). Note that God didn't inspire the writing of the Bible to fill our brains, but to transform our lives through living applications and preaching of his Word. Those of us who preach and present Bible studies must avoid being like a bad photograph (as in the old days when Kodak was king)—overexposed and underdeveloped.

Finally, to avoid these flaws and be a great preacher as a called and anointed servant of God, the preacher must possess an intense passion for Christ. She or he should have a genial personality, be lively, not passive, have a rich imagination, and love language. When it comes to a love for language, I often tell my students they should fall in love with words and romance them—treat them well so that when sent forth to do their bidding, they do not return empty or void. But even though words are important in declaring the truths of God, there is something even far more important. As someone once said, "Preach the Word and sometimes use words." Brennan Manning wrote, "What the world longs for from the Christian faith is the witness of men and women daring to be different, humble enough to make mistakes, wild enough to be burnt in the fire of love, real enough to make others see how unreal they are."[119]

As an anonymous author opined, a great preacher is a person who prepares his or her sermon as though it all depends on them and preaches as though it all depends on God. In his classic volume on preaching, Samuel D. Proctor, one of the great preachers of the past century, wrote that the essential characteristic of a preacher is not merely to interpret the past, foretell the future, or dissect the present, but to be a hearer and doer of the Word.[120]

John R. W. Stott[121] and other scholars describe a preacher as one who functions as a

Prophet (Hebrew *nabi*)—a mouthpiece or spokesperson of God (Jer. 1:5–10). This divinely ordained position has two important aspects:

1. *Foretelling*—as in the gift of prophecy demonstrated in the life and ministry of ancient biblical prophets and more recent Christians such as Ellen G. White.
2. *Forthtelling*—the preaching of a divinely anointed/appointed person who challenges the church and ministry by speaking truth to the powers of this violent, hedonistic, narcissistic culture and age.

Herald or announcer with the status of an ambassador who acts as an official messenger of his or her Master and King (2 Tim. 4:2; 2 Cor. 5:20).

---

[119] B. Manning, *Souvenirs of Solitude: Finding Rest in Abba's Embrace* (Colorado Springs, Co.: NavPress, 2009), p. 37.

[120] *The Certain Sound of the Trumpet.*

[121] See *The Preacher's Portrait: Some New Testament Word Studies.*

Teacher or resourceful presenter of God's inspired, relevant truths. He or she addresses real issues as well as the prophetic signs of the times with practical illustrations and applications, confident that God has all the answers and solutions.

Steward—a trustee, overseer, and caretaker of God's spiritual and material resources (1 Cor. 4:1, 2). She or he is never manipulative but performs with honesty and integrity, especially in the use of sermonic illustrations and commentaries.

Witness (*martur* from which we derive the English word "martyr") is one who has "heard . . . seen . . . looked at and touched . . . concerning the Word of Life" (1 John 1:1). John R. Stott wrote that "whereas a steward is a domestic metaphor that takes us into the house for the well-being of the household, and the herald is a political metaphor that takes us into the market place or street where she or he sounds the trumpet to gather people on behalf of the king, the witness is a legal metaphor that takes us into the law court of the world. There, Jesus is on trial at the bar of world opinion, where various verdicts are being passed on Him. The devil accuses Him with many ugly lies and false witnesses. The Holy Spirit is the 'Paraklete,' the counsel for the defense, and He calls preachers to be witnesses, to substantiate His case."[122]

Servant distinguishes himself or herself as obedient and faithful to Christ as he or she preaches and teaches Christ and him crucified (1 Cor. 1:23–25; 2:2).

Facilitator, or one who functions as a microphone in the conversation or dialogue between God and his people during the proclamation of the Word.

Poet, or one who speaks against the prose of the world.[123] By prose of the world, Walter Brueggemann, who created this phrase, means a world organized in settled formulae so that even pastoral prayers and love letters sound like memos. And by poetry, he does not mean only rhyme, rhythm, or meter, but language that moves,

---

[122] Ibid.

[123] *Finally Comes the Poet*, p. 3.

jumps at the right moment, and shatters old worlds with surprising and even abrasive language.

As long as God continues to entrust the great work of salvation to fallible humans, his church will have to face and solve problems. He has chosen to use preaching as a major source of guidance and solutions for those difficulties. However, the human preacher must interpret and expound the inspired text with such authenticity, authority, passion, and sensitivity that God's Word comes alive so that his people clearly hear his voice. Then, and only then, will they be persuaded to relinquish to God all rights to themselves through prayer and meditation on his Word.

CHAPTER 5

Preaching Definitions

Preaching is God's great institution for planting and maturing of spiritual life. When properly executed, its benefits are untold. When wrongly executed, no evil can exceed its damaging results.[124]

This book seeks to be a practical, user-friendly, resource of information to help readers avoid the pitfalls of proclaiming the Word of God in non-transformative ways. Therefore, helpful definitions of methods, forms, or types of preaching, plus the process by which the speaker prepares a particular sermon, is examined. This also includes the importance of distinguishing different ways in which sermons can be prepared and delivered, along with discussions of various combinations of methods, types, and styles as follows.

Expository Preaching. In the history of homiletics, almost every sermon has been taught, prepared, and preached as expository. Haddon Robinson asserts that all sermons are expository and wrote that "expository preaching is the communication of a biblical concept, derived from and transmitted through a historical, grammatical, and literary study of a passage in its context, which the Holy Spirit

---

[124] Unknown—quoted from http://www.christian-history.org/preaching-quotes.html.

first applies to the personality and experience of the preacher, then through the preacher, then through him to his hearers."[125]

Expository preaching is also defined as a method of research, form of preparation, and style of delivery. It opens up the meaning of a text of Scripture so that the preacher can apply it to the lives of hearers with passion, purpose, and power. It expounds Scripture by deriving both its main and sub-points from a specific text through a process of exegesis and interpretation that moves the ancient text forward with applications by the preacher to his or her audience. However, an expository sermon first covers the scope of the passage before applying it to the lives of the listeners.

At its core, such preaching is more a method or a philosophy that amounts to a set of commitments or convictions an expositor brings to the task of preaching. More than any other method or form, expository preaching promotes biblical literacy and leads to transformed preachers and congregations. It is, however, more than an exegetical lecture or discourse in that it is not a verse-by-verse preaching that squeezes every ounce of meaning out of the original biblical languages. Neither is it a commentary running from verse to verse without unity, outline, and pervasive drive. It is not pure exegesis that lacks a theme, thesis, structure, and development. Expository preaching allows the biblical passage to provide clues for shaping the sermon. In essence, it is not always a typically deductive three-point and proem method of preaching.

Textual Preaching. A miniature form of expository preaching that limits itself to just a verse, a few verses, or part of a verse (a sentence or two) or a chapter in which the speaker derives the subject and main divisions solely from the text. Involving a more intensive scrutiny of a limited passage, textual preaching is only a method, type, or form of preparing a sermon. Although there's no such thing as a textual style of delivering a sermon, it provides an effective vehicle for

---

[125] *Biblical Preaching: The Development and Delivery of Expository Messages*, p. 21.

1. exposition of some of the Bible's grand themes or statements, because it lends itself to more dramatic, rhetorical, and artistic development. It, however, does not allow preachers to turn elsewhere in Scripture for sub-points of a sermon and arrange them in ways that deliberately employ such artistic features as contrast, climax, storytelling, parallelism, refrain, and metaphor.

2. evangelistic preaching, because it allows a preacher to combine the benefits of exploration and exposition of a given text so as to leave the listener with a single passage that will serve as a reference point for reflection long after the initial hearing (e.g., John 3:16). Due to the fact that the passage is usually just one or two verses long, this reference point is something that a nonbeliever can grasp and remember. At the same time, as in an expository sermon, the preacher is free to cover key ideas with a variety of applications and illustrations.

Topical Preaching. This is also only a method, form, or type of preparing a sermon. There exists no such style of delivery called topical preaching, but it is the elaboration of a topic rather than a scriptural text or passage. Focusing on a particular subject or area of current significance, topical preaching has all the essential characteristics of textual and expository preaching, but it bears no analytical relation to any one particular passage of Scripture.

Topical preaching bases its message on two or more different biblical units that share a common subject and have at least three divisions:

1. Theological topical exposition that finds its subject in any subject addressed in the Bible, such as marriage, temptation, forgiveness, and so forth.

2. Biographical topical exposition that reveals a divine truth observed (for example, in the lives of Moses or David).

3. Contemporary issue exposition that finds its subject in the original author's intentional use of a biblical character as now

viewed in the context of current culture and then moves to Scripture to discover what passages address that specific issue, such as spiritism practiced by King Saul (1 Sam. 28:1–25).

Narrative Preaching, is also known as "the new homiletic." It is a method, type, and form of preparing a sermon that allows the congregation to draw meaning inductively without "preaching points" as the sermon unfolds. Also, it is a style of sermonic delivery as defined below. As a form or method, it presents a story—often a parable or series of stories—to dramatically make a moral point and convey divine truth. Points or lessons develop as the story unfolds. Because stories and imagery can powerfully shape us, narrative preaching taps into the wellspring of personal and communal meaning as the stories come to life through the power of narrative and imagination. Among the variety of narrative sermons are the following:

1. Pure narrative, in which the story is the preaching itself.
2. Frame narrative provides an introduction to the story in order to help the congregation understand its significance.
3. Multiple story narrative, where the preacher uses one biblical story to comment directly on another.
4. Fictional narrative sermon, in which the preacher creates a new story inspired by close reading of the biblical story.
5. Personal narrative, in which the preacher employs his or her own unique story or personal experience.

Prophetic Preaching. A method and style I revived in my denomination that is promoted by many homileticians as a highly effective means of reaching a twenty-first-century audience. It is an integral part of Black or African American preaching, as well as a powerful form of proclamation that exercises divine authority as it critically questions the status quo, offers theological/biblical insight into current situations, and challenges people to repent by presenting God's justice and compassion. See chapter 3 above for a more detailed discussion of this profound transformational preaching method and style.

Black or African American Preaching. Like jazz, the only music genre created in America, this unique method and style of preaching was born in America, raised through suffering, and today is copied, even mimicked, by many who seek to emulate the energy, imagery, alliterations, turns of phrases, and storytelling of this powerful, passionate, proclamation of the gospel. "It was the rhythmic use of language that enabled black preachers such as Martin Luther King Jr. to communicate the power beyond the literal word."[126]

Because it emerges from the experience of African slaves in their American diaspora, Black—or African American—preaching expresses, through protest and praise, the hope and vision of freedom from any sort of enslavement. According to Calvin B. Rock, "It's a homiletic art form born of faith, rooted in love, driven by hope, shaped in trial, nurtured by pain, mentored in suffering, and authenticated by time."[127] While elevating the centrality of the gospel and interpreting communal suffering, this method and style of preaching aims to teach, heal, and impart personhood to disenfranchised, discouraged hearers. Leslie Pollard, president of Oakwood University, wrote that Black preaching is "a unique sociohistorical method of pulpit discourse that was born, reared, and nurtured in the church of America's Black people."[128]

Biographical Preaching. Capable of being adapted to a narrative or expository style of delivery, this form and method focuses on a biblical character's life and traces his or her story through a number of passages. It can also explore a person or the preacher's story, from which the speaker draws out points/lessons from her or his own experience. However, the preacher should take great care to avoid giving too many details not germane to the salvation of others or

---

[126] Protest and Praise, p. 231.

[127] "Black SDA Preaching: Balanced and Binding or Betwixt and Between," *Ministry Magazine*, 2000.

[128] "Saga and Song," *Ministry Magazine*, 1995.

that may provide opportunity for worshippers to vicariously enjoy the fruits of sin.

Evangelistic Preaching. A style of delivery that seeks to convert large groups of nonbelievers to the Christian faith or to bring members who have strayed back to their previous faith. It is generally doctrinal in nature, using a more topical, deductive method of preparation and expository presentation.

Liturgical Preaching. Liturgy, by dictionary definition, is "a form of public worship, ritual, collection of formularies for public worship; a particular arrangement of services, a particular form of the Eucharistic service."[129] Unfortunately, today this word leaves the impression that anything related to liturgy involves a superior form of "stained-glass preaching" or "high church." Thus "liturgy becomes a negative word that implies worship is an arcane art that specializes in printed prayer books, set rituals, smells, and bells."[130] Additionally, "in contrast with defining worship as music only, some have regarded worship as preaching only,"[131] and this overemphasis or underplay is now part of the negative connotations associated with liturgical preaching. Because of the decade-long battles about "worship" that has led some to label it as "warship," liturgical preaching is needed today more than ever. Its importance rests in the fact that it is a method or type of sermon that explains the reason and intent for preliminaries and other aspects of the program during a worship service. It also underscores the meaning of ordinances or sacraments such as communion and baptism and why others, such as marriage ceremonies, are more often excluded from the main worship program.

Redemptive-Historical Preaching. A form, type, or "method of preaching that emerged from the Reformed Churches of the Netherlands in the early 1940s,"[132] takes into consideration the context of any given text within the broader history of salvation as

---

[129] *Preaching as Worship*, p. 41.

[130] Ibid.

[131] Ibid.

[132] http://en.wikipedia.org/wiki/Redemptive-historical_preaching.

recorded in Scripture. The "Bible is seen as the unfolding story of the coming of Christ . . . not as a collection of abstract moral principles, but rather as an anthology of the events of God's great works in history." Thus "the narratives are to be preached with a view of how the texts point to Christ."[133]

Illuminative Preaching. Also known as proems (preliminary comment, such as preface or prelude), illuminative preaching connects an apparently unrelated verse or religious question with a biblical festival, current cultural, or calendrical event.

Conversational or Relational Preaching. This genre of preaching is the most recent addition in homiletics and requires greater explanation. It affords preachers the privilege and challenge of proclaiming God's Word to a social and culturally diverse generation representing "every nation and tribe and tongue and people" (Rev. 14:6). This diverse contemporary community is generally categorized as composed of postmodern audiences, especially millennials. More and more, it is also being classified as the emerging generation, so called because they seem to know neither the Lord nor what he has done (Judg. 2:10). These internet-savvy, technologically literate, multitasking generations are generally disenchanted with organized religion.[134] If or when they attend church, they prefer interactive sermons with short, pithy phrases they can text and tweet to their friends and followers. Thus the importance of conversational or relational style of preaching.

It is notable that conversational or relational preaching is a risky endeavor that does not fit the demeanor or delivery style of every preacher because it reflects the manner in which most people communicate and use less of a loud, booming "preacher" tone. It is therefore generally referred to as "heightened conversation,"

---

[133] Ibid.

[134] In an article entitled "Relational Preaching: Conversation and Collaboration in the Postmodern Sermon (www.ministrymatters.com), Mary S. Scrifres proposed that emergent audiences are usually comfortable with the idea that truth is relative and that truth is more likely to emerge within the community than through one designated preacher.

meaning the "heightening" (not changing) of one's normal speech to communicate the biblical message. It is risky if or when the dialogue with the congregation becomes a debate, but is effective when another preacher or appropriately appointed person dialogues about a Scripture passage with the main preacher while drawing the worshippers into the conversation.

There are four types of relational preaching:

1. *The Teaching Sermon.* It uses many of the techniques noted for manuscript preachers, with the added freedom of observing and responding to listeners during the delivery.

Most teaching sermons involve a passage of Scripture or doctrinal issue the preacher explores or unfolds for the congregation. Since great teachers are good conversationalists and incredibly attentive to the reactions of their students, relational preachers are encouraged to use their freedom and techniques, such as paying attention to listeners and responding to their body language, to transform presentations from a lecture to a conversational mode. For instance, if the preacher notices a lot of raised eyebrows or wrinkled foreheads expressing confusion or concern, he or she should step back and restate the point in a new way. When the listeners' attention begins to wane, the speaker should recognize that they've learned as much as they are capable for that time and wind down the lesson.

2. *The Interactive Sermon.* The preacher asks questions of and invites responses from the congregation during the course of the sermon.

Walking among the people is a visual way of including them in the sermonic moment. However, these interactions must be managed with great care to remember the speaker is still the preacher with enormous power. Therefore, teasing can feel like bullying, and questions can seem like threats. The interactive preacher can ease some of these tensions by occasionally sitting on a stool or bringing himself/herself down to the audience's physical level. Questions and responses of the listeners are to be woven into the sermon as it evolves. The interactive preacher also listens as much as she or he talks so the sermon becomes more conversation and less "preachy."

3. *The Conversational Sermon.* Although this can be effective in large settings, it is easiest in small groups.

The congregation sits in a semicircle and listens as the preacher introduces the topic and Scripture. The conversation ensues more like that of a book club or study group. The preacher becomes the facilitator, offering wisdom from research or expositions from beforehand as the listeners wrestle with the subject matter. Even as he or she shares insights, there's expectation that additional or even new wisdom will emerge from the group as the Spirit speaks through the gathered community.

4. *The Questioning Sermon.* This is an effective conversational method when preaching to new Christians or seekers who are exploring various spiritual paths.

The worship service should be designed so that there's ample time to review questions and reflect for a few moments. The message time then centers on the questions and comments from the congregation. The preacher who uses this style must be familiar with Scripture in anticipation of potential questions or responses. Conversational or relational preaching is not for everyone, but it is another exciting way of communicating God's holy Word. Allowing conversation into preaching encourages new connections between listeners, preachers, Scripture, culture, and church.

Transformational Preaching. Promoted primarily by women preachers in the beginning of their public proclamation of the Word, transformational preaching emphasizes more of the speaker's responsibility to make the sermon an indelible, persuasive event that results in changes in the listener's heart, mind, and eventually, lifestyle. It conveys the commonly held belief that a sermon should be an experience that transforms the worshipper through life-situational preaching. Also, it embodies the fluidity of movement that embraces relationality, vulnerability, and all that enhances the creative powers and processes of preaching through the personal testimony of the speaker.

System-Sensitive Preaching.[135] Focusing on the vast differences that exist in the manner in which Christians process and approach ecclesiology and soteriology, it seeks to employ the eight categories of how humans handle information, especially religious materials, and can often raise one's ministry and preaching from despair to inspirational.

The Deductive Sermon. The oldest of preaching methods, "usually begins with a premise or an accepted truth out of which the preacher unpacks significance for the listeners. That is, the preacher states the main idea near the beginning and then develops that idea through the rest of the sermon. A deductive sermon is logical and linear as it develops a concept. Its reasoning begins with a general proposition and moves to the particulars."[136] While deductive preaching is best used when presenting doctrines of one's denomination or tradition, it can be more susceptible to the reading into or proof-text method of expounding Scripture. For example, the preacher may focus on certain Scriptures and interpret them in line with the views or traditions of his or her community of faith. Therefore, the sermon starts with a conclusion supporting that belief, then finds proof in the text while telling the listener what to do or believe. "In this day and age of narrative preaching, however,

---

[135] For more on this innovative concept regarding the eight concepts of systems thinking, see *Systems Sensitive Leadership: Empowering Diversity Without Polarizing the Church* by Michael C. Armour & Don Browning.

[136] *The New Interpreters Handbook of Preaching*, p. 375.

deductive sermons have fallen on hard times."[137] The result is that many preachers reject it or speak of it in pejorative terms. However, deductive sermons should not be abandoned out of hand, for they are invaluable when it comes to impressing the minds of hearers with biblical doctrines (2 Tim. 3:16).

The Inductive Sermon. Introduced by Fred Craddock during the 1970s in his classic volume *As One Without Authority*, it is a welcome alternative to the propositional deductive sermon that dominated preaching up until that time. "An inductive sermon based on a biblical text leads the hearer through form and movement on a journey of discoveries toward the answer to the question "What does this text mean for us today?"[138] An inductive sermon is often described as one "that begins with the specifics of experience and ends with a general conclusion" in contrast to "a deductive sermon [that] begins with a conclusion and supports it with specifics from experience and Scripture."[139]

Inductive sermons bring facts or evidence from the text that allows the listener to discover the application along with the preacher, leaving a personal, lasting impression. This involves the following:

a) Observation that approaches a text as a detective or FBI—Faithful Bible Investigator—with a magnifying-glass focus on Scripture, asking "What do I see?" while considering its context.

b) Interpretation, or what does it mean to the people by focusing on the content of the pericope.

c) Correlation, or how does this relate to the rest of Scripture in concert with the rule for Bible study expressed as "precept upon precept, precept upon precept, line upon line, line upon line, here a little, there a little" (Isa. 28:10).

---

[137] Ibid.

[138] Ibid., p. 390.

[139] Ibid.

d) Application, or what does it mean to me/us in a dynamic conclusion that engages "between text, preacher, and hearer, in which hunches are tested and played out through experience in a quest for the discovery of a biblical truth."[140]

Sermon Delivery Styles

Although various methods mentioned above do incorporate some particular styles of delivery, such as expository preaching, it is worthy of specific attention because it includes an interesting variety.

a) **The narrative delivery** emerged during the twentieth century with the advent of women in the pulpit. A single speaker who assumes the persona of a biblical character in a dramatic presentation is also referred to as a monological style of preaching. Often, preachers who use this style will enhance the sermon by wearing costumes appropriate to the period of the text and/or by using ancient artifacts to illustrate sermonic content.

b) **Extemporaneous delivery** of a sermon means it is impromptu—done without specific previous study and/or preparation. Having continuously and consistently studied Scripture, the preacher relies on the promise of Jesus that you shouldn't "worry beforehand about what you are to say, but say whatever is given you in that hour, for it is not you who speak, but it is the Holy Spirit" (Mark 13:10).

c) **Manuscript preaching style** employs verbatim notes (written word-for-word as the preacher would speak). Some outstanding preachers of the past—such as Spurgeon, Whitfield, and Martin Luther King Jr.—were manuscript preachers most of the time. Excellent preachers like the late Fred Craddock and contemporary pulpiteers such as Calvin Butts or Thomas Long use manuscripts for the majority of

---

[140] Ibid., pp. 390, 391.

their sermons, while demonstrating adeptness at occasional extemporaneous preaching.

d) The use of manuscripts strengthens one's grammar, literary, and writing skills while preserving the material for future publication and posterity. The danger, however, in using this style is that one can become bound to the manuscript and instead of preaching its content, will read it like a lecture.

e) **Memorization style** of delivery is exactly what the word indicates, because the practitioner writes a manuscript then commits it to memory, word for word. Although I sometimes use this style when I am nervous about speaking to some audiences—such as my fellow preachers, or professors who are trained to dissect and evaluate a sermon—I have observed a distinct weakness among those who consistently use this style. The delivery eventually becomes theatrical, lacking the authenticity of a natural speaking voice, or the demeanor of the preacher appears wooden and disconnected from the congregation.

f) **Noteless style** is preaching a thoroughly written sermon without taking the manuscript or notes into the pulpit. The speaker is not concerned about reproducing the sermon word for word. "The speaker without notes must have two things entirely at his [her] command—the Bible and his [her] mother tongue."[141] The danger inherent in this style is that the preacher often forgets important points intended to inspire the audience and is often tempted to tack such points at the end of the sermon or in a closing prayer.

g) **Outline delivery** style includes both memorization and extemporaneous preaching from a careful summary of the sermon that highlights the main points. I often write my outline on Post-it notepaper, then stick it to the page of the chapter of my pericope. It gives the appearance that one is preaching extemporaneously and provides maximum opportunity for good eye contact with the audience.

---

[141] *Disciples Indeed,* p. 52.

Notable Homiletic Terminologies

Preaching and singing are peas from the same pod, because they both use vocal cords to deliver the sound of words. Like professional singers, preachers should pay persistent attention to the protection, warm-up before use, and preservation of the voice—for no matter how great the content of a sermon, without clear vocal communication or expression, the delivery will be a dismal failure.

Rhythm and Cadence

Just as the human body functions by the rhythm of a heartbeat, so the preacher must deliver a sermon with recurrent, measured movement called rhythm or pattern of speech. Rhythm, suggests Michael Spencer, is "the 'residue' that gives preaching motion and momentum."[142] All styles of preaching must resonate with rhythm. The cadence of language, on the other hand, is a spontaneous, authentic flow of a sequence of sounds that involves a slight falling in pitch and general modulation of the voice more evident in Black or African American preaching, often with background organ accompaniment. Cadence is the tempo, pulse, and pace of the preacher's words that leaves room for the insertion of responses from the congregation. African American preachers of yesteryear described it thus: "You start low, go slow, climb higher, strike fire, then sit down in the storm."[143] Such cadence is a rhetorical device that employs well-known turns of phrases from everyday experience to paint pictures and bring the ancient texts to life. This often occurs through the expansion of syllables, with several tones corresponding to one syllable as the preacher presses to feel the emotions of words that transmit the vitality of the communication.

---

[142]   *Protest and Praise*, p. 150.

[143]   "The Musicality of Black Preaching: Performing the Word," in *Performance in Preaching*, p. 192.

Alliteration and Affectation

Dictionaries describe alliteration as the commencement of two or more stressed syllables of a word group either with the same sound or sound group. Consonantal alliteration uses words that begin with the same sound, such as "pulpit presence," while vocalic alliteration employs vowel sounds that may differ from syllable to syllable, such as "boys to men." By means of picturesque exegesis, attention to alliteration, storytelling, and masterful turns of phrases, the preacher can grip the congregation's attention and hold it in rapt suspense without prompting them to respond throughout the preaching moment.

Affectation is any artificial action, gesture, or speech; pretentious feelings; or movement designed and delivered to impress or manipulate an audience. It is evident in preaching when someone copies the vocalization, stage presence, and posture of another, especially an iconic preacher. Why, I often ask, would one strive to be even a good copy when the alternative is to be an authentic original? By all means, when preaching, we must avoid any behavior that is not natural to us or not genuinely felt, because it indicates an affinity toward mediocrity.

Illustration and Humor

To illustrate something is to illuminate or throw light on a subject in order to help an audience interpret what they hear and see in terms of what they already know from personal experience. In addition, illustrations help others to remember the message.

Jesus was an exceptional user of illustrations. He spoke of familiar things—such as bread, salt, light, water, patches of old cloth, a man digging for treasure, fishing, and farmers sowing seeds. The range of possible illustrations—such as stories, quotations, charts, pictures, graphs, and hands-on things—is endless. But one should be cautious when using illustrations. For instance, (a) never tack on one that has no relevancy to the message, and (b) never use an illustration that attracts attention to itself and away from the main truth. The preacher's personal stories or testimonies are the best illustrations. However, when doing so, avoid (a) putting yourself as the "good person," at the center of too many of them; (b) illustrations that require too much explanation; and (c) using too many PowerPoint or video clips during the sermon.

Richard Lischer describes the increasing dependence on technology as "The Gospel of Technology." He notes that the overuse "of such media serves to associate the sermon (and church and preacher) with the glamour, power, and authority of the same technology that rules the world." He asserted that "the retreat from the word was fueled by the ideology of a newly professionalized culture and the personal insecurities of the minister . . . [in] successful churches whose members would never dream that the light-shows, videos, and PowerPoint presentations that accompany the Sunday sermon represent a fundamental lack of confidence in the spoken word of God."[144]

Great preaching also employs humor—that is, good humor—to communicate the gospel and sometimes inspire laughter because "for the sorrowing, every day is evil; for the joyous heart, it is festival always" (Prov. 15:15). However, "laughter that is not the laughter of a childlike heart right with God can be terrible; it can be the laugh of scorn or ridicule or delight in evil. Such laughter is as the crackling of burning thorn. But the laughter of the joy-filled child of God is a delight to behold."[145]

While humor is an important part of human development, preachers must never strive to be comedians in the pulpit, although we should learn the art of timing and delivery from experts who make their living solely from the spoken word. Good humor—one of those qualities better experienced than defined—can be described as unaffected graciousness and sincere friendliness communicated

---

[144] *The End of Words*, p. 198.

[145] *Not Knowing Where*, p. 93.

through smiles, storytelling, and a general demeanor of pleasantness. Brennan Manning notes:

> Effectiveness in the ministry is enhanced by good humor. Through good humor, a Christian triumphs over the subtle form of egotism that would make him pose as a martyr or at least a victim. That makes him want to be noticed, consoled, or placed on a pedestal. And it makes community life richer and more delightful. Paul called good humor a charism and exhorted the Christian community in Philippi to manifest it: "Rejoice in the Lord always! Rejoice! Everyone should see how unselfish you are. The Lord is near. Dismiss all anxiety from your minds. Present your needs to God in every form of prayer and in petitions full of gratitude. Then God's own peace, which is beyond all understanding, will stand guard over your hearts and minds, in Christ Jesus" (Phil. 4:4–7).[146]

Verbal and Reading Punctuation

Punctuation is defined in dictionaries as "the practice or system of using certain conventional marks, spacing, signs, characters, and certain typographical devices as aids to the understanding and correct reading, both silently and aloud, of handwritten and printed texts." It is almost always used in reference to *reading*, and I am appalled at the very poor attention given to the reading of Scripture during public worship. Many readers do not practice reading a text before appearing before the congregation, where they mispronounce, misinterpret, and misrepresent the living Word. I always insist that anyone invited to read Scripture during worship, especially for the first time, either practices with me beforehand or demonstrates to me their proficiency prior to the moment of presentation.

---

[146] *Souvenirs of Solitude*, p. 105.

Verbal punctuation, or oral indications of emphasis, is the underscoring of a word or thought when reading. It is even more important in a sermon when introducing a new paragraph, sentence, and scene. The preacher accomplishes this through intonation, pitch, and pauses. Its lack is one of the most prevalent weaknesses in much of oral presentations nowadays. It can be corrected or improved by watching and learning from great orators, whether in politics or religion.

Voice Modulation and Projection

In music, modulation includes the change of key, pitch, or volume or the sound of a person's voice. Likewise, in preaching, modulation occurs when the preacher exercises control or adjusts what he or she is expressing by lowering the voice to a soft stage whisper in order to make a thought or statement more dramatic, emphatic, or mysterious—then raising it with dramatic fervor. Modulation in speech is like the natural gait of a horse that begins with the walk, increases to a trot, then a canter, and picks up speed into a gallop as the delivery reaches its crescendo or climax, also known as the moment of celebration in a sermon.

Voice projection, as in singing, indicates the strength of speaking, the passion applied to each word or sentence so that communication is clear, whether delivery is soft or loud. Breathing techniques, such as air flowing from the expansion of the diaphragm with well-balanced exhalation, is essential for proper voice projection. To accomplish this, preachers should direct their voice at the person(s) in the very back of the audience or room, not just by raising the volume but by throwing the voice, like a ventriloquist, in that direction.[147]

Voice Care

I cannot emphasize enough the importance of a preacher taking care of his or her voice just as professional singers do theirs. In a July

---

[147] For more details, see *Vocal Technique: A Guide for Conductors, Teachers, and Singers* by Julia Davids and Stephen LaTour.

2010 article entitled "How to Care for Your Voice: Eight Practical Suggestions for Preachers," Derek Morris stated that "most of us received little or no instruction in voice care during our college or seminary training. Many of our preaching professors assumed we all knew how to take care of our voices. They were wrong . . . Your voice is a miracle of creative genius. Your vocal cords are quite small . . . Your vocal cords vibrate hundreds of times per second when speaking. Continuous misuse or abuse will damage them, and sometimes that damage becomes permanent."[148]

In addition to this outstanding article, I also recommend the DVD that accompanies the volume *Performance in Preaching: Bringing the Sermon to Life (Engaging Worship)*. It not only offers some unique sermon delivery instructions, the DVD also features a variety of professionals demonstrating some of the best ways for preachers to protect and care for their voice.

Voice care should also include the correction of any idiosyncrasies of speech, dialects, and tone. For instance, "a short, discordant squeak, like a rusty pair of scissors, is to be gotten rid of at all hazards; so also is a thick, inarticulate utterance in which no word is complete, but nouns, adjectives, and verbs are made into a kind of hash."[149]

I once read, and I believe you would agree, that a vanilla one-flavor-fits-all voice is boring. It turns listeners off, while an expressive, energized voice keeps them tuned in and attentive. My recommendation for the best care and energizing of one's voice is to consult a communications expert and take classes or attend workshops or lessons from a professional vocal teacher/coach or check the variety of offerings on YouTube. I can personally attest to the value of such a move. Not only will your preaching be great, but also, your voice will last for as long as you need it.

[148] https://www.ministrymagazine.org/archive/2010/07-august/ how-to-care-for-your-voice.

[149] *Hints on the Voice for Young Preachers* by C. H. Spurgeon, http://www. spurgeon.org/s_and_t/voice.htm.

CHAPTER 6

Preaching the Literary Forms of the Bible

The Bible is not a book for the faint heart—it is a book full of all the greed and glory, violence and tenderness, sex and betrayal that befits humans. It is not the collection of pretty little anecdotes mouthed by pious little church mice—it does not so much nibble at our shoe leather as it cuts to the heart and splits the marrow from the bone. It does not give us answers fitted to our small-minded questions, but truth that goes beyond what we even know to ask.[150]

The Bible is a treasury or library of sixty-six books written during a period of almost two thousand years by forty divinely inspired, different authors. They hailed from three continents and wrote in three languages. Adding to that, it is the inspired Word of God with a human touch presented in a variety of literary forms that make the Bible a unique book. Yet "all Scripture is inspired by God and profitable for teaching, for reproof, for correction, for training in righteousness" (2 Tim. 3:16). Peter wrote, "But know this first of all, that no prophecy of Scripture is a matter of one's own interpretation,

---

[150] *An Arrow Pointed to Heaven*, p. 43.

for no prophecy was ever made by an act of human will, but men [and women] moved by the Holy Spirit spoke from God" (2 Pet. 1:20–21).

However, while the majority of Scripture is plain and relatively easy to understand, interpret, and explain, some parts are harder to grasp, even with the tools of hermeneutical theories and exegesis. The prophet Isaiah (Isa. 6:9) asserted that there are hard-to-decipher truths in the Word of God, and Jesus affirmed his assertion by quoting him (Matt. 13:13–15). Peter wrote that the apostle Paul's "letters contain some things that are hard to understand, which ignorant and unstable people distort, as they do the other Scriptures, to their destruction" (2 Pet. 3:16). Yet both apostles asserted that "all" Scripture—not just some chapters, verses, or passages, but all—are inspired. It means that the less interesting, less majestic, apparently less useful parts were all written under the Holy Spirit's inspiration and guidance.

Therefore, the whole of Scripture is a revelation of the one God, disclosing one single plan of redemption and one covenant of grace (Eph. 4:4–5). This means preachers can take an exemplarist approach, with the understanding that the biblical authors were under the same ethics and subject to similar experiences as ours. For instance, we can parallel God's call to Abram with our experience (Gen. 12:1–4), or Jeremiah's reluctant response to ours (Jer. 1:5–10). Their insecurities reflect our fears (Exod. 4:10–13), and their perplexities and aspirations are similar to ours (Esther 4:1–14). Not only are their fears ours (1 Kings 19:1–4) but often their cries (Job 1:21). It is instructive to show our congregations the shortcomings, the thrill of victory, and the agony of defeat of the men and women whom God used despite their flaws and failings. However, we must beware of cheapening God's grace in the process; otherwise, we will bring upon ourselves and our ministry the following divine charge: "'And now this commandment is for you, O priests [preachers]. If you do not listen, and if you do not take it to heart to give honor to My name,' says the Lord of Hosts, 'then I will send the curse upon you, and I will curse your blessings; and indeed, I have cursed them already, because you are not taking it to heart'" (Mal. 2:1, 2).

It is also important to note that God did not reveal himself all at once to his people. Instead, he gave a series of cumulative acts of self-disclosure by speaking in different ways and various manners (Heb. 1:1–2). Therefore, preachers today must study Scripture and preach the Word of God with the understanding of progressive revelation, also referred to as progressive light. This, however, should never be understood as the later revelation contradicting the earlier. On the contrary, it must not; but rather, some doctrines become clearer and more prominent in these last days (e.g., the emphasis on worship in Rev. 14: 7).

Augustine famously illustrated progressive revelation when he compared the Old Testament to a room fully furnished but unlit. The occupants couldn't see its contents because of the darkness, but they became visible in the light of the New Testament, and that light reveals nothing that wasn't there before. For example, David had a very clear grasp of the mercy of God (Ps. 51), but we find no indication that he saw that it would operate through the shed blood of One who was God's only begotten Son. Preachers can be conduits of progressive revelation to their congregations by learning the literary forms of the Bible.

Discovering Literary Forms of the Bible

Many consider the use of the Bible's literary forms as the most underdeveloped or neglected aspect of sermon preparation and biblical preaching. The literary form is the genre in which a passage is written and the rhetorical dynamic is the effect the particular literary feature produces in the reader or preacher. For instance, upon seeing Eve, his bride, for the first time, Adam said "This is now bone of my bones and flesh of my flesh" as he accepted and repeated the name given her by God. He declared, "She shall be called Woman [*isha*] because she was taken out of Man [*ish*]" (Gen. 2:23). The literary form is a song or poem he sang using God's words. If treated just as narrative, one will miss the fact of the divinely given names (*ish* for "man" and *isha* for "woman"), not Adam and Eve. It wasn't until after the Fall when

Adam (whose name comes from the Hebrew term *adama* meaning "earth" or "to be red") named his wife Eve (Gen. 3:20).

We can define genre as a conventional pattern recognizable by certain formal criteria, such as style, shape, tone, particular syntactic or even grammatical structures, and recurring formulaic patterns used in a particular society or in social situations governed by prescribed conventions. Broadly speaking, genre is a class or group of literary texts marked out by certain common features that permit us to distinguish them from other texts. It enables us to avoid reading texts flatly as something they are not. A genre may include a whole book, such as the Gospels or Epistles, within which other genres may occur, such as parables or hymns. Once we understand the genre, our quest is to discover how to read the text, then plan and preach sermons that emphasize Scripture's redemptive and historical messages.

Some readers, students, and even preachers of the Word often forget that, like any other book, the Bible must be understood according to certain rules. Thankfully, biblical scholars and homileticians "have augmented the methods of textual interpretation to include literary and rhetorical approaches, thereby expanding both the avenues of access to biblical texts and the range of possibilities for hearing the claims of those texts upon contemporary life."[151]

Thomas Long also created clear principles for discovering a deeper, fuller meaning of a text or passage of Scripture in his landmark book *Preaching and the Literary Forms of the Bible*. "Long argues that the literary form and dynamics of biblical texts can and should make a difference in the kinds of sermons created from those texts, not only because of what the texts say but because of how they say it. He presents a methodology for taking the literary characteristics of biblical texts into account in the text-to-sermon process and then applies that methodology in separate chapters on preaching psalms, proverbs, narratives, parables, and epistles."[152] In addition to the

---

[151] *Preaching and the Literary Forms of the Bible*, p. 11.

[152] Online publication description at www.amazon.com.

---

above literary forms, we must include miracle stories, apocalyptic writings, prophetic oracles, wisdom literature, law texts, and poetry.

In "The Approach—Part 1" of his book on literary forms, Thomas Long shares some invaluable insights for the biblical expositor. He asserts that the Bible consists of a variety of literary and rhetorical forms and, in the creation of sermons, preachers should develop a process of sermon preparation sufficiently nuanced to recognize and employ those differences. It means that it is inadequate to view biblical texts simply as "inert containers for theological concepts." Preachers should note that "form and content are equally important in appreciating the ménage of a passage from the Bible." To facilitate this process, Long formulates five helpful questions "that lead to a close analysis of the literary features in the texts and the rhetorical dynamics which are likely to take place *in front of* the texts, that is, between text and reader."[153] Those questions, followed by brief comments from other authors, are as follows:[154]

1. *What is the genre of the text?* In his *Theories of Preaching*, Richard Lischer explains that "the Bible includes many genres [and] . . . All of these genres embody characteristic literary patterns common to the literature of the cultures in which the Bible arose."

2. *What is the rhetorical function of the genre?* (What effects or impact are the literary features of a particular genre designed to produce in a reader?) For instance, Fred Craddock noted that "a parable does something to a reader that a psalm does not do, and vice versa."

3. *What literary devices does a particular genre employ to achieve its rhetorical effect?* Just as the previous question asks what does the text do to and for the reader, this one raises the issue of how the text can do what it does.

---

[153] *Creative Styles of Preaching*, p. 93.

[154] Ibid.

4. *How does the text under consideration, in its own literary setting, embody those characteristics and dynamics described in the previous questions?* Mark Barger Elliot quotes Nancy Murphy's answer to the question: "Turn to the peculiarities of a particular text to see how this text, while fitting the pattern of its genre, is nonetheless unique."

5. *How may the sermon, in a new setting, say and do what the text says and does in its own setting?* "The preacher's task is not to replicate the text but to regenerate the impact of some portion of the text." And Mark B. Elliott, quoting James Loder, commented, "If appropriate, the preacher might even select for the sermon a markedly different pattern." [155]

According to Thomas Long, his questions "provide a focus to our approach" and should be used for all Scripture so as to discover the literary form and genre of the text. The following are a few major genres in the vast array of literary forms extant in Scripture.

The Psalms

Reportedly one of the most referenced and read books of the Bible is that of Psalms. Its passages are popular pericopes in public and private worship, used for comfort during difficult trials, spoken when tempted, and proclaimed to comfort mourners or celebrate various anniversaries. The Psalms "cover a wide spectrum of human experience. Whether one faces pain or joy, deep theological concerns or great theological affirmations, failure or success, the continuum of human experience is found in the Psalms . . . Whether portraying creation, history, sin, man, the nation of Israel, the various writers

---

[155] Ibid.

of the Psalms call the people of God to find their full satisfaction in the LORD."[156]

Psalms are prayers and poetry sometimes put to music and sung as hymns during worship. Highly structured, they employ an extraordinary use of language that says more and says it more intensely than does ordinary language. For instance, Hebrew poetry makes extensive use of figurative language that conveys the idea or image by putting its common or plain sense to other usages through metaphor, simile, allegory, anthropomorphism, litotes (confirming truth by denying its opposite), hyperbole, and personification. The psalms also include different forms, such as parallelism,[157] didactic devices, and as Walter Brueggemann noted, liturgical, devotional, and pastoral approaches. They should be preached, not just occasionally from a verse but from an entire psalm, to declare the "whole purpose" or counsel of God. However, to preach from the psalms, one must understand the following principles and processes of Hebrew poetry.

First, while English poetry is a literary form distinguished by a strong sense of rhythm, meter, and emphasis on the interaction between sound and sense, "Hebrew poetry is characterized by brevity in line length, parallelism, and figurative language," wrote Robert

---

[156] *Preaching from the Psalms*, article by Dr. Robert V. McCabe, Professor of Old Testament, Detroit Baptist Theological Seminary, http://www.oldtestamentstudies.org/my-papers/other-papers/wisdom-literature/preaching-from-the-psalms/.

[157] This is the use of components or successive verbal constructions in a sentence that are grammatically the same or similar in sound, meaning, or meter. For example, in English, "Like father, like son" or "Easy come, easy go" and in Hebrew (especially psalms and proverbs), the words of two or more lines of text are directly related in some way. Hebrew poetry employs three distinct forms of parallelism: (a) the synonymous in which the same sentiment is repeated in different, but equivalent words (Psalm 19:1, 2). (b) The antithetical in which the parallel members express the opposite sides of the same thought (Psalm 73:26), and (c) the synthetical (aka constructive or epithetical), in which the two members contain two disparate ideas connected by a certain affinity between them (Psalm 24:3, 4).

V. McCabe, [158] who also noted that "the literary idiom of the Psalms is lyric poetry." He explained, "A lyric poem is characterized by its abbreviated nature . . . such as Psalm 1."

Second, McCabe pointed out, "through the use primarily of thematic elements that are shared between psalms as well as certain literary features, we can more precisely classify the lyric poems of the Psalms [into] six basic genres." These are (1) lament, the expression of grief, sorrow, or regret that is a dominant feature of more than one third of the psalms; (2) praise hymns, identifiable by their joyful, exuberant tributes to God; (3) thanksgiving, filled with expressions of gratitude to the Lord for his response to requests of individuals or groups; (4) kingship and covenant psalms that celebrate and affirm loyalty to God, the theocratic King, and his covenant; (5) songs of trust that emphasize confidence in God as well as the security it produces; and (6) wisdom psalms possessing a definite didactic nature emphasizing the Torah as fundamental for blessings.

Third, McCabe noted, "is an evaluation of the historical setting of a psalm" and the "two areas that the preacher should examine." They include the superscriptions that head a number of psalms, such as the one that begins Psalm 3. It "informs us that this psalm comes from the time when David fled from Absalom" and provides the sociocultural as well as emotional context for the preacher. "The second area," continued McCabe, "would be from the other biblical data from within the psalm itself and from any other place in the canon," whether Old or New Testament.

"The fourth principle," McCabe elaborated, "focuses on the three-part structure of lyric poetry"—i.e., subject (generally contained in the first few verses), development of the subject (the major part of the poem's structure), and conclusion or rounding off of the psalm in the form of summation (e.g., Ps. 1:6).

The fifth principle "examines the structure of the psalm" and "expands on the preceding principle of the poem's three-part

---

[158]   *http://www.oldtestamentstudies.org/my-papers/other-papers/wisdom-literature/preaching-from-the-psalms.*

structure . . . Poems are built on the guideline of theme and variation." And "having established the poem's theme, the preacher should seek to discover how each part of the poem contributes to the theme." McCabe further proposed that "there are eight types of structural material in the Psalms," including descriptive, expository, narrative, dramatic, emotional, repetitive, logical, and catalogue structural materials.

The sixth and final "principle relates to analyzing a psalm's poetic texture." This, he affirms, deals with the details of the poem under consideration, such as its rhetorical devices and figurative language. "Two questions should be asked of the details in the poem," he instructs. "Why is this figure or device used here? What is the logic of this figure or device in its context? In analyzing the poetic texture of a psalm, it is best to go through the text progressively, unit by unit."

Approaching a psalm from a literary perspective augments the preacher's hermeneutical, applicational and exegetical process, bringing the ancient words to life for the contemporary audience.

The Parables

Thomas Long asserted that "preaching on a parable is a novice preacher's dream but often an experienced preacher's nightmare." He explained that "the beginning preacher walks into a parable with a confident gait, striding boldly over what appears to be familiar terrain . . . But the more we get to know the parables, the less confident we become of our understanding of them." In fact, "the experienced preacher knows that the parables—so beguilingly simple on the surface—are, like a field with a hidden treasure, rich in meanings easily overlooked."[159]

Although he affirms Long's conclusions, Craig L. Blomberg argues, in the outline of his own approach, that preaching parables can be made easier if the preacher is aware that "Jesus's parables made one main point per main character." He further proposed that "the

---

[159] *Preaching and the Literary Forms of the Bible*, p. 87.

forty or so parables of Jesus exhibited only six different structures when one examined the number of main characters in each and the relationships among those characters."[160]

Long offers three ways of approaching parables:

a) "The code [which] was perhaps the earliest and certainly the most enduring way of understanding the parables. To view a parable as a code is to say that the parable symbolizes the kingdom of God allegorically."[161] Mark Barger Elliott has commented that "when we view a parable as a 'code,' we understand each aspect of the parable as referring to a deeper, hidden meaning. The task of the preacher is interpreting these meanings and deciphering the hidden allegory. For example, after reading the parable of the tenants in the vineyard, we might 'decode' the text and conclude the tenants represent Israel and the beloved son is Jesus."[162] He suggests that by breaking the code, we will "confirm [the] status of the readers as insiders. Outsiders receive the literal meaning of the coded parable, but only an insider sees the fully symbolic meaning."[163]

b) The imagery of vessels is Long's second approach. He noted that "in the nineteenth century, the code was largely replaced by an understanding of parables as vessels—that is, as containers of concepts, general truths, or theological ideas."[164] Elliott explained that this approach "focuses on creating a simile rather than an allegory. It pushes us to image what something is *like* and therefore discern a previously unknown truth. The goal of the parable as vessel is discovery, not confirmation."[165]

c) Then, according to Long, "more recent students of the parables have replaced the vessel image with a view of the parables as objects of

---

[160]   *Preaching the Parables: From Responsible Interpretation to Powerful Proclamation*, p. 15.

[161]   *Preaching and the Literary Forms*, p. 95.

[162]   *Creative Styles of Preaching*, p. 97.

[163]   *Preaching and the Literary Forms of the Bible*, pp. 96, 97.

[164]   Ibid., p. 95.

[165]   *Creative Styles of Preaching*, p. 98.

art." And "like other art forms, parables are not pedagogical devices but aesthetic creations which engage readers in eventful encounter and invite new ways of seeing and understanding the human situation." Elliott suggests that "with the text presented as an object of art, the preacher invites the listener by an act of the imagination to wander through the parable." He also includes three "helpful suggestions on how to preach a parable as an object of art." They are as follows:

1. "First, allow the central metaphor to guide decisions as to what to include in the sermon." In other words, quoting another author, he proposed that the preacher "'find images or metaphors that shed enough light on the original metaphor that you can play one against another.'"
2. "When recreating the experience of the parable," Elliott noted, "'tell the story from one perspective.'"
3. Finally, "consider 'telling the story of the parable in modern dress.'"

The Epistles

Thomas Long wrote, quoting William G. Doty, that "even though in its preaching and liturgy, the church has tended to place its greatest emphasis upon the Gospels, the epistle is the dominant literary form found within the Christian canon." He adds that "at least twenty of the twenty-seven books in the New Testament present themselves as letters, and two other books include material in epistolary forms (Acts 15:23–29, 23:26–30; Rev. 2–3)."[166] He recommends "several good reasons to revive the practice of epistolary preaching" because (1) preaching on the Epistles helps to correct the overreliance on narrative preaching, and (2) it allows the sermon to depict the Christian faith not simply as a series of experiences or a collection of doctrinal affirmations, but as a way of life grounded in specific and coherent practices. (3) Furthermore, it permits sermons to help hearers in their quest to find meaning in the various relationships and

---

[166] *Preaching and the Literary Forms*, p. 107.

commitments of their lives. By using Thomas Long's five-question approach, mentioned earlier, to any or every epistle, the "sermons will be rescued from being either abstract theological essays or op-ed pieces on the cultural issues du jour. They will address the great questions that have always troubled the human heart, and they will do so in ways that build up real churches facing concrete problems and trying to heal actual conflicts."[167]

How then should we preach from epistles? First, avoid interpreting each verse or passage of an epistle as though they were independent paragraphs with no connection to the rest of the letter. Second, remember that they are someone else's mail written to specifically address needs present in the churches to which they were addressed and may not be concerns of the modern-day reader. Third, keep in mind that epistles are what Gordon D. Fee and Douglas Stuart describe as "occasional documents,"[168] because they arise out of and are intended for a specific situation. Fourth, read the epistle repeatedly to reconstruct the historical background to understand the community and circumstances being addressed so as to discover the original readers' situation to which the author was responding. Fifth, after recovering the historical situation or event in which an epistle is embedded or the circumstances that prompted its composition, trace the argument of the epistle. Sixth, pay attention to its structure, main and minor propositions, and logical argument. Seventh, once you have a working knowledge of the central idea and the reasoning of the epistle, you are ready to extrapolate and communicate its meaning to your congregation.

The Narratives

A narrative is a written or spoken account or story of connected events and experiences. "There are two odd things about the Bible stories," Thomas Long noted. "The first odd thing about biblical

---

[167] Ibid.

[168] *How to Read the Bible for All Its Worth*, 3rd edition, p. 58.

stories is that there are so many of them. There are battle stories, betrayal stories, stories about seduction and treachery in the royal court, stories about farmers and fools, healing stories, violent stories, funny stories and sad ones, stories of death, and stories of resurrection. *In fact, stories are so common in Scripture that some students have claimed, understandably but incorrectly, that the Bible is exclusively a narrative collection"* (emphasis mine). "The second odd thing about the Bible and stories has been expressed by Adele Berlin," Long wrote. And he added, "'It is ironic that, although telling is so important in the biblical tradition, there is no word for story. There are words for songs and oracles, hymns and parables . . . [but] there is nothing to designate narrative *per se*.'"[169]

Des Cummings Jr. provides "three process goals if you choose to preach a narrative passage . . . first, experiencing the story; second, interpreting the story; and third, relating the story. Each of these goals is achieved by one or more procedural steps," such as to "identify" and "fill out the dynamics," while the procedural steps for interpreting the story include "biblical research" using the following techniques: "(a) Interaction analysis . . . that aids the expositor in thinking theologically. . . (b) Check conclusions—it is vital that the passage determine the message . . . (c) Record the sources."

Cummings suggests that the best ways to relate the story are to "construct a logical flow; design the bonding—[this] is the point at which the hearer makes a conscious choice to allow God to live out this truth through him/her . . . Select the illustrations [and] write out the sermon."[170]

To wrap up this introduction to preaching the literary forms of the Bible, let us look at two narratives with multiple genres. For instance, the feeding of the five thousand (represented as A below) is rife with Hebrew literary genres and appears in all four Gospels: Matthew 14:13–21, whose Gospel speaks primarily to the Jews; Mark 6:33–44, whose focus was a Roman readership, in occupation

---

[169] *Preaching and the Literary Forms*, p. 66.

[170] https://www.ministrymagazine.org/archive/1984/08/narrative-preaching.

of Judea, which made them familiar with Jewish culture; Luke 9:12–17, the only Greek or Gentile author who was not an eyewitness, but one recording the testimonies of eyewitnesses; and John 6:1–14. Luke's Gospel emphasizes the divinity and humanity of Jesus since it primarily addressed a Greek audience, particularly the intellectually minded, whose literature and art featured a search for the perfect man. John wrote for everyone, and the things he reported sought to establish that Jesus was indeed the eternal God who became man (John 1:1–14).

The feeding of the five thousand took place among a Jewish audience at Bethsaida on the western side of the Sea of Galilee (Luke 9:10). However, the later feeding of four thousand (recorded only in Matt. 15:32–39 and Mark 8:1–9, represented as B below) took place in Decapolis, a region occupied mostly by Gentiles on the eastern side of the Sea of Galilee. Jesus's main lesson in both narratives was to teach his disciples that he was indeed the bread of eternal life, and he was enough to feed and satisfy both Jews and Gentiles everywhere. The locations and audiences of both narratives are distinguished and identified primarily by the following literary devices.

(A) The feeding of the five thousand had four miracles:

i.   The first miracle took place in the "desolate place" or desert identified as such by all the authors (except Luke). [171] All who reported this event used a Hebrew poetic device referencing (or literally quoting) Psalm 23:1, 2—a well-known, popular

---

[171]   Although the Greek *ereimon* means a desert, desolate, uninhabited, lonely, solitary, or remote place deprived of people, because it was spring, John wrote that "there was much grass in the place" (John 6:10). The miracle appears to be that grass was found in this desolate place. It perhaps was the site chosen by Jesus for this retreat from the busy highways of Galilee, where he demonstrated that he is indeed the Good Shepherd (Psalm 23) who, by grace, transforms spiritually desolate places into plentiful resources for everyone. Just as the arrival of spring refreshes the desolate place to produce green grass, so the presence of the Messiah replenishes the spiritually dry hearts of humanity with abundant love, forgiveness, and acceptance.

psalm of their day. For instance, Mark noted that the hungry crowd looked like "sheep without a shepherd" (verse 34) and were commanded to sit down on green grass (verse 39). Matthew remarked that Jesus was "ordering the people to sit down on grass" (verse 19), while John used *chortus polus* to emphasize that the newly grown spring grass was abundant, plush, and green (verse 10). This poetic phraseology would evoke images in the minds of a Jewish audience and point them to the fact that Jesus is indeed the Messiah for whom they longed and of whom Scripture prophesied that when he appeared, "the wilderness and the desert will be glad . . . and blossom like the crocus . . . they will see the glory of the Lord, the majesty of our God" (Isa. 35:1, 2). Also, "they will say, 'This desolate land has become like the Garden of Eden; and the waste, desolate, and ruined cities are fortified and inhabited'" (Ezek. 36:35).

ii. The second miracle was that Jesus transformed "barley loaves" (noted only in John 6:9) into good bread after he eulogized it (blessed by speaking well of it publicly—Matt. 14:19). He did so because in those days, barley was the ordinary, coarse black bread of Galilean peasants and members of the poorest classes. People considered it an inferior kind of grain good only for animal fodder (1 Kings 4:28). "While all other meat offerings were of wheat, that brought by the woman accused of adultery was to be of *barley*, because, as her deed is that of the animals, so her offering is the food of animals."[172] According to Vincent's Word Studies, "Barley (*krithinous*), a detail peculiar to John, occurs in the New Testament only here [John 6:9] and John 6:13. An inferior sort of bread is indicated by the term." Pliny [the Elder] (AD 23–79), a Roman author, naturalist, and philosopher, as well as some Jewish writers, describe barley as food fit primarily for beasts. Suetonius speaks of a turgid rhetorician as a barley orator,

---

[172] *The Life and Times of Jesus the Messiah*, vol. 1, p. 681.

inflated like moist barley; and Livy relates how cohorts that had "lost their standards were ordered barley for food."[173]

In light of this cultural view of barley, after "ordering" or making the crowd to "recline" on carpet-like, plush green grass as if they were princes and princesses, it would be anticlimactic—perhaps even insulting—to feed them bread they knew to be relegated to the poorest classes even though they were used to it in private consumption. So Jesus, the true *bread of life* (John 6:48), lifted the barley loaves before them and may have said a traditional blessing for a meal in his day that went something like this: "Blessed are you, O Lord our God, King of the world, who brings forth bread from the earth" or "What God has cleansed, no longer consider unholy" (Acts 10:15). Whatever Jesus said, it transformed the barley (perhaps in the minds of the people) into delicious, rich loaves of tasty bread.

iii. The third miracle is the multiplication of the five barley loaves (small flat bread about the size of a common roll) and two small fish donated by a poor lad. It was an incredible miracle, especially since Scripture notes that "there were about five thousand men who ate, besides women and children" (Matthew 14:21), who received a good, healthy portion, not fragments. Such a crowd of poor people, who were unsure of their next meal, may have stashed a few extra pieces to consume later. Some scholars suggest that, all together, close to twenty thousand ate that day; yet the multitude were all filled and satisfied. Greek has two words for "satisfied"— *empiplemi* ("to fill or satisfy," used only in John 6:12) and *chortazo* ("to satisfy," which comes from the root meaning "grass," employed by Matthew, Mark, and Luke). They chose this particular word as a metaphor to conjure up images of people filled, satisfied (like cattle who would lie down to

173 www.sacred-texts.com/bib/cmt/vws/joh005.htm.

regurgitate and chew the cud), and relaxed as they reminisced about the miracles they had just witnessed.

iv. The fourth miracle was the filling to the brim of the twelve disciples' baskets with the leftover pieces of loaves and fish. "Each of the Gospels use the same word here for baskets (*kophinos*), a wicker-basket, called "coffins" by Wycliffe."[174] Here, a word indicates that the audience was a Jewish one, because they commonly used this particular kind of basket and it is distinct from the soft and frail reed *sphuris* used primarily by Gentiles.

(B) The feeding of the four thousand (Matt. 15:32–39 and Mark 8:1–9) had only two miracles:

i. The first was Jesus's multiplication of seven loaves and a few fish to feed "four thousand men, besides women and children." As with the five thousand, Jesus had compassion on the people, but we find no miraculous demonstration using the desolate place, Hebrew poetic mention of green grass or that Jesus ordered them "recline" on the ground. Perhaps this was due to the fact they would not be familiar with the imagery of Psalm 23. Instead, He gently "directed them to sit down on the ground" where the grass would be parched at that midsummer time of the year. In reporting the event, neither Matthew nor Mark used Hebrew poetic allusions to indicate that Jesus was the Messiah or referred the Gentile audience to psalms or Scripture they would not have known. The account does not report the kind of bread or who provided the loaves and fish, facts not important to a multitude of very hungry Gentiles, but both Matthew and Mark mention that the multitude ate and were all satisfied (*chortazo*).

---

174 *Word Pictures in the New Testament*, vol 1, p. 118.

ii. The second miracle was the seven large baskets filled to the brim with leftover broken pieces—not scraps, crumbs, or fragments—of loaves and fish. However, both Matthew and Mark used a literary genre to identify the audience as Gentiles by distinguishing the baskets as *sphuris* (a round basket or hamper made from reed, not wicker, that could be rolled, twisted, or folded, and is sometimes large enough to hold a man, as in Acts 9:25).

Later, when the Gospel writers reported that Jesus referred to the two miracles, both authors noted that he employed the two words for baskets—*kophinos* (Matt. 16:9 and Mark 8:19) for the twelve baskets, and *sphuris* (Matt. 16:10 and Mark 8:20) for the seven large baskets—that would have distinguished the different audiences as Jews and Gentiles.

The authors, not Jesus, were making a point through the literary form, because his main goal was to convince his disciples, who were then lacking in understanding, that he was indeed the bread of eternal life and that there was plenty enough for all people (John 6:35), whether Jews or Gentiles.

PART THREE—PRAXIS

CHAPTER 7

Preaching and Worship

All Scripture is inspired by God and profitable for teaching, for reproof, for correction, for training in righteousness; so that the man of God may be adequate, equipped for good work. I solemnly charge you in the name of God and of Christ Jesus, who is to judge the living and the dead, and by His appearing and His kingdom: preach the word, be ready in season and out of season; reprove, rebuke, exhort, with great patience and instruction.[175]

Preaching the Word of God has always been central in the life of God's called-out people. Such proclamation is distinct from giving a speech, even if that speech is eloquent, authoritative, and godly. As previously noted, proclaiming the Word actually began with God himself when he spoke to the Israelites (Exod. 20:1–17). The Hebrew word for proclamation (*qara*) actually "denotes primarily the enunciation of a specific vocable or message . . . customarily addressed to a specific recipient and is intended to elicit a specific response."[176] It also means to call or read aloud, and captures the

---

[175] 2 Timothy 3:16, 17; 4:1, 2.

[176] *Theological Wordbook of the Old Testament*, vol. 2, p. 810.

---

essential definition of preaching in the Old Testament. It was used when God said to Moses, "I Myself will make all My goodness pass before you, and will *proclaim* the name of the Lord before you . . ." (Exod. 33:19).

The same word appears in Sanballat's letter to Nehemiah: "You have appointed prophets to *proclaim* in Jerusalem concerning you . . ." (Neh. 6:7). And it also appears in the Lord's command to Jonah: "Arise, go to Nineveh, the great city, and *proclaim* to it the *proclamation* which I am going to tell you" (Jon. 3:2) (emphasis mine). Additionally, to demonstrate that preaching was not a unique phenomenon to the newly minted Christian faith, the apostle Peter noted that it goes as far back in human history to Noah, whom he called "a preacher of righteousness" (2 Pet. 2:5).

The Greek word *kerusso* "signifies (a) to be a herald, or in general, to proclaim . . . publish . . . to preach" (Rev. 5:2); (b) to preach the gospel as a herald (Matt. 24:14); (c) to preach the word (2 Tim. 4:2) as well as (of the ministry of the Scriptures, with special reference to the Gospel)."[177] In New Testament times, a herald was one who preached or proclaimed a message or paved the way for a promised event or person. John the Baptist was such a preacher (Matt. 3:1). The leper whom Jesus healed "began to proclaim" (Mark 1:45) what he had done despite the stern warning not to (verse 42). Jesus announced that the Spirit of the Lord anointed him to preach the Gospel (Luke 4:18), and in his last command to his disciples, he told them to "go into all the world and preach the gospel to all creation" (Mark 16:15). After his ascension, they did just that. "And every day, in the temple and from house to house, they kept right on teaching and preaching Jesus as the Christ" (Acts 4:32).

A vast array of historical evidence indicates that preaching was a significant part of the life of the early church. *The New Schaff-Herzog Religious Encyclopedia* (available online)[178] reports that exegetical, polemic homilies became a staple of the church during the period of

---

[177] W. E. Vine, *An Expository Dictionary of New Testament Words.*

[178] https://books.google.com/books?id=pZJAAQAAMAAJ, p. 159.

AD 200–800. There we learn that "Origen, the great thinker and scholar of the Greek Church, is the father of the sermon as a fixed ecclesiastical custom, to whom can be traced the theological-practical exposition of a definite text as well as the homily." The report continues, "It is noteworthy that at that period of the separation of the divine service into homiletical-didactic part and a mystical part, the sermon was missionary and apologetic in type and suited to instruct the catechumens" or neophytes, persons under instruction in the rudiments, elementary facts, and principles of Christianity in the early church. Sermons then "took the form of explication and application of the text, using particularly the method of allegory, which from that time on became prevalent and controlled the homiletical use of Scripture until the Reformation."

But it was John Chrysostom (349–407), whose Greek name means "golden mouthed," who put preaching on the map. Archbishop of Constantinople and numbered among the early Church Fathers, he was, perhaps, the first celebrity and prophetic preacher who become known for sermons denouncing the abuse of authority by political and ecclesiastical leaders. Later, when Augustine (354–430) came on the scene, he "was distinguished for his energy and tirelessness as a preacher." However, his sermons were "strong in the elements of experience, witness-bearing, dialectic, and practical applications . . . more infused with the Gospel."[179]

The separation of the sermon from the rest of the worship service (something we've inherited) may have begun in the Middle Ages. For, while some elements were done in Latin, "the sermon required the use of the vernacular of the region"[180] and created the sense that some parts of worship (i.e., preaching) were more important than others. However, with the proliferation of mass media communications and a renaissance in worship, preaching reached its zenith as the main portion of worship in the mid-twentieth century. During that worship resurgence, churches devoted more than half the time spent

---

[179] Ibid., p. 160.

[180] Ibid., p. 161.

in worship to preaching. But the last decades of that century until now has seen a tremendous paradigm shift in worship style and content as music, drama, praise dancing, and video presentations usurped the centrality of preaching. It's as if the proponents of this change felt that "when sermons are regarded as primary, worship is reduced to plying musical ability and arranging service elements appropriately"[181] to fit in as "preliminaries."

But those opposed did not surrender and sit silently as the movement toward music gathered strength and popularity. Some, like the very conservative evangelical author Albert Mohler, retaliated in articles, saying, "Music fills the space of most evangelical worship, and much of this music comes in the form of contemporary choruses marked by precious little theological content. Beyond the popularity of the chorus as a musical form, many evangelical churches seem intensely concerned to replicate studio-quality musical presentations."[182]

The worship style changes, and opposing opinions, such as Mohler's, "have sadly contributed to friction and sometimes even divided churches, causing some preachers to become understandably wary." As an example, in an October 2014 online article, T. David Gordon confidently predicted "The Imminent Decline (not disappearance) of Contemporary Worship Music,"[183] and gave the following eight reasons summarized below:

1. Contemporary worship music hymns not only were/are comparatively poor, they had to be. One generation cannot successfully "compete" with fifty generations of hymn writers. It would need to be fifty times as talented as all previous ones to do so.

---

[181] *Preaching as Worship,* p. 32.

[182] http://www.albertmohler.com/2013/08/19/
expository-preaching-the-antidote-to-anemic-worship/.

[183] http://secondnaturejournal.com/the-imminent-decline-of-contemporary-worship-music-eight-reasons.

2. Early on in the contemporary worship music movement, many groups began setting traditional hymn lyrics to contemporary melodies and/or instrumentation. The writers quickly realized how difficult/demanding it is to write lyrics that are not only theologically sound but are appropriate, memorable, and edifying (not to mention metrical).

3. As a result, the better contemporary hymns (e.g., "How Deep the Father's Love" and "In Christ Alone") have been overused to the point that we have become weary of them.

4. It is no longer a competitive advantage to have part or all of a service in a contemporary idiom (probably well more than half the churches now do so), so now we've reached what Malcolm Gladwell calls the "tipping point."[184] (Gordon also asserted that contemporary worship music no longer marks a church as hip or forward-looking because many/most churches now do it).

5. As with all novelties, once the newness wears off, what remains often seems somewhat empty. In a culture that celebrates what is new (and commercial culture always does so in order to sell the latest releases), most people will constantly look for only what is new.

6. While ostensibly created "for the young people," the driving force behind contemporary worship music was always my own sixties generation of anti-adult, antiestablishment, rebellious Woodstockers and Jesus freaks, who are beginning to die off.

7. Praise teams generally accompany contemporary worship music, and they have frequently (but by no means always) been problematic. It has been difficult to provide direction to them due to the inherent confusion between whether they are *participants in* the congregation or *performers for* it.

8. We cannot evade or avoid the "holy catholic church" of the Apostles' Creed forever. Even people untrained theologically have some intuitive sense that a local contemporary

---

[184] See *The Tipping Point: How Little Things Can Make a Big Difference.*

congregation is part of a global and many-generational (indeed eschatological and endless) assembly of followers of Christ. Cutting ourselves off from that broader catholic (universal) body may appear cool for a while, but we ultimately wish to commune with the rest of the global/catholic church.

Gordon further asserted that "contemporary worship, to me, is an oxymoron," adding, "basically, worship is what angels and morning stars did before creation." Such observations are challenging, thought-provoking, and conjure up uncomfortable feelings. Some of them have become fighting words proclaimed by a diverse group of conservative opponents of the new trend in worship. Like a shot over the bow, or throwing down the gauntlet for a duel, these discourses are enough to raise the hackles of those who promote contemporary worship. In fact, truth be told, worship has already become so controversial that someone commented that it "should be spelled 'warship,' and tragically, the term *worship wars* describes conflict, sometimes bitterly splitting congregations over worship styles."[185]

The situation is not much better or peaceful in more traditional churches in which the musical style continues to be hymns and choirs. The pressures to conform, plus the dwindling attendance and declining financial support, is causing many to surrender, under duress, to the new wave of worship style in which music is more dominant than preaching. Yet make no mistake—such worship wars are not new.

Even before the establishment of his church, the woman at the well wrangled with Jesus about where to worship. She observed contentiously, "Our fathers worshipped in this mountain, and *you people say that in Jerusalem is the place* where men ought to worship" (John 4:20, emphasis mine). Note his response; one that, upon reflection, should cause the warriors of worship to lay down their arms. "Woman, believe Me, an hour is coming when neither in this mountain nor in Jerusalem will you worship the Father. *You*

---

[185] *Preaching as Worship,* p. 30.

worship what you do not know, we worship what we know, for salvation is from the Jews. But an hour is coming, and now is, when the true worshippers will worship the Father in spirit and truth; for such people the Father seeks to be His worshippers" (John 4:21–23, emphasis mine).

Jesus made it clear then that "the worship of God will be emancipated from the bondage of place,"[186] but can we anticipate that it will be loosed from the conflict over music? However, do not miss his tone when he said "salvation is from the Jews." It's not an assertion of fact but a sarcastic challenge of her theological presupposition, because the Bible clearly states that salvation is from Jesus alone (Acts 4:12). Then he put the cap on her argument, saying "you worship *what* you do not know" and "we [the Jews] worship *what* we know" on their presupposition that salvation is from them and their forefathers like Abraham (emphasis mine). Notice that he underscores the fact that both nations worship "what," not "who"— necessitating the explanation that the hour is coming, and now is, when all will worship "who"-- the Father.

Since *proskuneo*, the word for worship, means "to make obeisance, do reverence to" (from *pros*, 'towards,' and *kuneo*, 'to kiss') and "is used of an act of homage or reverence" in the battle between preaching and music, both the protagonist and antagonist are worshipping "what." For instance, on one side, usually composed of so-called conservatives, they worship what they do not know; and on the other are those categorized as liberals, who worship what they know. And neither worship *who* they know—because if they did, they would not allow such controversy to detract his church from its mission to seek and save the lost.

The "hubris that plagues the act of preaching" has not helped to heal the wounds caused by these controversies. Unfortunately, "rightly convinced of preaching's importance, preachers can wrongly become self-important. Investing all their effort in sermon-making and claiming its importance for proclaiming the gospel (Rom. 10:9),

---

[186] Word Pictures in The New Testament, vol. 5, p. 66.

they can sideline worship as a secondary matter," Michael Quicke proposed. He wrote that "Charles Rice mischievously described such an attitude as viewing the sermon as 'a kind of homiletical ocean liner, preceded by a few liturgical tugboats.'"[187] As another example of such "hubris," Quicke also quotes John Killinger, who declared that "there is no substitute for preaching in worship. It provides the proclamatory thrust without which the church is never formed and worship is never made possible."[188]

Quicke describes the problem of pastors who relegate all but preaching to the bottom drawer of "preliminaries" better than anyone I have had the privilege of reading. He suggests that such attitudes are the result of myopic views of preaching and worship. "Myopia," he argues, "is defined as 'a visual defect in which distant objects appear blurred because their images are focused in front of the retina rather than on it—nearsightedness. Often unaware how limited its vision has become, myopic preaching misses out on God's long-range worship perspective, on the details of life."[189] He also notes that "myopic preaching is marked by ten characteristics"[190] briefly highlighted as follows:

1. Faulty Definitions. "How people define worship shows its relative value to them"—whether it's only music, preaching, liturgies, pragmatics, maintenance, or what happens in church on the day one worships.
2. Thin Theology of Worship.
3. Nondirective Use of Scripture.
4. Liturgical Amnesia.
5. Feeble Community Formation.
6. Naiveté about Culture.
7. Ambivalence about Music.

[187] Ibid., p. 28.

[188] Ibid.

[189] Ibid., p. 39.

[190] Ibid., pp. 40–59.

8. Not Living in God's Narrative.
9. Isolated Preparation.
10. Worshipless Sermons.

Since preaching is increasingly playing a supporting role to music and other contemporary additions to worship, how can those who have never known Christ hear without the preached Word of God (Rom. 10:14, 15)? Another question is "Why should preaching have the dominance in worship when music has the power to touch the soul with such astounding emotions and accuracy?" Let me propose the following:

1) Perhaps preaching is significant in worship because God (a) created the world with his word (Gen. 1; Heb. 11:3); (b) revealed himself to the world as the Word (John 1:1); (c) revealed himself to humanity by the inspired Word (1 Tim. 3:16; 2 Pet. 1:21); (d) performs his works (John 9:4) of redemption, re-creation, reconciliation, and restoration by his Word (Matt. 9:22; Mark 5:8; Luke 4:39; John 11:43); and (e) converts people (changes hearts and lives) by his Word (1 Pet. 1:23).

2) A 2002 US-based survey by the Barna Research Group concluded that participants in the "worship wars" have ignored the real issue regarding worship. The major challenge "is not about how to use music to facilitate worship as much as it is to help people understand worship and have an intense passion to connect with God . . . Most of the church people who fight about their musical preferences do so because they don't understand the relationship between music, communication, God, and worship." Furthermore, "church leaders foster the problem by focusing on how to please people with music or how to offer enough styles of music to meet everyone's tastes rather than dealing with the underlying issue of limited

interest in, comprehension of, and investment in fervent worship of a holy, deserving God."[191]

3) Although preaching of the Word is a necessary and customary part of worship, the twenty-first-century Christian church has had a dearth of great preaching. Many of the outstanding homileticians and proclaimers are either retired or dead. Thus, there's a desperate need in preaching for what Susan Scott describes as "fierce conversation." This is not "menacing, cruel, barbarous, or threatening" language. It does not sound "like raised voices, frowns, blood on the floor, no fun at all" discourses. "The word *fierce* has the following synonyms: robust, intense, strong, powerful, passionate, eager, unbridled, uncurbed, untamed."[192] Fierce conversation is the backbone of prophetic preaching, in which speaking truth to power and challenging the status quo nurtures, nourishes, and evokes relevance and creativity that would balance the prevailing model of "contemporary worship."

4) Life abhors a vacuum, and when one develops, it finds something to fill it. If preaching continues to retreat or be relegated to the status of "preliminaries," a whole host of innovations will rise up to take its place. Today it's contemporary music, but who knows what tomorrow will bring? However, fighting each other for power or prominence of our preferences in worship is not the Holy Spirit–anointed answer to resolve such tensions. Only through prayer and fasting—the foundation, launching pad, and sustenance of preaching and worship—can we deal with such problems.

5) Worship was intended to please God, not humanity. Contemporary worship is very anthropocentric rather

---

[191] https://www.barna.org/barna-update/article/5-barna-update/85-focus-on-qworship-warsq-hides-the-real-issues-regarding-connection-to-god#. VWXfJ2RgYlw.

[192] *Fierce Conversations: Achieving Success at Work and in Life, One Conversation at a Time,* pp. 1–12.

than theocentric or Christocentric. We have no biblical evidence that God inscribed (on tablets of stone like the Ten Commandments) the Genevan order of worship developed by John Calvin and practiced by many conservative Protestant churches today. Nor is there scriptural support that anyone's traditions, instincts, favoritisms, or experiments are divine commands for the content and exercise of worship. Though believers are called to worship God, he has given no rules or regulations regarding style or content. Consequently, in our obsessive, anthropocentric clime, we want what pleases us. When we "come together as a church," wrote Paul as if he were a member today, "I hear that divisions exist among you, and in part I believe it" (1 Cor. 11:18).

6) Worship—Walter Brueggemann suggests—is a conversation between God and his people. We cannot and must not eliminate or undermine preaching in order to substitute entertainment for evangelism under the guise that we must make worship interesting and exciting so the unconverted will come to church. The call for entertainment is seductive and appealing because we all want to see many who live beyond the choir brought to faith in Jesus. But, in the words of Robert Godfrey, "we must remember that entertainment is not evangelism, and evangelism is not worship." No matter how great or professional they are, a comedian in the pulpit, a group of praise dancers on the platform, or a big-band sound of music in the sanctuary will not convert people, and neither will solemn hymns played and sung like a funeral dirge. It's by the gospel of Jesus Christ. "For by grace you have been saved through faith; and that not of yourselves, it is the gift of God; not as a result of works, so that no one may boast," the apostle Paul declared (Eph. 2:8–10).

Finally, on one hand, traditional Protestant worship has always been strong on reverence and may seem mechanical, formalistic, and without emotion to some in our media-driven, action-obsessed culture. On the other hand, others may view contemporary worship, with its enthusiasm and joy, as being focused on fun and excitement at the expense of reverence. But how do we know that this isn't part of the "new thing" (Isa. 43:19) God has promised to do in the last days?

I recommend that proponents of both approaches (a) ask and answer whether the content of their worship achieves a biblical balance in which preaching is the lamp to the worshippers' feet (Ps. 119:105) and the music/songs recount and guide them to God's saving works of redemption, reconciliation, and restoration. (b) Put an end to the "warship" by beating ideological swords into plowshares (Isa. 2:4), to cultivate a new era of Christian preaching and worship so that the world will know Jesus is Lord because of our love for one another (John 13:35).

CHAPTER 8

Women in the Word—Preaching a Spirit of Collaboration

We may be debarred entrance to many pulpits (as some of us now are) and stand at the door or on the street corner in order to preach to men and women. No difference when or where, we must preach a whole gospel.[193]

One of the biggest injustices in the Christian Church—in its more than two-thousand-year history—is its devaluation of the spiritual gifts of women, especially when it comes to preaching. "The bias against the use of their formidable gifts for communicating the gospel is one of the most appalling ethical failures in all of Christian history. Even with the World Council of Churches' designation of the 'Ecumenical Decade of Churches in Solidarity with Women' (1988–1998), it may not now be assumed that the right of women to preach is an idea whose time has fully come."[194] Without a doubt, while the trend has been definitely moving toward the acceptance of women in the pulpit in the twenty-first century, we still have a long way to go to be fully integrated in ministry. But it will come.

---

[193] Quoted in *Daughters of Thunder* by Bettye Collier-Thomas.

[194] *Concise Encyclopedia of Preaching*, p. 510.

"The agitation for change is enhanced by the fact that many of today's Protestant seminaries have student bodies that are nearly half female. Added to this is the pressure of federal laws enforcing the equality of women in every aspect of secular life. *No denomination will likely survive far into the twenty-first century without finding some way to conform to the popular doctrine of equality and to the word of the apostle Paul, who said that in Christ there is neither male nor female* (Gal. 3:28)"[195] (emphasis mine).

The presence of women in the pulpit provides more than the ethical requirement of equality or political parity. For instance, it should remind us that God created both male and female in his image. Regrettably, for centuries, the Christian Church has presented only one side or aspect—the masculine—of the face of God. Yet Scripture does not support such a position. Richard M. Davidson, Professor of Old Testament Interpretation, wrote:

> Genesis 1 teaches us that male and female participate equally in the image of God. "So God created man (Heb. *ha'adam* 'humankind') in His own image, in the image of God created he Him; male and female created He them." This foundational passage (and surrounding context) gives no hint of a divine creation order, with no subordination of one to the other. We find that this description of the relationship between man and woman holds throughout Scripture and beyond. No inspired writer—not Moses, Jesus, Paul, or Ellen White—teaches the creation headship of man over woman.[196]

Additionally, we are now living in the fulfillment of God's promise given through the prophet Isaiah, who wrote, "Look, I am

---

[195] Ibid., p. 511.

[196] "Seven Reasons the Bible Supports Ordination/Commissioning of Women as Pastors and Elders," in *CURRENT Magazine*, Vol. 2, p. 8.

about to do something new; even now it is coming. Do you not see it?" (Isa. 43:19, Holman Christian Standard Bible). Part of that "new thing" is the restoration of women to the position to which he originally created and intended us to function—as co-priests—with increasing influence in the gospel ministry, especially in the pulpit.

The prophet Joel continued the divinely designated refrain of something new, saying, "It will come about after this that I will pour out My Spirit on all mankind; and your sons *and daughters* will prophesy" (Joel 2:28, emphasis mine). This was fulfilled on the day of Pentecost when 120 men and women disciples gathered together in one place (Acts 1:14–15), the Upper Room in Jerusalem. Peter preached a powerful message and quoted from Joel (Acts 2:16–21) to affirm that the prophecy was being fulfilled then and continues to our day as more women are being divinely appointed to preach the Word until Jesus returns to literally, physically receive us to himself (John 14:3).

From the beginning, God intended women to be an integral, equal partner in the priesthood of all believers. Davidson wrote:

> Although indeed the terms "male" and "female" connote sexual (biological) differences, there is no hint of ontological superiority/inferiority or functional leadership/submission between male and female. To the contrary, both are explicitly presented as "equally immediate to the Creator and His act." In the wider context of this passage [Genesis] (1:26, 28), both the man and the woman are blessed. Both are to share alike in the responsibility of procreation, to "fill the earth." Both are to subdue the earth. Both are given the same co-managerial dominion over God's nonhuman creation. "Both have been commanded equally and without distinction to take dominion, not one over the other, but both together over the rest of God's creation for the glory of the Creator."[197]

---

[197]   *Flame of Yahweh: Sexuality in the Old Testament*, p. 22.

While affirming our divine call to proclaim the gospel alongside our brothers in ministry, this chapter does not focus on the pain women in the pulpit have encountered, suffered, endured, and survived. Rather, it seeks to equip those called and anointed women to rise above such adversity, rejection, or vilification to preach the Word with power. It offers tips, advice, and even instructions on how to be the best preacher God has endowed us to be at a time when the contributions of women in the world and, slowly, in the Word are receiving increasing attention and recognition. But before getting down to some basics of "how to" prepare and preach as women, let me address how women can minister more effectively.

A Desperate Need for Role Models

First and foremost, we need role models. In recent years, the number of women responding to the divine summons to "preach the word" (2 Tim. 4:2) has increased exponentially. While "sobering figures point to overall enrollment decline" in North America, according to a recent study,[198] seminaries across denominations report record-high registrations of women. For instance, according to the Association of Theological Schools, during the 2012–2013 school year, women accounted for approximately 37 percent of Protestant seminary students.[199] Many of them are older professional women who have left lucrative careers to prepare to preach and teach the gospel. Yet despite the proliferation of books, journal articles, and YouTube sermons by women, there still remains a shortage of role models and mentors in local seminaries and churches.

A female role model for women in ministry is very important because, according to Carol Noren,

> seeing another woman in the pulpit has the effect of raising a sort of mirror to the woman preacher. It

---

[198] http://www.intrust.org/Portals/39/docs/IT413wheeler.pdf.

[199] http://www.ats.edu/resources/publicationspresentations.

causes her to compare her own work with this other person who is like her and yet not like her, to reflect on how she has grown and what she may become. *A feminine role model can demonstrate what a masculine one can only parody.* The way a woman's laughter, solemnity, tension, and other moods come across over a public address system is something only a woman preacher can show another.[200]

Noren's comments hit the mark, including this: "When a woman who is a role model testifies to the divine, enabling grace at work in her own life and ministry, her successors learn to claim its sustaining power for themselves."[201]

I had the good fortune of being the first Black female pastor, the first female senior pastor, and the first female professor of preaching in my denomination. It has, at times, also been a misfortune, in that I didn't have other female role models to help me work through or understand some of the challenges or opportunities as I matured as a minister in each position. For instance, when I became senior pastor of one of our larger congregations in North America, the men who had been used to decades of hearing the amplified monotone of their male senior pastor complained vociferously that I screamed when I preached. It was an insight from the Holy Spirit that enlightened me to realize that it offended their eardrums when I raised my voice, in moments of exuberance, because they were unaccustomed to hearing the amplified voice of a woman preacher. Now, as a role model for women in the Word, I share tips with other women on how to strengthen their voices so that it doesn't sound screechy or nagging when amplified.

For example, I once read that Ellen White developed her voice—in the days when microphones were not as available as they are today—by going into the woods to practice projecting her voice.

---

[200] *The Woman in the Pulpit,* p. 30.

[201] Ibid.

Since I viewed her as one of my role models, I too went into the woods near our church and preached loudly to the trees. I still claim that there's a forest of converted trees in Maryland, where I preached and projected with such passion that it often brought sweat, if not blood. The result was and is that my vocal cords developed a strength and resonance that has engaged listeners and, according to their testimonies, changed the minds of many who were opposed or objected to women preachers. Today, I highly recommend tools found in the video accompanying the book *Performance in Preaching: Bringing the Sermon to Life (Engaging Worship)* by Childers and Schmit.

There's also a desperate need of role models for women preachers in nonverbal, self-disclosure and communication. In fact, there's no limit to which I would have striven to be told or taught what Carol Noren wrote:

> This is more than a matter of commenting on what is aesthetically pleasing or conventional. Nonverbal communication is a theological issue. By it the preacher reinforces or negates sermon content. Consciously or unconsciously, the woman preacher models for the congregation what she believes to be important and unimportant in her message. Through clothing, posture, face, and gesture she discloses her understanding of being created in the image of God, female, and called to ministry. Nonverbal communication, like the first-person reference or story about other women, is linked to gender expectations in our culture."[202]

Women preachers need female mentors for self-disclosure in attire, gestures, facial expressions, voice control, body language, and a host of other unspoken expressions that accompany preaching the Word.

---

[202] *The Woman in the Pulpit*, p. 77.

Wanted: Meaningful Mentors

But such mentors must be real. Women are not looking for other women who just pay lip service to the process of mentoring, but those who will bring meaning and faithfulness to the role. I once heard a preacher say that the word *mentor* could be defined as "men touring the life of another." Since I grew up in England, where queens refer to themselves as "the prince" or "the king," and since there is a female king in Ghana,[203] I don't feel compelled to be politically correct and gender inclusive when I use that phrase to underscore the need for "wo-men-touring" the life of another woman in ministry.

When I mentor women, I first ask for a written paragraph or two of what such mentoring means to the mentee and what are some of the measureable outcomes or competencies they anticipate at the end of the process, for mentoring is not a lifetime appointment or a game people play. I also invite mentees to spend a day or more "touring" my life, because some things are better learned through observation than conversation. It means that they accompany me in the classroom or when I go shopping for clothes, personal necessities, and groceries— during which I'm always stopped by other shoppers for a variety of reasons, but seldom about fashion or politics. They also go with me to the gym, social gatherings, my study as I deliberate over sermons, and in worship as I deliver what I prepared. It helps them to understand the importance of being as normal as possible in an extraordinary situation, such as the high calling to ministry.

Some of the other areas in which mature women in ministry can mentor those new to the role include dress, general decorum, pulpit presence, deportment, and speech (such as finding one's preaching voice and proper posture). No matter how supportive of women in the pulpit a man may be, he cannot successfully help in these areas with balanced sensitivity and diplomacy.

---

[203] See story of the American secretary who became a female king in Nigeria at http://www.cnn.com/2013/01/31/world/africa/king-peggy-otuam-ghana/.

The absence of female mentors is not just a difficulty for women in ministry. It has been recognized as a problem in all professions as more women break through the glass ceilings of sports, business, politics, and religion. However, "though positive role models are useful for theological, professional, and personal maturation of anyone in ministry, a general shortage of feminine models means that *a woman must be intentional about identifying and claiming those who will help equip and sustain the maturation process.*" Additionally, "because models serve differing functions at various stages of ministry, the woman preacher will do well to discern which ones are needed at a given time, which have outlived their usefulness, and which, if not set aside, may actually impede her development" (emphasis mine).[204]

To avoid "a common hazard: the danger of overidentification with a model at the expense of one's individual integrity and gifts,"[205] when selecting a role model or mentor, women in the Word should be very discerning. Never recoil from vetting a potential mentor or role model. Be observant regarding the temperament and attitude of such a candidate. Is she overbearing, controlling, emotionally needy, desperate for approval, eager for acceptance and approbation? Does she practice what she preaches and teaches? In a contemporary Christian culture in which Jesus sells more than he saves, and where the prosperity gospel has penetrated almost every pulpit, does she use the Word of God as an avenue to fame and fortune or as a source of inspiration to transform others?

The lack of consistent, accessible role models and mentors for women in the pulpit inspired me to create a preaching model for women in my Doctor of Ministry dissertation at Boston University School of Theology.[206] It invites "feminists, womanists, and women of other faiths to focus on common threads of faith so that the

---

[204] *The Woman in the Pulpit,* p. 43.

[205] Ibid.

[206] *Theleia Theology: A Preaching Model for Women,* 1998.

religious dialogue of reconciliation may be engaged and expanded in earnest" through our preaching and teaching ministries.[207]

A Few of My Role Models (whom I've never met)

"Although women who preach have not been, and still are not, widely recognized in mainstream Christianity as the equals of male preachers, they have continued to come forth and to pursue the prize—the pulpit."[208] Many of them have been incredible wordsmiths, prophets who spoke for God, and iconic preachers/teachers who've left indelible legacies across the rocky road that women in ministry tread. Some, like me, had no mentors, but paved the way for those who follow in their footsteps until Jesus comes. It was to these role models from the past that I turned to obtain the guidance I so desperately needed, especially in the early years of my ministry. Although the list is too long to include all those from whom I drew strength, wisdom, understanding, and professional guidance, and although I never had the privilege of personally meeting them, the following women have been a blessing in a variety of ways. They also continue to have a great deal of influence on my life and ministry.

Ellen G. White (1827–1915) was a founder, formative leader, and prolific author of my denomination, the Seventh-day Adventist Church. She "has been largely ignored" in homiletics and religious literature of mainstream Christianity despite her prophetic writings or the fact that "471 [of her] sermons are known to exist from the period of 1865 to 1915, the majority [of which] deal with the subject of Christian faith and life. The rest cover a wide range of topics, such as ministry (65), education (39), medicine (31), miscellaneous topics (28), health and temperance (20), and publishing (4)."[209]

From the beginning of my divine call to preach and teach the gospel, I believed women can do aspects of ministry that men cannot

---

[207]   Ibid.

[208]   *Daughters of Thunder*, p. 11.

[209]   *Concise Encyclopedia of Preaching*, p. 502.

accomplish. Ellen White, a strong supporter of women in ministry, confirmed this when she wrote in *Words to Lay Members*:

> The Lord has a work for women, as well as men. They may take their places in His work . . . and He will work through them. If they are imbued with a sense of their duty, and labor under the influence of the Holy Spirit, they will have just the self-possession required for the time. *The Savior will reflect upon these self-sacrificing women the light of His countenance, and will give them a power that exceeds that of men. They can do for families a work that men cannot do, a work that reaches the inner life. They can come close to the hearts of those whom men cannot reach.* Their labor is needed (emphasis mine).[210]

Rev. Dr. Ella Pearson Mitchell (1917–2008) was the first woman dean of Sisters Chapel at Spelman College. She taught at the American Baptist Seminary West and Claremont School of Theology. But her greatest influence on my preaching life and ministry came through *Those Preaching Women*, a five-volume collection of Black women's sermons she edited, as well as *Fire in the Well*, a joint autobiography with her husband, Henry, the acknowledged father of Black, or African American, preaching.

From her I learned to avoid mediocrity at all cost and to embrace a consistent "practice of excellence," especially "as a means of dealing with those who would despise" or oppose women who respond to the call of God to preach. "Excellence," she insisted, "transcends its detractors. And in the end, it will conquer, moving past opposition to be used by God."[211]

To accomplish such a professional goal of excellence, and to be recognized for it, women in ministry have to be academically and

---

[210]   *Welfare Ministry*, p. 145.

[211]   *Those Preaching Women*, vol. 2, p. 14.

homiletically ten times better than male colleagues, as was Daniel and his three friends (Dan. 1:15). "There is a sense in which this is an unjust load," Dr. Pearson observed. "But there is another sense in which this may be used of God to save the church for which Christ died. God did not wish that we women be so burdened, but God reserves the right to wring from this cross a blessing for us, as well as for the church. In a day when the church is more threatened than ever, it may be that it requires more dedication and preparation than ever."[212]

Congresswoman Barbara Jordan (1936–1996) was a lawyer, educator, politician, and the first African American congresswoman from the Deep South. The daughter of a Baptist minister, Jordan served as a US congressional representative from Texas. She was the first and, to date, the only African American woman to deliver the keynote speech at a national political convention. From my early teens, I was a logophile (lover of words), but it was from Barbara Jordan that I learned their full importance, power, influence, and value. I observed how she articulated and gave life to each expression so that her words not only left a lasting impression, but also, like cherished servants, always fulfilled their mission. Her opening statement to the House Judiciary Committee proceedings on the impeachment of Richard Nixon, given on July 25, 1974, riveted the nation and changed my attitude forever when it comes to the use of words, the coining of phrases, and the elocution of a speech or sermon. Her demeanor was authoritative, her emotions tempered, her timing impeccable, and her voice was like a bell that jarred the nation awake from an uneasy slumber. A voice crying out for justice in the wilderness, she spoke with authority in a manner that all—great and small—could hear and understand. From that day, I dared to dream of speaking like Barbara Jordan.

Although I do not subscribe to every aspect of feminist theology, the early writings of pioneers such as Rosemary Radford-Reuther, Elizabeth Schussler Fiorenza, and Letty Russell opened the eyes of

---

[212] Ibid.

my understanding in ways worthy of being paid tribute.[213] Feminist theology had its genesis in the twentieth century, during the period of increasing public recognition of society's exploitation of women and the protests led by proponents of the feminist movement that took America and the world by storm. Their public outcry against marginalization of women, as well as centuries of injustices perpetrated by "patriarchal" societies and religion, led to some significant changes in church and national polity. A natural outgrowth of feminist theology is feminist preaching, described as the voice or religious proclamation with the central theme of addressing the oppression, violence, and inequity created by the contemporary social realities of gender prejudice and dehumanizing "isms," such as handicappism, ageism, sexism, classism, and so forth.

Christine M. Smith, one of the early feminist authors, said, "Preaching from a feminist perspective involves solidarity and oneness, not elite detachment and individual power. It is not talking about solidarity; it is about creating it by the very act of proclamation."[214] And because our society rears women to compete against each other more than network with each other, the emphasis on or call for solidarity among women in ministry is a challenging but exhilarating one.

Womanist theology and preaching is an extension of feminist theology from which I've learned a great deal about looking at a biblical narrative without preconceived notions. The term's creator, Alice Walker, Pulitzer Prize–winning poet and novelist, says *womanist* is indigenous to African American folklore. She defines *womanist* as "a black feminist or feminist of color" who is "responsible, capable," and "emotionally flexible."[215]

Delores Williams, a professor at Union Theological Seminary and one of the most productive womanist authors, defines it as being unapologetically concerned about the well-being of African American

---

[213]   See *Weaving the Visions: New Patterns in Feminist Spirituality.*

[214]   *Weaving the Sermon: Preaching in a Feminist Perspective,* p. 56.

[215]   *In Search of Our Mother's Garden: Womanist Prose,* p. 41.

---

women, yet as very "committed to [the] survival and wholeness of entire people, male and female," adding that "womanist is to feminist as purple is to lavender."[216] Williams supports her position by stating that, since the pre-Civil War, the black woman's experience has been mired in coerced and then postbellum voluntary surrogacy; therefore, the "image of a surrogate God" cannot have salvific power for black women in a world still dominated by white male rule. It was in response to the repeated use of the term "white male rule" in womanist theology that I coined the term "leukosanerocracy" from three Greek words: *leukos* ("white"), *aner* ("man" or "male"), and *cratos* ("rule").

"How to" Preaching Tips for Women

It is a known fact among homileticians that women excel in discovering or drawing fresh insights from Scripture. The reason is that we do not stand outside a text and analyze it. We step into its world and see, taste, and smell its texture before concluding exactly what it means. This kind of hermeneutic, as mentioned previously, is experiential. Yet despite our prowess in Scripture, the consistent lack of available role models often leaves some in a quandary over simple social standards.

For example, one of the most-asked of me questions by women, especially the younger ones in ministry, is "How should I dress, particularly when preaching?" The reason, I believe, is due to the rapidly changing mores in dress as the world becomes more casual in terms of public appearance. For instance, unless you are a member of the emergent generation, you might remember the days when a female lawyer couldn't appear in an American courtroom wearing pants—not even if it was part of an expensive, classic, well-fitted suit. Today, women lawyers can, like men, dress in pantsuits.

Worshippers now wear anything comfortable, from shorts to spaghetti strap dresses for church. Some appear like a woman I saw

---

[216] *Sisters in the Wilderness: The Challenge of Womanist God-talk*, p. 243.

in tie-dyed jeans at an announced formal dress banquet. Although I do not wear them in the pulpit during our Sabbath morning service, more and more women, who may not be robed, are wearing pantsuits. However, my recommendation is to exegete your audience to know when and where a dress is acceptable or expected. Thank God that—like the disappearance of requirements for only suits with skirts by female lawyers—such a dress code for female preachers is "gone with the wind."

Another question that ranks at the top is how to find one's voice. The human voice is the vehicle for the message and the best indicator of who is the presenter. "Without a dynamic, natural voice, it is difficult to obtain and maintain the attention of the listener."[217] Yet among preachers, it is the least understood, worst protected or cared-for instrument of communicating the gospel. "Naturally, without any special effort, the voice is easily manipulated up and down the pitch range, altering between loud and quiet, fast-paced and leisurely, and modulating quality to add variety. This control over the many dimensions of sound should be treasured."[218]

To begin to find and treasure one's voice, the preacher must be able to distinguish between the habitual and natural voice. The habitual voice is what a person grows up using; but it may not be natural because when one is anxious or distressed, it squeaks or becomes tinny and screechy. However, the natural voice is sometimes lower or higher than the habitual and can stretch without strain. Finding one's natural voice gives the preacher confidence and the audience pleasure in listening to the message. Sometimes, when students preach, their habitual voice slips into a lower register and sounds unnaturally raspy, guttural, or husky. Or it can also express itself at a higher register that sounds whiny, sharp, hyper-nasal, adenoidal, and unpleasant, like fingernails on a blackboard.

Preachers can distinguish between their natural or habitual voice or discover their natural voice by practicing the following:

---

[217] *Concise Encyclopedia of Preaching*, p. 495.

[218] Ibid.

1. Breathing exercises emphasize the use of the diaphragm instead of the throat for vocalization. "Breathing for speech differs from ordinary breathing employed during sleep or other nonvocal activities. Speech utilizes expiratory air, which vibrates the vocal folds and produces sound. Common breathing problems of the minister include (a) speaking too long without a pause for breath, (b) pausing long enough for short gasps only, and (c) placing too much attention on breathing by using shoulder and neck muscles rather than the efficient abdominals, resulting in strained, unnatural voice."[219]

2. Pitch can be the bane of a woman's voice when amplified before she learns how to control it. The pitch is "determined by the length, mass, and balance of tension in the vocal folds. For example, a small woman would have smaller vocal folds and therefore produce a higher pitch than a large man. Thus our natural pitch is inherent since it is related to gender and body frame. But other factors, such as stress or stage fright, add tension to the vocal folds and can result in an elevated, strained voice."[220]

To help my students, especially women, discover their natural voice and appropriate pitch, I regularly invite specialists in speech therapy and other aspects of communications to demonstrate and guide them in the development and proper use of this treasure called voice. "Understanding and nurturing the voice are essential to the longevity and effectiveness of a minister's livelihood. Developing a natural and dynamic style of speaking will ensure a voice that will be reliable and effective for a lifetime."[221] Vocal resonance and great articulation when speaking, particularly in English, will help

---

[219] Ibid.

[220] Ibid., p. 496.

[221] Ibid., p. 497.

congregants with hearing challenges better understand what the preacher is saying.

Here is a question seldom asked but deserving of attention: "How do I acquire the art of storytelling?" I have observed that women have difficulty telling stories or giving testimony without meandering. For example, we like to include every little detail of who said what and when, such as "On the way to the market a mile from the hair salon, I ran into Margaret, and she said, 'How are you?' And I said, 'I'm fine,' and she said 'You do look fine,' and I said . . ." ad infinitum. My recommendation is to write out your story or testimony and edit, edit, edit until you find and use the most descriptive words, the shortest sentences, and the best turns of phrase to grab and hold the listener's attention. Always remember that the shorter and more concise a story, the greater the impression it will leave in the minds of your audience. As previously mentioned, preachers, like comedians, make their living with words; therefore, to understand verbal punctuation and how to use it effectively, every preacher, female or male, should observe and learn from them.

To become a better preacher also includes paying attention to demeanor and decorum. Although the following are not exclusively feminine traits, please make every effort to avoid picking at invisible lint, nervously straightening clothing, touching your face, picking your nose, licking a finger to turn pages, and scratching one's head. Check to make sure a skirt, especially a flowing one, isn't longer in the back than the front, or vice versa. Make sure underthings with shoulder straps are well hidden and that slips are not showing below the hem; and if, by chance, you wear a short skirt to sit on a platform elevated above the sight line of the audience, never forget your seated posture. It means that, for dressing, an extra moment before a full-length mirror is not only necessary, it is required! Unless we make ourselves aware of such things, some women preachers, who don't have pockets to jingle coins in like men, will inadvertently slip into such awkward-looking antics when feeling anxious or nervous.

Feel free to use feminine phrases or jargon. In the early years of feminist theology, female God language brought words such as "weaving, sewing, patterns, pregnant, and birthing" into sermons. Such new language was blazed across the covers and generously sprinkled through the pages of feminist books and articles. Rita M. Gross defended the feminine God language when she wrote:

> Let me say immediately that I am quite aware that God is not really either female or male or anything in between. I only wish the people who argue to retain solely male imagery were as aware that God is not really male as I am that God is not really female. I am talking about the only thing we can talk about— *images* of God, not God . . . All the words used in the religious enterprise are, in the long run, analogous and metaphorical. Every statement contains bracketed "as if" or "as it were." Statements about God cannot be taken literally. They do not exhaust the possibilities at all. Rather, they are the best that can be done at present by means of an imperfect medium. They have inherent finality, no ultimate truth, no unalterable relevance. They are tools—linguistic conventions. Such are the inherent limitations of language about God . . ."[222]

Today, even men use this language in the pulpit, as some speak of being impregnated by the Holy Spirit and the inspiration of birthing a sermon.

Women Can and Should Create New Rituals

I once read an article about "Finding Comfort After a Miscarriage," in which the author wrote, "Jewish women who find that the tradition does not provide rituals to sacrilize the events of their lives have turned back to the tradition for the tools to create

---

[222] "Female God Language in a Jewish Context" in *Womanspirit Rising,* pp. 168, 169.

new rituals."[223] I had just received a phone call a few days prior from a young mother whose firstborn child had died in her seventh month of pregnancy. She and her husband were distraught and wanted me to do a funeral for the baby, whom they had lovingly named. As we laid that tiny child to rest in the cemetery in a specially designed box, the parents' grief was palpable. Watching them cling to each other in their loss, I remembered the above quote and decided at the graveside that I would introduce a new ritual into the life of my congregation.

Within a few weeks, we held our first service for parents who had lost infants. During the service, I urged them to name their unborn or prematurely deceased child or children. We invited others than our regular church members, and to our surprise, the service was packed that morning. Members made a small cradle and placed it at the foot of the cross on our platform, and I preached a sermon about Christ's love for little children, followed by a litany I composed that allowed parents to express their grief and mourn their loss. Near the end of the service, we suggested that participants write the name of the child or children they'd lost on a card prepared for the occasion. Also, we instructed them to place the card in the cradle at a specific time during the service. Then we prayed for all those children, calling out their names before God and our congregants as we joined in the families' grief. There wasn't a dry eye among the worshippers by the end of the service. Many expressed then, and weeks afterward, how cathartic and healing an experience it had been for them.

After the service, an eighty-something-year-old wife of a retired missionary to China took me aside and told me her story. The woman had been in her twenties when her first child was stillborn in a strange land far away from home. She never had the opportunity to see him, touch him, name him, and express her feelings of loss, because the body was whisked away and interred in an unmarked grave. Several years later, she had visited that location and walked the grounds, searching and praying for an opportunity to grieve and release the pain of loss. Now she affirmed how blessed she was to

---

[223] *In Our Own Voices*, p. 150.

have participated in this new ritual, saying, "Where were you sixty years ago? I have carried this pain for so long, and only today have I been able to release it after I named my firstborn and emotionally laid him to rest."

As pastors, we encounter these and many other painful transitions and occasions, but they provide opportunities to introduce rituals to relieve the distress some may have carried for years. "There are no traditional prayers to recite over a miscarriage. There is no funeral or mourning ritual to follow. After suffering a miscarriage, a woman does not even routinely recite the prayer said after coming safely through a dangerous experience . . . something all women can do after giving birth."[224]

Ladies, let us exercise the privilege to create rites for these and other important passages in the lives of the members of the body of Christ whom we serve. For this, too, among the diverse opportunities to preach and teach, we have been called and sent by our Savior to exercise a spirit of collaboration.

[224] Ibid.

CHAPTER 9

Preaching to the Contemporary Mind

> *Every few hundred years in Western history, there occurs a sharp transformation . . . within a few short decades, society rearranges itself—its worldview; its basic values; its social and political structure; its arts; its key institutions . . . Fifty years later, there is a new world and the people born then cannot even imagine the world in which their grandparents lived and into which their own parents were born. We are currently living through just such a transformation.[225]*

The world and its people have changed—and so must our preaching! The cultural and philosophical shift from modernity to postmodernity requires it. The millennial generation—who sees and understands the world differently from previous generations and who vote with their purses, feet, and diminishing presence in organized churches—demands it. Therefore, contemporary preachers and books on homiletics must ask and answer the question, "How can we preach to this generation?" First, let's review the following.

---

[225] Peter F. Drucker, *The Post-Capitalist World*, *http://www.nationalaffairs.com/doclib/20080709_19921096thepostcapitalistworldpeterfdrucker.pdf.*

Process of Generational Identification

Generational identification is neither a science nor an art. It's not merely a question of demographics or world events, nor is it a matter of identifying cultural touchstones. Rather, it is a process invented, as well as initiated, by advertising agents, business consultants, and lifestyle trend journalists. The American public, however, and the watching world it infects, tend to buy into such generational schemes by accepting and treating their prognostications as genuine science. Having said that, and since we have no suitable alternative categories, and because we are conditioned to accept it, let us continue to use them so as to understand better those we intend to reach.

Among the most respected and popular authors of generational studies are Neil Howe and William Strauss.[226] They describe themselves as authorities on generational change in American history. Their work has many scholarly characteristics, but it also shrewdly combines marketing, business consulting, and lifestyle trend journalism. According to their theory, the United States has witnessed the following five generations during the past century:

1901–24 GI Generation
1925–42 Silent Generation
1943–60 Boomers
1961–81 Thirteenth Generation to know the US flag
1982–2002 Millennial

The *Boston Globe*'s *Brainiac Guide* blog argues that Howe and Strauss's identification is flawed because there were actually several more generations born during the past century.[227] The following is the Brainiac's Guide to America's Recent Generations:

1884–93: ~~Lost Generation~~ The New Kids

---

[226] See *Generations: The History of America's Future, 1584–2069*.

[227] http://www.boston.com/bostonglobe/ideas/brainiac/2007/12/the_socalled_si.html.

1894–1903: ~~Lost Generation~~ Hard-boiled Generation
1904–13: ~~The Greatest Generation~~ Partisans
1914–23: ~~The Greatest Generation~~ The New Gods
1924–33: ~~The Silent Generation~~ Postmodernist Generation
1934–43: ~~The Silent Generation~~ Anti-Anti-Utopian Generation
1944–53: Baby Boomers
1954–63: ~~Baby Boomers~~ OGX (Original Generation X)
1964–73: ~~Generation X~~ PC Generation
1974–83: ~~Generations X/Y~~ Net Generation
1984–93: Millennials
1994–2003: ~~Millennials~~ TBA

Somewhere between the two concepts of generational categories lies the truth, but since I am not an expert in this area, I will continue our discussion using extant literature and information as above. Note that the *Brainiac Guide* identifies those born between 1994–2003 (and, by inference, anyone born after that date) as TBA (to be announced).

Phyllis Tickle[228] says that whatever we may think or say about this generation, we must agree that there has been a noticeable shifting and reconfiguring of itself in such extraordinary ways as to defy any final assessment or absolute projection of its final form. She suggests that every five hundred years, such a major shift occurs in religion—the current one possibly dating to September 11, 2001, when terrorists attacked and destroyed the Twin Towers and took more than three thousand innocent lives. However, Tickle also suggests a more subtle genesis a few decades prior to that catastrophic event, and since we are not even midway through the five hundred years, we should call this generation "emerging," because no one knows what it will be at its culmination. Other generational observers predict that we are the first generation in three hundred years to go through a distinct cultural change and paradigm shift in religion.

---

[228] *Emergence Christianity: What It Is, Where It Is Going, and Why It Matters.*

Decades ago, Francis Schaeffer, the late American theologian, philosopher, and apologist, was concerned with the transformation in epistemology (what we know). In a conversation in which he expressed his concern about the proliferation of the postmodern philosophy, he reportedly exclaimed in exasperation, "We are no longer living in a Judeo-Christian culture. We are living in a post–Judeo-Christian culture." Since then, with the violence of extremist Islam, it has become evident that in these last days, we are no longer living in a post–Judeo-Christian culture, but actually in an anti–Judeo-Christian worldview and culture. Several generations influenced by or embracing a postmodern ideology coexist today; therefore, it seems plausible to define the following.

Modernism. A late nineteenth- and early twentieth-century movement, sought the following:

a. From a humanistic perspective, to break with traditional and classical forms in the arts, character, or quality of thought, expression, and technique.

b. From a religious point of view, theology tended to accommodate traditional religious teachings to contemporary thought and practice, especially in the downplaying of supernatural elements.

In the Roman Catholic Church, its proponents attempted to modify traditional beliefs in accordance with contemporary ideas, creating major theological conflicts.[229]

Postmodernism. A theory or philosophy involving a radical reappraisal of modernism assumptions about culture, identity, history, religion, and language. It has morphed into a contemporary movement of thought that developed in the 1970s. Reacting to the rejection of the dogma, principles, or practices established by modernism through its denial of the possibility of objective knowledge, postmodernism is therefore skeptical of truth, unity, and progress as defined by

---

[229] See *The Condemnation of Modernism* by Cardinal Mercier—http://www.cfnews.org/Mercier-Modernism.htm.

modernist interpretations. For example, whereas the church (Roman Catholic and Protestant) accepted that Jesus said "I am the way, *the truth*, and the life," (John 14:6, emphasis mine), people embracing postmodern assumptions do not understand "truth" the way those who reject postmodernism do.

For instance, we were trained to discover truth based on the five foundational Protestant principles of (1) *sola scriptura*—by Scripture alone, (2) *sola fide*—by faith alone, (3) *sola gratia*—by grace alone, (4) *solo Christo*—through Christ alone, and (5) *soli deo Gloria*—glory to God alone. But today, the Western world has seen a significant change in this concept of truth, for postmodernism holds to no objective truth. Rather, truth is not to be discovered but created. This means that, from a postmodern perspective, whatever you think is truth, is truth. It doesn't matter what an author wrote, especially in the ancient books of the Bible or in Judeo-Christian writings today. Postmodernists tend to favor the concepts of alternate reality called *uchronie*[230] (counterfactual theory), concluding that perception is everything. It means that whatever you perceive to have happened is just as true as what actually did take place. Thus their motto is

---

[230] A genre of fictional literature called "alternative history." It consists of stories that ask "what-if" questions in which real records of past events are recreated to determine how different life would be in the present experience. Contemporary novels using alternative history are called *uchronie*, based on the prefix "u" as in *utopia*, a place that doesn't exist, and "chronos," Greek for *time*. Thus, "uchronie" has become a buzzword for a time that doesn't exist, and that's exactly what alternative history offers—times and things that do not exist. Yet scholars from major universities have joined other secular authors to produce essays ranging from serious scholarly efforts to fanciful, satirical portrayals. Some in the entertainment industry use time travel, such as the *Back to the Future* movies, to replace what actually exists and show how the world would be "if" something had taken place differently in history. Today, some of the most explored themes in these popular genres of "What if the past had happened otherwise?" include "What would life be like if the Nazis had won WWII? What if Christopher Columbus hadn't made it to America? What if the Confederacy had won the American Civil War? And what if 9/11 never happened?"

"Don't impose your values one me—let me determine what is right or wrong for me."

As a result, we have (a) not a postmodern generation but, rather, overlapping generations who wholeheartedly embrace and live by the postmodern philosophy; (b) generations who no longer have the ability to discern right from wrong because they have lost the truth about the person, character, and nature of God; and (c) generations with postmodern ideologies, thinking Christianity is false because it emphatically claims to be true and declares all other religions that do not accept Jesus Christ as Savior as invalid.

Generations Raised Under Postmodernism

The March 4, 1966, edition of the *London Evening Standard* published an article titled "How Does a Beatle Live?" It presented a behind-the-scenes look at the internationally popular musical group. The article contained a number of musings, remarks, and random thoughts from a conversation with the late John Lennon, member and lyricist of the Beatles. When asked about his personal view of the current state of religion, he replied, "Christianity will go. It will vanish and shrink. I needn't argue about that. I'm right and I will be proved right. *We're more popular than Jesus now.* I don't know which will go first, rock 'n' roll or Christianity. *Jesus was all right, but his disciples were thick and ordinary. It's them twisting it that ruins it for me*" (emphasis mine).[231]

When the report reached the United States, thousands of American Christians not only resented the sacrilegious nature of Lennon's musings, but some worshippers launched a "Ban the Beatles" campaign and protested with placards outside the concert venues of their US tour later that year. It's been more than four decades since that statement rattled the cage of the sleeping giant called American Christianity, and little did they know how prophetic

---

[231] http://www.beatlesinterviews.org/db1966.0304-beatles-john-lennon-were-more-popular-than-jesus-now-maureen-cleave.html.

were those words. For look at the state of Christianity among our largest generation, the one now labeled millennial.

A February 2010 article entitled "Religion Among Millennials" by the Pew Research Center reported:

> By some key measures, Americans ages 18 to 29 are considerably less religious than older Americans. Fewer young adults belong to any particular faith than older people do today. They also are less likely to be affiliated than their parents' and grandparents' generations were when they were young. Fully one in four members of the Millennial generation—so called because they were born after 1980 and began to come of age around the year 2000—are unaffiliated with any particular faith. Indeed, Millennials are significantly more unaffiliated than members of Generation X were at a comparable point in their life cycle (20% in the late 1990s) and twice as unaffiliated as Baby Boomers were as young adults (13% in the late 1970s). Young adults also attend religious services less often than older Americans today. And compared with their elders today, fewer young people say that religion is very important in their lives.[232]

When one reads the entire article, it is obvious that it uses the term *religion* as a synonym for *Christianity*, and even clearer that, regardless how we feel about John Lennon's now ancient remarks, they are being fulfilled in front of our very eyes. Revisiting those ominous words alongside recent statistics about the drastic drop in attendance at Christian worship and the enrollment in seminaries is like a clarion call from Jesus saying, "Are you still sleeping and resting? Behold, the hour is at hand, and the Son of Man is being

---

[232]   http://www.pewforum.org/2010/02/17/religion-among-the-millennials/.

betrayed into the hands of sinners. Get up, let us be going; behold, the one who betrays Me is at hand!" (Matt. 26:45, 46).

The time has definitely come for Christians to talk less about being true and right or having the truth and instead aggressively and passionately evangelize this generation with the story of Jesus Christ and his incredible love and amazing grace. Additionally, as previously noted, we must now preach to a diverse overlapping of generations, five of which I have identified as follows:

First, *baby boomers* (1944–1953). They came of age during the anxious era of the Cold War and its threat of apocalyptic nuclear war. Second and third are (a) the *Original Generation X* (1954–1963) and (b) *Generation X*, also known as the *Politically Correct (PC) Generation* (1964–1973). Both came of age when, on the home front, African Americans were challenging segregation, a new youth culture was emerging, and sociologists, social critics, poets, and others were critiquing American society, all in an atmosphere charged with paranoia on the political front. Their protests led to the rejection of the GI generation's rules without content but unfortunately threw out God with the unwanted rules.

The fourth is *Generation X/Y*, called the *Net Generation* (1974–1983). Currently in their thirties, they are the most racially and ethnically diverse generation, greatly influenced by the rapid expansion of the internet, cable television channels, satellite radio, and other such technological advances. Some have referred to them as "the lost generation," because they are the first group of "latchkey" kids and single-parent families exposed to lots of divorce and day care. They are also characterized by a reputation for violent computer games and high levels of skepticism because they choose a church to attend as they do their movies—with an attitude of "what's in it for me?"

The fifth generation are the *millennials* (1984–2002). The term was coined in 1988 as they entered kindergarten, anticipating their high school graduation date of 2000, the first year of the new millennium. Also called the emergent generation, they are largest in the United States (more than 80 million strong), eclipsing baby boomers. They avoid conventional churches and worship, resulting in a significant decline in their presence, regardless of the denomination. Reportedly, their main reason for rejecting Christianity is because it claims to be the only true religion while declaring all others to be false. The result is that they are a generation who has lost the truth about the person, character, and nature of God, along with the ability to discern right from wrong from an organized Christian perspective. Current church growth statistics indicate that 80 percent of the millennial generation who become Christians are converted not because Christianity is true and Christ is Lord and Savior, but because it's the best thing that has come along at that particular time. Therefore, as soon as something appears that they think is better, they will drop out of church.\

Experts in social studies suggest one should not neglect the emerging Generation Z. They are characterized by four marks: (a) Recession, (b) Wifi enabled, (c) Sexually fluid and (d) Post Christian attitude.

How then can we reach and teach these diverse groups, especially the emerging generation that embraces a postmodern mind-set and worldview? How can we preach the gospel to those who know "neither the Lord nor what He had done"? (Judg. 2:10). Here are a few recommendations:

Preaching must be biblical. I have already defined biblical preaching in a previous chapter. However, a brief observation is fitting because this means that preachers must be fully immersed in the Word of God every day of the week so that when they open the inspired text, they are in communication with God and are therefore able to interpret and expound Scripture with authenticity, authority, sensitivity, and passion. "There are three ways in which we can responsibly receive communications from God: by giving deliberate thoughtful attention to the Incarnation; by identifying ourselves with the church [not a building, but the *ekklesia*—called out, living body of believers [cf. Eph. 1:23]; and by means of Bible revelation."[233]

---

[233] *Approved Unto God*, p. 15.

Unfortunately, preachers today suffer from a spiritual vacuum arising from either believing in Him, but not believing Him, or from refusing to treat Him seriously or to do His will faithfully. I believe that's why, in the words of Oswald Chambers, "The majority of orthodox ministers are hopelessly useless, and the unorthodox seem to be the only ones who are used" by God nowadays. "We need men and women saturated with the truth of God who can restate the old truth in terms that appeal to our day."[234] This alone will cause the Word to come alive and God's voice to be heard clearly when the audience is drawn into a conversation with Him as they listen to the preacher and are transformed or persuaded to obey Him.

Preaching must be relational. I have also presented a description of relational preaching and the four major categories, including (a) the teaching sermon, (b) the interactive sermon, (c) the conversational sermon, and (d) the questioning sermon. In addition, the deductive preaching of doctrines, in a commanding voice with a pointed finger, that prescribes how to think and what to believe does not resonate with the millennial generation. Large numbers of them no longer seem to need to or will readily attend "command performances" in organized churches with hard pews lined up behind one another as a didactic preacher shouts at them during a deductive sermon. They get their news, watch sermons, and listen to a variety of values-oriented presentations from handheld digital devices, or they attend large arenas in which someone presents poetry and music to a diverse audience with promises to improve or develop its spirituality. This means that, in order to attract and retain their commitment, conventional churches must change their preaching styles to include more inductive, relational sermons that deal with relevant issues and less deductive sermonizing. Finally, preaching to the contemporary mind must be prophetic.

---

[234] Ibid., p. 19.

CHAPTER 10

Preaching Beyond the Choir

Perhaps no other phenomenon of the twentieth century has provoked more discussion, inquiry, and argument than the rapid proliferation and exploding technology of the modern mass communications media throughout the world. Elaborate and expensive research studies are conducted by the hundreds each year, heated disputes are conducted, glowing reports are heard about the media's potential, and sobering protests are made about the many calamities and damage being wrought by the media upon society. Religious mass media users also seem fascinated by the marvels of the new technology. Some acclaim the media as a modern-day miracle wrought by God, while others seem adamantly unconvinced that they can be used effectively in religious work.[235]

Preachers are famous for preaching to the choir. The phrase means they persistently commend an opinion to those who have already accepted it. Preaching to the choir clearly refers to the pointlessness of preachers who repeatedly attempt to convert those who are already

---

[235] B. E. Davis, *Mass Media in Missions, http://web.ovu.edu/missions/guidelines/ chap8.htm#top.*

converted and who, by their consistent presence, demonstrate their faith in the doctrine and mission of the church. Using this definition to evaluate sermons today, it seems that the large number seek to cajole, manipulate, coerce, and sometimes inspire the choir. How then can they preach beyond it? First, we must identify the audience we seek and then, without apology or reluctance, use the current technology of mass media to broadcast the gospel of grace to them.

"The world population (the total number of living humans on earth) was 7.244 billion as of July 2014, according to the medium fertility estimate by the United Nations Department of Economic and Social Affairs Population Division, and it is projected to reach 7.325 billion by July 2015."[236] Only a mere 2 billion embrace the Christian religion, and that number is declining, according to David Barrett and George T. Kurian, editors of *The World Christian Encyclopedia: A Comparative Survey of Churches and Religion.*

Today, in the early decades of the twenty-first century, many denominations in America are stagnant and have far less impact on our unbelieving culture than we are willing to admit or accept despite the vast number of buildings labeled as churches across our nation. Personal observation has led this author to conclude that there exist two groups who are "beyond the choir": children inside the church and those who are not believers outside, and are not being influenced by Christianity as they could or should be.[237] It means our preaching must reach both inside to win the hearts and minds of the spiritually disenfranchised as well as beyond the walls of our churches to transform the lives of those to whom the postmodern culture has bequeathed a legacy of apathy and indifference to Christian values and virtues.

---

[236] http://www.worldometers.info/world-population.

[237] This does not include our faithful, God-fearing practitioners of the Jewish or Muslim faith, for whom I have a deep love and respect.

How Can We Preach to Reach Children Inside Our Congregations?

Recently, I was shopping in a supermarket. In front of me was a mom with a toddler who couldn't be more than two years old. To my amazement, instead of struggling to hold a bottle to his mouth (as would have been normal in the past), the child was gripping an iPad Mini in one hand and intently watching/scrolling through programs. It was as if I had an epiphany, because I immediately realized that the Christian Church, in general, and my denomination, in particular, is far behind the times when it comes to reaching this group that is languishing, spiritually speaking, in our midst and yet is far beyond the choir. Imagine, I thought, what a difference it would make if we invested in iPad Minis and invited children to draw or watch a Bible story as we narrate it to them during our long worship services? Or what if we captured their attention and nurtured their rich imagination with cartoon Bible stories on any of those innovative devices? We could take a page from the display of iPads in the lounges at New York's LaGuardia Airport.

However, despite the proliferation of handheld devices, storytelling in person is still one of the best ways to hold children's interest and help them grasp those values that will help them cope successfully with life. Additionally, every sermon should have something, in the form of a video slide or a story, to which the children in a congregation can relate. The problem is that ministers and members are still fumbling and mumbling through stories during the "children's lesson" in weekly worship events. If I had a dime for each time I cringe during a story, I could retire as a wealthy woman today. I am exasperated by those who turn their backs to the children gathered in front and speak as if their assignment was to interest or entertain the adults. You know the story is going south when he or she grabs a microphone, stands up instead of stooping or sitting at the level of the children, turns to the congregation with his or her back to the children, and begins with "Boys and girls, I'm not a good storyteller, but . . ." or "I'm going to tell you a true story." Churches should be very selective about who receives the privilege of ministering to children during worship, but many are not. After carefully choosing such persons, they must be trained and equipped for such a life-transforming task.

My mentor and friend, Pastor Throstur Thordarson, reminds me regularly that children are not abstract or theological but are concrete in their thinking. They respond in unquestioning acceptance as they follow a story. Therefore, those who minister to children must own and feel the emotional value of the story in their hearts so that they do not present it mechanically. They are to remember the power of old fairy tales that taught them moral lessons and now present elemental truth in such a way that it becomes part of the child as she or he grows up.

While many are not natural-born storytellers, some find it easier than others, especially when it comes to telling a story to a group of children diverse in age and culture. Eric B. Hare, master storyteller and prolific author of children's stories, suggested that, to allay fear and nervousness, the speaker should present truth to children in the guise of images based on three primary principles: (1) simplicity, (2) directness, and (3) virility of character.

A. W. Spalding, another author and storyteller who often collaborated with Hare, wrote, "I am not a natural storyteller. My mind runs to other forms of thinking, and stories slip away from me. I have to keep practiced to meet the demand."[238] He suggests the following seven essentials in storytelling:

1. Select your story.
2. Know your story.
3. Feel your story.
4. Analyze and outline your story.
5. Modify your story as necessary.
6. Tell your story simply, directly, and expressively.
7. Have an aim and a climax.

---

[238] *Christian Storytelling*, p. 9.

Here are a few key elements of a good story:

1. Something must happen.

    a) Every step in each story is an event.
    b) They are all closely connected.
    c) There are no gaps in the plot—keep it simple.

2. Each event presents a distinct picture.

    a) Each picture is simple in its structure.
    b) Each picture is either familiar or a mystery.

3. There is often a fair amount of repetition.

Some of the great children storytellers agree that the storyteller must be acquainted with at least seven important tools: (1) imagination, (2) facial expressions, (3) body movements, (4) voice modulation and intonation, (5) verbal punctuation, (6) nervousness and tension, and (7) confidence. Such individuals will practice telling the story again and again prior to the moment of delivery. He or she will memorize and use integrated sentences that children can relate to or understand; and, more than anything, *never* interrupt the story to explain or illustrate a point believed to be complex or unclear. The storyteller's own mood must be ready at the moment of delivery because it and the direction of the story must be clear, authoritative from the beginning, and spoken without throat-clearing hems and haws. Spalding and Hare wrote:

> The storyteller, in coming to the little child, must hear a voice as from a burning bush: "Put off thy shoes from off thy feet, for the place whereon thou standest is holy ground." Here is the untrodden field of a soul fresh from the hand of the Creator; here is the temple of life opened to the service of consecrated priest.

With what reverence must the teacher approach one whom the Master used as a symbol of the kingdom of heaven! Out of the turmoil and strife of the world the storyteller steps into the presence of the child as into a sanctuary of innocence and peace. The altar with its eager fire is waiting for the incense . . .[239]

Here are a few additional noteworthy points every children's storyteller should observe:

1. Carefully plan your first words because it is important to pull the children immediately into the heart of the story with the opening sentences.
2. By no means begin with (a) "The name of my story is . . ." (b) "I heard this story years ago when . . ." (c) "I'm so glad to be with you today" (c) I'm not a good storyteller but . . ." or (d) "Now, boys and girls, this story . . ."
3. Instead, begin with "Buddy was a top dog. When he walked down the street, all the other dogs just moved out of the way" or "Jesus took a vacation. Did you know that?"
4. Know the story; possess and feel its message, various steps, and climax.
5. Flesh it out by the practice of telling and retelling it.
6. Memorization is useful, but avoid the pitfall of sounding like a wooden speaker or a robot.
7. As much as possible, according to the environment, seat the children close together in a half-circle (but don't be in the center), because they tend to be mentally close if they are physically close.
8. Create the mood, then tell the story with drama and zest.
9. Speak well, clearly, and loudly, using simple words joyously. No one can thoroughly enjoy a story clouded with theological or technical words that convey no meaning to them.

---

[239] Ibid., p. 12.

10. A child is adept at make-believe, but such imagining is, as a rule, practical and serious. It is credulity rather than imagination that helps children make-believe.

The telling of Bible stories follows the same rules as above, but you should do so using language and imagery that children can readily understand. It is also the responsibility of the storyteller to analyze and think about the story so as to articulate it clearly with passion and purpose. A big danger is to assume you know the story and then, under pressure during the delivery, forget important points. Here are a few tips to adapt a story for children: (a) carefully analyze the elements of the story, (b) decide which steps are needed to reach the climax, (c) include only a few characters for simplicity, and (d) change technical or theological terms into plain ones, as well as complex images into familiar ones. To further enhance or improve your storytelling skills, I have included several outstanding books in my bibliography.

How Can We Reach Beyond the Choir Outside Our Churches?

Whether you preach to a hundred or to thousands at a time, the best prospects of reaching unbelievers outside your community of faith is via social and other mass media. It consists of a diversified variety of formats and technologies that touch large audiences. This vast array falls into at least four categories:

1. Technologies that transmit information electronically, such as radio, recorded music, film, and television
2. Outdoor media, comprised of billboards, signs, and placards on or inside commercial buildings, sports stadiums, shops, and buses
3. Print media, including newspapers, books, pamphlets, flyers, magazines, comics

4. Digital media, composed of both internet and mobile devices for emails, websites, blogs, podcasts, YouTube, Twitter, Instagram, and others.

The Power of Digital Mass Media

We are living in a media-driven culture. Media marketing expert Phil Cooke wrote:

> I once heard it said that if an alien from another planet were to examine the United States and write an evaluation of our religious habits, he would probably conclude that Oprah is America's pastor, the vestments of the twenty-first-century church are manufactured by Nike, the communion table is poured by a barista from Starbucks, and in the children's department, a clown from McDonald's is certainly more widely recognized than Jesus of Nazareth. Today, people confess their sins on daytime television, purge their guilt by donating to TV evangelists, and seek redemption through the story arc in an action movie.[240]

Some preachers often underestimate and underuse the power of the global digital media as they fail to realize that such readily available forms of mass communication have changed our world more than any other technological advances since the dawn of time. Likewise, these formats have also impacted preaching, or how the Word is heard and received, but in a different way, more than any cultural force since the beginning of the early church. For instance, according to the A. C. Neilson Company, "The average American watches more than 4 hours of TV each day (28 hours/week, or 2

---

[240] *Branding Faith: Why Some Churches and Nonprofits Impact Culture and Others Don't*, p. 25.

months nonstop TV-watching per year). In a 65-year life, that person would have spent 9 years glued to the tube."[241]

Such viewing bombards people with more than three thousand advertising messages per day. The average family watches television and accesses the internet five to seven hours a day, and by the time children reach eighteen, they will have spent the equivalent of half a year consuming the mass media by watching television, listening to an iPod, talking on a cell phone, and surfing the internet. It means that this generation values their digital media space more than their people space and interaction. In fact, they would rather send a text message than endure a face-to-face conversation.

I once witnessed this in a California restaurant in which a couple sat across from each other, both feverishly texting, never saying a word or making eye contact, their attention focused on their handheld devices. Later, I discovered from the waiter that they were actually texting each other. All this means that while preachers speak to the choir one to two hours a week, those beyond the choir are consuming mass media five to six hours per day. Ask yourself, "Who has the most influence in their lives?"

Because some preachers do not use digital mass media as much as the public, the sad result is that we are barely, if at all, reaching those beyond the choir. So the question is "What can we do about this?" Are we, as B. E. Davis noted, going to join the heated disputes about the many dangers the media inflicts upon society? Will we continue to denounce those who bring and focus on such devices during worship, or are we going to learn to properly use such resources to preach the gospel so as to reach and transform this generation beyond the choir?

Keys to Understanding or Using Digital Mass Media

I must confess, although it's perhaps already obvious, that I am an admirer of Phil Cooke, author of several books about the importance

---

[241] https://www.csun.edu/science/health/docs/tv&health.html.

of Christians producing high-quality media programs. He taught me the following four significant keys in understanding and using digital mass media.

1. **The power of branding.** A label or identity indicated by a distinctive characteristic such as a stamp, graphic design, name, or trademark, it represents the story or reputation that surrounds a person, product, or organization.

Cooke emphatically asserts that identity is what makes one church different from the thousands clamoring for the attention of those we wish to reach with the gospel message. For example, decades ago, grocery stores and shops stocked only one brand of every item. Some may remember those days when people called toothpaste "Colgate," and facial tissue was known as "Kleenex." Today's supermarkets offer thousands of items of the same kind, and their producers pay millions of dollars to highlight their own distinctive characteristics, known as "branding" a product. For instance, at least twelve kinds of chocolate cookies with a white creamy center are marketed, but there's only one "Oreo" cookie. We may find several kinds of cola sodas on the supermarket shelves, but only one "Coca Cola." That's due to branding!

"Whether you agree with their theology or not," Phil Cooke wrote, "in most people's minds: Billy Graham is the *salvation guy*. Robert Schuller is the *motivation guy* . . . Rod Parsley is the *Pentecostal guy*. James Dobson is the *family guy* . . . Joel Osteen is the *inspiration guy* . . . And on the female side: Joyce Meyer is about *enjoying everyday life*."[242] That's the result of intentional branding.

In this "information-rich and time-poor" media-driven culture in which we find ourselves overwhelmed by the available choices, branding, according to Cooke, is about helping people cut through the clutter to make you, the preacher of God's grace, their top selection. Branding, he assures, is vital, because of the fact that (a) visibility

---

[242]   Ibid., p. 18.

is as important as ability, (b) you can't brand a lie in this generation that cries out for authenticity, (c) and being different is everything. Too often, we tend to copy others instead of being our unique selves.

While Cooke underscores the positive power of digital media, he also cautions preachers about the downside that could cause them to focus more on the "branding" at the expense of promoting the power of the Word. To emphasize his warning, he repeatedly quotes James B. Twitchell, saying, "What does religion look like from a marketing point of view? Mind you, I'm not talking about God. *That's a belief, not a brand.* A brand is a story that travels with a product or service or, in this case, a concept. In the beginning of Christianity was the Word, and as I'm sure you've already guessed, *the Word was the Brand*"[243] (emphasis mine).

2. **Everything we knew about the media yesterday has changed significantly.** For instance, people are no longer limited to three major television stations or a few dominant radio broadcasts. They can now record exactly what they want to see or hear and when they want to. Also, within seconds, they can surf through and choose from thousands of programs.

Nowadays, many churches are investing in cameras and live-streaming worship services or sermons on the internet and television. When compared even to the homemade videos on YouTube done by amateurs beyond the choir, some of these presentations are so poorly packaged they are actually branding Christianity as a mediocre religion. The outcome is that our viewing audience is consistently a small fraction of those of other sources. That's where experts like Phil Cooke—recognized as one of the top religious media consultants in America today—are most valuable. He once told me that it takes two to three seconds for people to decide what program they will watch as they surf the thousands of available channels. Also, he

---

[243] *Branding Faith,* p. 14.

cautioned that search engines are not just about seeking and finding information—they are about reputation management because what is stored there, when exposed to the viewership of millions, can make or break a person's reputation. And it has, when one considers the fall of mega-church pastors featured in internet exposures such as Ted Haggard and others in "10 Evangelist Preachers Who Fell From Grace," Bishop Eddie Long in "5 'God Soldiers' Who Fell From Grace," and the popular family values program on TLC destroyed by the revelation of a nineteen-year-old sexual misconduct by its then thirty-seven-year-old star of *Nineteen Kids and Counting*.

The lesson, therefore, is that in our media-driven culture, preachers and pastors must strive to live transparent lives so that they are above criticism, especially by those who desire to damage the Christian faith or profane God's name.

3. **Take note of and respond to the greatest generational change in the world's history.** Although I have already discussed these generational changes in "Preaching to the Contemporary Mind," when it comes to reaching them through mass media communications, Cooke discusses this matter as well as anyone I have heard or read.

He asserts that this generational change has seriously affected leadership styles. For example, first-generational preachers (in the 1950s and early 1960s) were very purpose driven, creative people. Encountering the greatest period of change in US culture, they confronted it with hard-and-fast rules. But many are now either deceased or retired. Their leadership style was more deductive, and they told people what to believe in religion or watch on television or movies, as well as how, when, and where to worship. However, those types of individuals—in attitude or action, if not age—who are still active in ministry today, are woefully behind the times.

Second-generational preachers have heralded a new wave of leadership styles. Not as driven as their parents, they are team-oriented leaders who better understand the power of technology and digital mass media. They grew up under what they considered to be rigid first-generational rules without content, and in response, they have created a "generational switch" in leadership style that engages rather than confronts the culture. The biggest evidence of this is in their attitude toward Hollywood. Whereas first-generational preachers emphasized the evils of and in Hollywood and confronted it with protests or boycotts, this second generation is using the honey of engagement rather than the vinegar of confrontation to change and shape culture. Some are even producing or financing mainstream movies. Because millions, especially those beyond the choir, are using it, they have concluded that media does matter and that preachers must use it to have any impact on the world around them.

4. **Understand the power of design in this media-driven culture.** Design is the outline, pattern, motif, sketch, artwork, or graphic of a logo, website, stationary, and business card that preachers and pastors use to promote their ministries.

Cooke asserts that design matters because humans are wired to create and appreciate great art. Therefore, we should always aim for excellence in the visual expression of our ministries since it's the first thing people see. It means that we should hire professionals to design how we want the public to see and know us. He adds emphatically that if we are determined to reach beyond the choir, preachers should "dump from their visual presentations something they all seem to love very much: globes, doves, flags, and flames." He asserts that not only are these symbols overused, but many of those we want to reach associate them with negative experiences or simply just don't know what they mean.

Finally, if we are going to reach the culture, beyond the choir, for Christ, ministers of the gospel must observe the following:

a. Use language others understand instead of theological terms that sound "like Greek" to them. Avoid speaking like the dictionary of theological terms in "Christianese" that one author refers to as "the pesky cultural gap" between people grounded in the Christian faith and those who are not. For instance, "just think about the word *conversion* or the big three—*justification, sanctification, glorification.*" While they have powerful and poignant meaning for us who have studied the Bible and its ancient languages, read volumes on the subjects, interpreted and preached on such matters, they are like a foreign language to those who are discovering and responding to Christianity for the first time. "Bridge the gap by either explaining or translating" wrote Luke Cawley. And he added, "We can easily bridge the understanding gap by providing explanations of concepts such as 'sin' or 'salvation.' This means that we can keep the previously misunderstood word but infuse it with a new meaning for those with whom we are communicating."[244]

b. If you are uncomfortable with any or all of the four categories of mass media communications noted above, I recommend (in addition to the one cited) two other books in my bibliography by Phil Cooke.

c. Have a clear vision of what God wants you to do, then discover how mass media communications can assist in successfully achieving it.

Speaking of a clear vision, Phil Cooke once told me a story about Walt Disney. He said after creating Disney Land, Walt had a vision of establishing Disney World, but before its completion, he passed away. The opening day was filled with parades, plenty of movie stars, and majestic entertainment. While the spectators were waiting for the ribbon-cutting ceremony, an assertive young executive who had worked on the team organizing the event sat next to Walt Disney's widow. As the program progressed, he leaned over to Mrs. Disney and said, "Too bad Walt isn't here to see all this."

---

[244] http://evangelism.intervarsity.org/how/conversation/how-not-speak-christianese.

She graciously leaned toward him and whispered, "Walt saw it. That's why it's here!"

One thing, however, we must always keep in mind: media matters, but we must never forget that it's meaningless without Christ as the center and circumference of all that we create and produce to reach beyond the choir.

CHAPTER 11

Illustrating the Word

A sermon . . . is an act of creation with real risk in it, as one foolhardy human being presumes to address both God and humankind, speaking to each on the other's behalf and praying to get out of the pulpit alive . . . A good sermon does not stop when the preacher sits down, but goes on posing questions and evoking responses long after it is over.[245]

I teach and am very emphatic that a great twenty- to thirty-minute sermon requires at least twenty to thirty hours of preparation—not per week but from the moment an idea strikes through the process of researching and exegeting the pericope. What amazes me, however, is that despite putting in the time, listeners remember many sermons for only as long as it takes them to get from the sanctuary to the parking lot.

I believe that preaching is the only profession that puts so much time in producing a product that is almost immediately forgotten. In fact, some sermons are like the paper bulletins some churches continue to produce. They are useful during the worship service but

---

[245] Barbara Brown Taylor, *The Preaching Life*, p. 70.

are discarded and forgotten immediately after worship, never to be retrieved again. Countless books and articles offer a variety of steps to prepare excellent sermons, but few that include or underscore what it really takes for a sermon to leave a lasting impression. I have come to the conclusion that what is most necessary to ensure sermons will last in the congregation's memory is the ability to make effective illustrations. Sometimes, years after preaching a particular sermon, someone will invariably remind me of that sermon by repeating an illustration.

Sermon Illustrations and How to Use Them

The internet is both a blessing and a curse for preachers. It is a blessing in that one can access volumes of information in minutes and contact thousands in seconds. But it is a curse in that almost every illustration imaginable, unless one writes or creates it for oneself, has already been seen or read and forwarded to millions. Consequently, unless it is a personal one, by the time a speaker begins to tell a story, invariably others in the audience have already heard or read it, thus robbing the preacher of the surprise element or original impact of that particular illustration.

However, because I was born and raised in Jamaica in a remote village at a time when it had no electricity, radio, or television, and my grandmother's nightly stories were our main source of entertainment, I have an incurable love of stories as sermon illustrations. When I became a Christian and discovered that Jesus frequently used illustrations through his parables and narratives, I was overjoyed. Also, I recognized that the greatest orators and preachers favored stories to make their messages clearer. I am now convinced of the importance of illustrations to introduce or end sermons despite acknowledging the obvious drawbacks to retelling a story already spreading like a virus across social media.

In an article about *The Priority of Preaching*, John Cheeseman noted that illustrations are especially important when preaching doctrinal sermons dealing with abstract truth that need to be illuminated by concrete terms. Illustrations also highlight a profound truth, relaxes the mind, deepens the understanding of complex issues, and relieves the heaviness of solid blocks of truth. I recommend that preachers discover how to tell compelling stories by reading books such as *The Art of Storytelling* by John Walsh.[246]

In his article ("5 Types of Sermon Illustrations and How to Use Them"), Eric McKiddie wrote:

> While a fourth grader can get away with one brush in art class, anyone beginning to take painting seriously knows she needs brushes of various breadths and sizes. It is the same with the preacher beginning to take illustrations seriously. Some sections of the sermon call for thick brushes like stories while others require only a thin dab from an analogy. The question, then, is which illustrations are most effective for which parts of the sermon?[247]

Here are five types of illustrations recommended by McKiddie, with my additional comments about how to use them effectively to consistently preach nothing but the best:

1. "**The story.** This is what most people think of when it comes to sermon illustrations. Examples include personal experiences, accounts from world history, current events," as well as news reports, famous people's lives, and incidents from your own personal experience:

    > One-paragraph stories work well for transitioning from exegesis of the passage to application of it.

---

[246] *The Art of Storytelling: Easy Steps to Presenting an Unforgettable Story,* Moody Press, 2014.

[247] https://www.thegospelcoalition.org/ article/5-types-of-sermon-illustrations-and-how-to-use-them.

Anything much longer and your audience might forget the point you were trying to drive home. But longer stories can be effective for conclusions, when you're trying to pull together the points you want your church to take home. No matter the length, stories work best when the problem or conflict of the story raises the need for a solution the passage provides.[248]

For instance, the following news report is an excellent introduction to sermons about the poor or homeless and the community care of those whom Jesus said we would always have with us (Mark 14:7):

Stop me if you have heard this before. Two police officers approached a Black teen in Barnesville, Georgia, on the campus of Gordon State College. I bet you think you know where this is going. But you don't. Officers Dicky Carreker and Maria Gebelein were responding to a concern about a tent on the college campus. They found Fred Barley in the tent. After talking with him, "the officers became aware of his humility and determined him to be a driven student who had nothing and who was dedicated to his education and to finding a job." See, Fred Barley is a homeless teen, and he rode his younger brother's bicycle more than six hours to the campus to register for his second semester of classes. When he isn't in his tent, he can be found riding his bike around trying to find a job. As the story continues, "Inspired by Barley's determination, officers Carreker and Gebelein gave him the money they had in their wallets and took him to the Sun Inn Motel, where they each paid for a night's stay." But it didn't stop there. Members of

---

[248] Ibid.

Barnesville's community soon heard about the story and have brought Barley gift cards, clothes, and food. He was even given a job at the local pizzeria. But what is even better is through a GoFundMe page started by a resident of Barnesville, they have raised more than $184,000 to pay for Barley's education and his dream of attending medical school. As Officer Carreker said, "It's just beautiful how our community has come together to help someone in need. Barnesville is the epitome of a small town with a big heart."[249]

2. "**The word picture.** This illustration elaborates on something figurative or metaphorical in the passage in order to show its significance."

For example, I recently preached a sermon entitled "Walk His Way" based on Ephesians 2:1, 2. I opened with the following experience:

It was a Martin Luther King birthday celebration breakfast in the Boston civic center. I was invited to sit at a front table directly in front of and almost under the stage occupied by notable politicians, priests, and other famous people. As we savored the eggs Benedict and listened to the speeches, a fashionably late group of people sauntered in and sat at what must have been reserved as the head table. All eyes turned to them as they took their places. One woman stood out. She was dressed in a white finely pleated skirt that fanned out like the wings of a swan as she graciously slipped into her seat. And although I was fascinated by all that I saw, what caught and held my attention were

---

[249] News That Illustrate—http://www.preachingtoday.com/.

her shoes. They had red bottoms, and this long before Jimmy Choo became a household word!

Well, since I consider myself to be a shoe queen, I was determined to find an opportunity to ask her where she purchased them. So I watched and waited, and when the opportunity came, I followed behind her. She entered the ladies room, and I graciously waited until she exited the stall then quickly approached her. She caught my reflection in the mirror and whirled around like an angry cat, eyes blazing with contempt. Before I could utter a word, she raised her hand to stave me off or silence me and spoke arrogantly, "Don't say a word to me!" And she stalked out. She gave me no chance to tell her how I admired her fabulous shoes. I was ticked, to say the least. As she swished past me, I became aware that a part of the back of her skirt was caught in her waistband, exposing her to ridicule. I thought for a moment that I should say something. After all, I am a Christian and a pastor. Then I remembered how she spoke to me. I shook my head and whispered under my breath, "Nah! I'm not that good a Christian," and watched as she walked past tables rippling with laughter.

That experience taught me a profound lesson my grandmother used to say repeatedly: "A haughty spirit goes before a fall." I also came to the conclusion that her action and attitude reflects that of the world; therefore, believers in Christ must avoid walking that way and walk his—Christ's way—by being imitators of God as his beloved children.

3. **"The analogy.** Analogies in general highlight points of comparison, but the best analogies end with unexpected punch lines that draw out a surprising connection. Forrest Gump is famous for this kind of analogy: "Life is like a box of chocolates—you never know what you're gonna get." The surprise punch line sticks with the listener.

Analogies compare an idea or thing to something else that is quite different. It aims at explaining a thing by finding resemblances to something else that is familiar. Metaphors and similes are tools used to draw an analogy, such as "I feel like a fish out of water," indicating I am not comfortable in my current environment or situation. "Analogies are especially effective for communicating cultural aspects of biblical times that would be lost on readers today," wrote McKiddie, adding, "I once heard David Helm say, 'When God tells Joshua, "Take off your sandals," he's saying, "Don't track your dirt on my carpet."' Again, the key is a good punch line."[250]

4. **"The list of examples."** These "illustrate contexts where your church can apply the sermon. Instead of giving steps for application (they won't remember them anyway), provide a quick list of examples to show how one might apply the message in various contexts. Your church can work out the steps themselves if you show them where the passage can bring change in their lives."[251]

McKiddie also counsels that "the key with lists is not to be cliché, superficial, or painfully obvious. Don't say, 'This applies to lust, finances, and impatience.' Those are examples, but they are not illustrative examples. Instead say, 'This applies when an attractive coworker walks into the break room, when the calculator won't give

---

[250] Ibid.

[251] Ibid.

you the numbers you need for your budget, and when your kids are setting a world record for the slowest meal ever eaten.'"[252]

5. "**The split story.** An effective way to bookend your sermon is by telling one half of a story in your sermon's introduction and then the other half in the conclusion. In the introduction, cut off the story before the problem is resolved. Then connect the unresolved conflict to the main spiritual need the passage addresses."

"This approach," McKiddie counsels, "leaves your audience under the assumption that the story doesn't have a happy ending, compelling them to listen in order to avoid a similar fate. Then, in your conclusion—to everyone's surprise—tell the happy ending your church didn't anticipate. This technique is effective because it gives a satisfying closure to the sermon. We are wired to desire a happy ending to stories. Even better, you give listeners who still think they can't change an example of someone who overcame a seemingly insurmountable problem. Hopefully, this illustration will help convince them that—with God's help—they can change too."[253]

In addition to these very effective types of sermon illustrations, great preachers experiment with quotations, charts, pictures, graphs, videos or movie clips, short dramatic narratives, impersonation of biblical characters or persons from history, the element of surprise, style of clothing, the appearance of unexpected special guest(s), prearranged "surprise" interruptions, the sparing use of statistics/surveys, and giving the audience something to touch or hold.

However, never overdramatize an illustration. For example, years ago, my associate joined me in preparing a surprise illustration one Easter. We made a paper-mache tomb in the center of the platform, and early the Saturday morning of Easter Sunday, before the congregation began to arrive, I hid him—dressed like Jesus in a

---

[252] Ibid.

[253] Ibid.

resplendent white robe—in the tomb with lots of dry ice to provide a smoky effect. The plan was that at the end of my sermon, when I declared "He is risen," my associate would burst from the tomb. And he did. Only it was such a surprise that a few of our very elderly members passed out and ruined the best-laid plans as people rallied to provide emergency medical assistance. The object lesson: remember to exegete your audience and never overdramatize an illustration.

Finally, despite this warning, "before you resign yourself to being a preacher who doesn't bother much with illustrations," observes Eric McKiddie, "experiment with the different types. You might find illustrations to be more effective than you think."[254]

Don't forget. Inspire your congregation to strive to reach their fullest potential, and offer our Savior and his people nothing but the best.

---

[254] Ibid.

PART FOUR—EPILOGUE

CHAPTER 12

The Preached Word

Type: A Prophetic Sermon

Title: "Don't Sell Your Birthright to Satisfy a Bellyache"

Scripture: Genesis 25:27–34

Theme: Speaking truth to power regarding gender inequality in my denomination (*delivered at a Seventh-day Adventist Women's Clergy Conference*)

An article in the September 16, 2009, *Washington Post* newspaper began with these words: "The king folds her own laundry, chauffeurs herself around Washington in a 1992 Honda, and answers her own phone. Her boss's phone too." The article was about Peggielene Bartels, a secretary in the Ghanaian embassy in Washington for thirty years. She grew up in a small city of about seven thousand before coming to America. Then thirty years later, when the ninety-year-old king died, the elders performed an ancient ritual to determine the next king. They prayed and poured schnapps on the ground while they read the names of the king's twenty-five relatives. When steam rose from the schnapps on the ground, the name that they were reading at that moment would be the new king—and that was exactly what happened when they came to Peggielene's name.

So now she's a king! In Ghana, she has a driver, a chef, and an eight-bedroom palace. She has power to resolve disputes, appoint elders, and manages more than one thousand acres of family-owned land. When she returned for her coronation, they carried her through the streets on a litter, and she even wore a heavy gold crown.

Paul Schwartzman, author of the article, wrote, "In the humdrum of ordinary life, people periodically yearn for something unexpected, some kind of gilded escape, delivered, perhaps, by an unanticipated inheritance or a winning lottery ticket."

Peggielene got the unexpected, and so will we, by right of our new birth in Christ. Yet so few will actually enjoy or utilize the privileges that come with our high calling as women in ministry because they will sacrifice or sell their birthright to satisfy a bellyache. To avoid such a disastrous decision, let's learn from the story of Esau in which he sacrificed his birthright to satisfy a bellyache, according to Genesis 25:27–34.

One of the saddest figures in the Bible is Esau. The firstborn son of Isaac and Rebekah, twin brother of Jacob, he was beloved of his father and admired by his people as a skillful hunter. Yet he traded the riches of his birthright for a bowl of pottage that promised immediate satisfaction and thus earned himself the designation in Hebrews 12:16 as an immoral, godless person.

It's as if Esau's story has been preserved for such a time as this, when we who are called to the gospel ministry cannot avoid bellyaches about justice and equality for women in ministry, as many face the daunting prospects of paying off bills created in their quest for knowledge to serve God but with little or no prospects of employment as ordained pastors in our denomination. Esau's story is also a strong reminder that no matter how dark the days ahead, no matter how desperate you may feel, how caustic the criticism or how bleak the future may seem—don't ever sell your birthright to satisfy a momentary bellyache, because God has a plan for your life.

Now I'm using *bellyache* as a metaphor for any injustice or prejudice that causes vexation or annoyance and displeasure to burn in one's heart and mind. For instance, one of my bellyaches, or pet peeves, is the poverty of great preaching in our pulpits. Some say that it indicates the lack of the presence and power of the Holy Spirit in our churches. Many of us may have to confess that high on our list of bellyaches is the issue of ordination of women in our denomination. So now that we have a working definition of a bellyache in this context, what exactly is a birthright?

The term *birthright* originates from the Hebrew *bakar* (to be born first). It included physical advantages, such as a legal claim to a double portion of the inheritance of a father's legacy. Imagine, Esau's inheritance would have been incredible when you consider how much he eventually received despite his foolish act of bargaining away his birthright. As the firstborn, he was also automatically entitled to receive his father's blessing as well as authority over other members of his family, including siblings from whom he would also obtain preferential and deferential treatment. The birthright also included spiritual advantages, such as the firstborn being anointed as patriarch and priest of the family on the death of his father. As the new patriarch, he would receive the threefold blessing of Abraham recorded in Genesis 12:2, 3.

While most strictly adhered to these birthright rules and regulations, we do find a few noteworthy divine departures from them. For example, God chose Abel, the younger, over Cain, his older brother; Joseph was selected over his eleven older brothers by both his earthly and heavenly fathers; and Israel was called the Lord's firstborn among nations to occupy a position of leadership and privilege in the world above all the other ancient nations.

The birthright was later bestowed upon spiritual Israel, or the Christian church of the Firstborn, who is none other than our incomparable Savior, Jesus Christ our Lord. In Colossians 1:15, the apostle Paul describes him alone as "the firstborn of all creation." He alone is the firstborn from the dead, according to Colossians

1:18. And Romans 8:4–18 tells us that he alone is the only begotten firstborn among many brethren who are partakers of his birthright.

Our birthright includes, but is not limited to, salvation by grace through faith; the power and presence of the Holy Spirit; all the rights and responsibilities of citizenship in the kingdom of God, including ordination and equal pay for equal work; not having to face the judgment; being caught up to meet the Lord in the air at his second coming; and an invitation to the marriage supper of the Lamb and a seat at the table where we'll be served by Prince Emmanuel himself. Thus, when I speak of our birthright, I'm underscoring the special privileges that automatically belong to believers, regardless of gender, race, ethnic origin, or culture, who are called and anointed children of the most-high God; who were born, not of blood, nor of the will of the flesh, nor of the will of man, but of God. And he has a plan to preserve and protect our birthright, according to a stunning story tucked away in Numbers 27:1–11 and repeated in Joshua 17: 3–5.

In the days of Moses, even if they were the firstborn or the only children of their parents, women could not inherit the birthright simply because they were females. But God commanded Moses to enact a new law that if a man who only had daughters died, his inheritance must pass to them and not to some distant male relative. This new rule allowed the daughters of Zelophehad to receive their inheritance, and I am convinced that one day soon, God is going to do for women in ministry today what he did for our ancient, disenfranchised sisters. So don't let the tyranny of church politics, or the temptation to justify your call, cause you to sell or sacrifice your birthright to satisfy your bellyache.

One commentator made a chart and added up all the numbers of the tribes, noting that out of 601,730 men counted, only six who were not heads of clans or tribes were named, and five of them were women. We hear of that one man only because of the five women listed in a census that didn't even count women in the first place. How and why did their names receive any recognition?

We find out the moment the census was over that it was due to the courage of the daughters of Zelophehad. They are Mahlah, the firstborn, whose name means "a sickly or weak one." Her name didn't describe her nature, because she demonstrated tremendous inner strength as leader of the pack. Noah, whose name means "to comfort or cheer to dispel sorrow," was obviously given a man's name by parents who desperately wanted a boy. Hoglah—which means "partridge," a bird with a plump body, short chest, and buffy head—was the moniker bestowed on the middle child and, apparently, the plain Jane of the bunch. Milcah means "queen," and she was the grandest of them all. She was followed by Tirzah, the baby of the family, whose name means "pleasantness or delightfulness," indicating that she, above all, was cute as a button and a favorite of her family.

As these five women stood on the plains of Moab with everyone else from the twelve tribes who were about to take possession of the Promised Land, they realized that the system and its policies were set up in such a way that they were going to be left out of the promise from the very start. They were together with their people in mind, soul, and body, on the edge of the wilderness, but what the census made clear was that they didn't count for anything—that they were invisible, like immigrants washing dishes in the back of the restaurant, like prisoners tortured away from the media, like children sold in the shadows as sex slaves, like women in Adventist ministry who have to be triply smart and work five times harder than most men to be accepted and respected. When everyone else crossed over, they would remain forever on the far edge, disconnected from the land of promise.

They didn't have to go halfway around the world to witness the existence of injustice. No, they saw it right where they were because whatever so-called equality existed, whatever inheritance was about to be celebrated, it didn't include them simply because they were women. While the rest of the group was mobilizing itself through the census to determine if it had sufficient forces to combat unknown enemies and capture and claim their birthright on the other side of the Jordan, the five sisters saw a battle to be fought right where they stood, within their own community, in which property rights were passed on only through males.

Their father had died on their sojourn in the wilderness, and if they had been sons, they would have inherited his portion of the land. Had they had brothers, they would have been able to share in their brothers' land. If they had been married, they would have gone to live on their husband's land. Or had they been widowed, their husband's family would have taken care of them. But since they had no father, no brother, no husband, and no in-laws, they had no rights to any land; and having no land in an agrarian economy meant being utterly marginalized and disenfranchised.

As women without men, the five sisters had the most to lose should the community reject them; and rejection was quite likely. Mahlah, Noah, Hoglah, Milcah, and Tirzah had no forum to voice their grievance in. Unlike us, women in their society had no opportunity or authority to enter the public square, much less to speak there. A woman's place was barely above that of a male slave, and to cross that threshold, what one female preacher called "that heavily guarded *frontera*"—to act outside of that system was an audacious act with huge risks. Yet these five sisters, with no precedent, no rights, no authority, and no testosterone to go with them, took action regardless of the outcome. It was the power of the presence of God with them, plus their strong relationship with one another, their shared grief and anger over being expected to settle for no settlement, that gave them collective strength. Above all, it gave them the courage to go before Moses in the most public forum possible and boldly take on the system.

It would have been far less risky to approach Moses in private and plead with him to work out some special deal for them, but like so many brave women in ministry who preceded us and on whose achievements we now stand, these sisters were not simply trying to get a piece of the pie for themselves alone. Their public petition was not only intended to effect change for themselves, but it was on behalf of the whole community as well, especially sisters who would come after them. For where there exists injustice for one, it diminishes the power and witness of all. So, they went forward to meet Moses at the entrance of the tent of meeting in the presence of Eleazer the priest, the leaders, and the entire congregation, to ensure that their petition would be heard and a permanent record of their selfless act would be available for posterity. You can bet that everyone was listening as they spoke up.

To do what they asked would require major policy changes in Israel's bureaucracy, but these sisters were clever and creative. You know, we can learn a lot from their attitude and action. For instance, they didn't confront or threaten Moses, nor did they picket the leaders with public protests. Instead, they appealed to the self-interest of the patriarchal mind-set they wanted to change, saying, "Why should our father's name be lost to his clan just because he had no sons?"

It wasn't because of their audacity and political acuity that their individual case served to change the rigid inheritance law to include women. Rather, it was because they took their case to God first, and he affirmed, empowered, and encouraged them to present it to Moses and the leaders. We know this to be so because the same Spirit of God worked on Moses, for instead of striking them down with leprosy or sending them to their tents without manna, Moses brought their case before the Lord. And the Lord spoke to him, declaring, "The daughters of Zelophehad are right in what they are saying. You shall indeed let them possess an inheritance among their father's brothers and pass the inheritance of their father on to them. Furthermore, it shall be for the Israelites a statute and ordinance, as the Lord commanded Moses."

Sometimes when we add up what we're up against and see the odds we face, it can be discouraging, especially when we hear provocative proclamations from those who are against giving us our birthright. Such comments and the numbers of those opposing us do matter; but, according to the book of Numbers, which ought to know something about numbers, they matter less when you factor in our God, who promised that it's not by might or power but by his Spirit that such matters will be resolved. So, I say to you now, the day will come when God will cause justice to roll down like waters in our denomination. The day will come when women will be ordained and recognized as equal partners in the mission to seek and save the lost. The day will come, and it's sooner than we think, when all God's children created in his image will be able to stand on this side of the Promised Land and shout, "Equal at last, equal at last! Thank God Almighty we are equal at last in the Seventh-day Adventist Church!" So be patient, my sisters. Don't get caught up in the politics of ordination or spend all or most of our precious moments together debating an issue already decided in our favor by God. And definitely don't let your buttons be pushed by negative prognosticators to sacrifice or sell your birthright to satisfy your bellyache.

For when the plight of those sisters was invisible to the multitudes of Israel, the One who counted every hair on their five beautiful heads put it in their hearts and minds to stand for their rights and stood with them. When their situation didn't count for anything in the census, He who promised to pour out his Spirit on all humanity, including those daughters, gave them strength and courage to step forward and speak about their grievance. When they took their public protest and petition before the leaders, He who promised that when his spirit is poured out on all humanity, even female servants would prophesy with divine authority—that One told the leaders that the sisters were right and commanded them to change the laws in their favor.

That same One knows what it means to be of no account, for he came on the scene in the midst of another census and was only greeted by a few no-account shepherds. That same One came to his own, and those who were his own did not receive him. That same One has provided men and women to press this issue on our behalf to its just conclusion, for never before have we had so many men in our church leadership willing to put their reputations on the line and risk their positions to speak publicly in favor of a change in the conventional policy that denies equal rights to women in ministry. So be patient, my sisters. Remember that, as daughters of God in

Christ, we have already obtained our divine birthright—not due to our courage but to his command, so that we can set our hope on him and never sell our birthright to satisfy our bellyache.

The book of Numbers doesn't record the reaction of the sisters when they won their case, but I think we know what it was. They must have danced with great joy. One day soon, when our reluctant leaders respond positively to God's command to ordain women in ministry because it's right, we will dance too. So be patient, my sisters. Don't sell your birthright to satisfy your bellyache and miss being part of that big celebration. Be a light when all other lights around you are going out. Be strong and courageous where weakness seems to be the norm. Go preach the Word with power, and when negative comments come your way, be an evangelist who shares the love of God in a world blinded by hate. And remember, laid up for you is a crown of righteousness that the Lord himself will award you and all who have waited for his appearing. Just don't sell your birthright to satisfy a bellyache!

Type: An Expository Sermon

Title: "A Wide Door for Effective Service"

Scripture: 1 Corinthians 16:8, 9; Acts 19:8–10

Theme: Baccalaureate challenge to graduates to change their world

A woman became very lonely after the unexpected death of her husband. Since she had made up her mind not to remarry, she determined that the best thing was to get a pet. She decided against a cat, because she thought they were too independent, and against a dog, because they are too high-maintenance. When she visited the pet shop, the owner quickly convinced her that what she needed was a talking parrot. Even though the price was much higher than she'd planned to spend, the woman took the parrot and drove home happily, thinking that she would be blessed with a very talkative new companion.

To her surprise, after a week of silence, she returned to complain to the pet shop owner. He asked her if she had placed a mirror in the parrot's cage, to which she answered in the negative. Purchasing the mirror, she rushed home to install it in the cage, but a week of silence sent her back to the pet shop. There she told the pet shop owner how the parrot seemed to love the mirror, always bobbing in front of it, but still it spoke not a word. The man convinced her that what the parrot needed was a swing, which she bought. The bird seemed to enjoy looking in the mirror and swinging on his swing, but it still said nothing.

Again, she returned to the pet shop, angry and frustrated that the bird would not speak to her. The pet shop owner pointed out the problem as being that the parrot did not have a ladder. She almost literally flew home with one.

The bird looked in the mirror, jumped on the swing, and ran briskly up and down the ladder, repeating the action several times; but still it said nothing. As she started toward the cage to cajole the parrot to speak, to her surprise, it fell from the ladder and lay shivering on the cage's floor. Picking it up, she started to press it lovingly to her cheek. Suddenly, the bird stiffened and died.

In anguish, she rushed to the pet shop to report what had happened.

"Did the parrot not say anything before he died?" the pet shop owner asked.

"Oh yes, he did," the woman replied. "He said, 'Madam, don't they sell any food at the pet shop?'"

Congratulations, graduates, and welcome to a world with many mirrors vividly reflecting every human image; yet for now, we can only see the image of God in a mirror dimly. Your legacy is a Christian church in which doctrinal pluralism has us swinging from one extreme to the other, yet seldom settling in a healthy, balanced middle where Christ is our all in all and our hope of glory.

Yours, my friends, is a church and world busy clamoring after and climbing up the ladder of success with little direction and even less purpose. Yet in spite of all their gadgets and gimmicks, people are starving to death for the real bread of life—Jesus Christ, our Lord.

Outside of God, Google is the next place I turn to for answers. Here is how Google describes our twenty-first-century world you have been prepared to engage and are being called to conquer. It is a world that promises to produce more but names everything less. For instance:

Our communication is called wireless
Our dress is topless
Our telephone—cordless
Our cooking—fireless
Our youth—jobless
Our food—fatless
Our labor—effortless
Our conduct—worthless
Our relations—loveless
Our attitude—careless

Our feelings—heartless
Our politics—shameless
Our education—valueless
Our follies—countless
Our arguments—baseless
Some bosses—brainless
Most jobs—thankless
Many salaries—much less

Some would say that I have painted a depressing picture of a church in confusion and a world in chaos, but I see it as potential paths not clearly marked, roads less traveled. And your education represents a passport to change and a ticket to cut a wide swath and blaze new trails. For you, men and women graduates, it's a wide door for effective service.

Every person of spirit, every graduate with energy, is on the lookout for openings. Many doors stand open for those who have eyes to see, but not all are for effective service that has eternal rewards. The doors for effective service are always open through God's providence. Revelation 3:8 says, "Behold, I have put before you an open door which no one can shut." Why? "Because you have a little power, and have kept my word and have not denied my name." Such doors are God's signal to advance, but—in the words of one anonymous author—"know that the future lies before you like a field of driven snow. Be careful how you tread it, for every step will show." Here's how the apostle Paul handled his opportunities and challenges, as you must on your next phase of the journey you are about to embark on. (Read 1 Corinthians 16:8, 9.)

Even though many others were calling him to leave Ephesus—some with very persuasive voices—Paul wasn't swayed because he took his orders from God, not humanity. Your education has prepared you for effective service to humanity; but when you leave this campus, you will be entreated by many persuasive calls, some sounding like the very voice of God, to abandon that vision. Take a word of caution from this woman who has had the privilege of going before you—don't make hasty decisions. Wait for that powerful, anointing presence of the Holy Spirit to guide and convict you in the ways of the Lord.

If you are among those who see God as your copilot, you will be persuaded to proceed prematurely. For if God is your copilot, it means you are the driver—you are in his seat. To avoid leaning on your own understanding, immediately change seats and let him be the pilot of your life. Then and only then will you be able to see life from his perspective, with his Word as the lens through which you view and review all things.

An open door is a fit image to express the opportunities and challenges that await you. But notice that, in spite of the magical mirrors in Ephesus or their reputation for indulging their sensuality on the swings and ladders of immoral seductions, Paul didn't focus on those as hindrances. Instead, he underscored the wide door for effective service. Why? Because it was clear to the aging apostle that it was the still small voice of God saying "There's still more work to be done here."

Paul knew that the will of God never takes a child of God to places where grace cannot provide or protect. So he was willing to delay immediate gratification for future glorification! And so must we modern messengers of God.

Be it known to you—as I had to discover upon leaving this center of training and equipping for effective service—that where there are great opportunities to serve, there are also many adversaries, some intensely organized in their opposition. They may manifest themselves in the form of open hostility, as in Ephesus. Or they may come in the garb of a false friendship, that "friendship of the world" which is "enmity with God." However they may appear, this is the danger in our time the most to be feared. But since, like Paul, we know that great service is not defined by resistance or reward but by God who is the pilot, you must go from this place and press on through the wide door for effective service. Press on through paths strewn with thorns of opposition. Press on through stony roads where adversaries lie in ambush. Press on, for your success is guaranteed in heaven, if not on earth, as long as you are true to the Spirit of Christ.

We admire people of courage and high spirit. People always ready to do and dare—to imagine and act for a great cause—like MLK, Bono, and recently, George Clooney. For them, difficulty seems to be an incentive and danger a great challenge. We pride ourselves in the fact that this is the spirit of our nation, a daring and adventurous attitude. So you shouldn't shrink from or be shocked by a wide door of opportunity amidst intense adversaries.

If you haven't already learned, you will discover it when you leave this august institution, that there's no gain without some pain. So even when pain eclipses pleasure, stand firm, knowing that what lies behind or before you is nothing compared to who is in you! For the Word of God says, "Greater is He that is in you, than he that is in the world!"

About twenty-five years ago, I sat where you are now sitting. I also felt the thrill of victory at graduation that almost compensated for some of the long winters of despair, but I didn't come here to process pain or preach to the choir. This morning, I want to talk to you about the wide door for effective service that awaits your energetic advance, and to share with you some important characteristics from the apostle Paul's experience in Ephesus that will equip you for success in the years to come. They are found in Acts 19:8–10. (Read the passage.)

First, Paul practiced speaking out boldly (verse 8). I believe it was Dr. Seuss who said, "Be who you are and say what you feel, because those who mind don't matter and those who matter don't mind." There has never been, nor will there ever be, a closet Christian of great influence.

When I was a little girl, I used to jump rope to this saying: "Speak the truth and speak it ever; cause it what it will!" Little did I know that it would become the motto of my life as a preacher. Regardless of your academic discipline, your career choice, your professional goals, speak out boldly, reasoning and persuading others, not about the latest gossip on church leaders or the foibles and failures of politicians, but about the kingdom of God as you've personally experienced it. The world is full of opinionated people pressing their perspectives from things they read or heard in a lecture, when people are starving for some real truth coming from a heart surrendered to Christ and intimately acquainted with the suffering of a life well-lived in and for him.

You know the truth. Your education was immersed in it. You are already five- and ten-talented people in the things that matter to God. So be bold in those eternal things. You are better equipped for life than at least 90 percent of the people you will encounter on the other side of that wide door for effective service. You have the answer for the cure of terminal illnesses. You have the resources not only to reach for the moon, but to capture the stars! So, don't be afraid, but be bold in the truth. The test of true faith is not in its silent assent but in its assertive tendency.

And don't just sit there and say, "I can't do that." In the words of Marianne Williamson (often misattributed to Nelson Mandela):

> Our deepest fear is not that we are inadequate. Our deepest fear is that we are powerful beyond measure. It is our light, not our darkness, that most frightens us. We ask ourselves, "Who am I to be brilliant, gorgeous, talented, or fabulous?" Actually, who are you not to be? You are a child of God. Your playing small does not serve the world. There is nothing enlightened about shrinking so that other people won't feel insecure around you. We are all meant to shine, as children do. We were born to make manifest the glory of God that is within us. It is not just in some of us; it is in everyone. And as we let our light shine, we unconsciously give other people permission to do the same. As we are liberated from our fear, our presence automatically liberates others.

Second, Paul practiced what he preached (verse 9). Throughout his ministry, Paul taught his converts and disciples not to associate with any so-called brothers or sisters in the church who were immoral and false witnesses. When he encountered such people in the church in Ephesus, he promptly withdrew and separated himself from fellowship with those whose minds had hardened against spiritual things. He refused to throw his pearls before swine and removed himself and his disciples from those who spoke evil of the Way—that is, the gospel, the movement, and the followers of Christ. And so must you, if you are to be authentic agents of truth.

Make no mistake, my friends—it takes a lot of courage to stand for what you believe in. But be sure that when you stand, it is for Jesus Christ! For this is not an inducement to excommunicate others or to separate yourselves from those with whom you disagree, as the former usurps the authority of God and the latter weakens the body of Christ. What it teaches us is the lesson my grandmother insisted I learn from one of her favorite sayings: "If you play with puppies, they will lick your mouth." Or, as I have heard almost all my life, "Bad company corrupts good morals." It means that when you come across people who would tear down your faith and ridicule your beliefs, walk away, separate yourself, and instead find eager ears hungry for the Word of truth and teach them the story of Jesus.

Finally, Paul practiced patience even as he was persecuted (verse 10). Even though there were many adversaries attacking him in Ephesus, he remained and served there for two long years. Instead of focusing on his detractors, he devoted himself to teaching and revealing the grace of the gospel so that all who lived in Asia heard the transforming word of the Lord.

Life does not force action on us, but rather, it sets openings in our way that are ours to enter. You must never fall into the black mood of thinking that an iron fate that leaves us no real freedom of action controls things. Neither must you rest in an easy optimism that declares that all must inevitably go well for you because of the sheer power of God's will for your life. Fatalism, whether it is pessimistic or optimistic, is the antithesis of the Christian spirit. Wide doors for effective service are open before you, but they require your participation, for it is you and only you who can enter them yourself.

I hope that when you leave this university, you will speak out and walk boldly through the door that God, in his providence, set before you.

I hope that you will never leave the Christian faith or the church to become another statistic of generational apostasy.

I hope that when all is said and done, your great achievements in life will be that you remained faithful even under painful pressure, if not persecution—that you fought a good fight and finished the course set before you by God. That you risked your reputation for that which is fair and just, and that you left this world and church of gadgets and gimmicks much better than you found it.

I hope that your dreams take you to the highest of your hopes, to the wide doors of your opportunities for effective service, to the most special places your heart will ever know, and most of all, to the bosom of Jesus Christ today and forevermore. It can be done! "Not by my might, not by your power, but by My Spirit," says the Lord of hosts. Amen.

Type: A Textual Sermon

Title: "A Gratitude Brunch"

Scripture: 1 Corinthians 11:23–26

Theme: Communion service reminder that Jesus shines in all places

Have you ever been the recipient of a gratitude brunch or lunch? It's both a humbling and uplifting experience. I read that once every three months, Michelle Stevens takes Jermaine Washington to what she calls a "gratitude lunch." And it's with a good reason too. You see, Washington saved Stevens's life when he donated a kidney to her. He described Stevens as "just a friend" whom he met at work, where they used to have lunch in the company's cafeteria. One day, as he sat at the same table with Michelle, she wept as she spoke about waiting on a kidney donor list for eleven months with little or no prospect of ever getting a call. She told him how she was being sustained by kidney dialysis, but suffered chronic fatigue and blackouts while being plagued by joint pains. Sometime later, as Jermaine thought about Michelle's situation, he couldn't stand the thought of watching his newfound friend suffer and die slowly; so in a rare act of kindness, he gave her one of his kidneys. After her successful surgery and recovery, once every three months, regardless of Jermaine's protests, Michelle takes him to a gratitude lunch.

We celebrate and serve communion once every three months, and since it's neither breakfast nor lunch, today I'm calling it a gratitude brunch, because we are gathered to offer Jesus thanks for giving more than a kidney to save humanity. We've come to express our gratitude to him for loving us so much that he gave his life so that we may live—not just a few more years on this old earth, but eternally with him in the earth made new. To better understand that our partaking of these communion emblems is indeed a gratitude brunch, please turn to 1 Corinthians 11:23–26. Embedded in it, we find some of the most familiar but misunderstood words about this most sacred ritual in Christian worship. (Read text.)

Why, I asked myself, from all the wonderful, miraculous, incredible events in the life and ministry of Jesus, did the apostle Paul pick and underscore "the night in which he was betrayed"? Was it only to fix a date or focus on the failure of friends at that table? It may have been so, but today, as we look a little deeper, we see that Paul had something more profound in mind. He wasn't focusing on a time, date, or the disciples' foibles. Instead, he was painting a poignant picture in which we can place ourselves to experience the real reason a communion service is a gratitude brunch. You see, to Paul, that meal was a portrait of Jesus in all his grace and glory, not just in relation to the times in which he lived, the circumstances in which he moved, and the men and women who crowded around him. Paul pointed to the night Jesus was betrayed as the background of human life—with all its trials, treachery, and troubles—to show that there's no place or problem where Jesus does not shine. Whether he's at a marriage feast like the wedding at Cana or in a simple home in Bethany in which Mary washes his feet with her tears and dries them with her hair, Jesus shines. Whether he's in a violent storm in a boat battered about on the lake or in a graveyard where a legion of demons confronted him, Jesus shines. Whether he's weeping outside the tomb of a dead friend or kneeling at the bedside of a little girl whom he's about to raise from the dead, Jesus shines, for he is the resurrection and the eternal life. There's no place where Jesus does not shine!

The Gospels give us a great portrait of Jesus against an ever-changing background of human life, and in every situation, some rare aspect of his grace shines forth and provides the key to his mastery over deception and death. But there is one occasion in which he's at his best, in which he gives the fullest revelation of his nature, in which all that is in him comes to a flashpoint and his whole personality, love, and grace find release. That is the night of his betrayal, in which the world was at its worst as Satan, sin, and some religious leaders plotted to bring him down to destruction and death.

The world is at its worst today. We see it when sin, evil, hatred, and cruelty gathered to assassinate nine martyrs in a church last week. We see it in the gruesome terror attack in France yesterday. We see it gathered in churches today, where leaders demonize others who differ in belief and behavior. Yet here we also see Jesus at his greatest graciousness, under the shadow of the cross, against the background of Calvary, "in the night in which he was betrayed," as he exercised one of the most magnanimous acts in human history. You see, when Jesus took the bread, he remembered how he declared confidently that he himself was the bread of eternal life. And when he had given thanks, or expressed gratitude, to God the Father for entrusting him with such a powerful assignment, he broke the bread and reminded his disciples, saying, "This is my body, which is given for you. Do this in remembrance of me."

What other aspect of Christ's life and ministry stands out and evokes our gratitude as much as this sacred service in which we imagine him at our table, breaking bread and giving it to us, his disciples? Look at the scene in your imagination. Note the ones present on the same night in which he was betrayed—not by his enemies, but by his friends, as he gave this most gracious covenant of sacrifice and love.

Judas, one of his inner circle of closest friends, sat at that table. We need not focus on the psychology or pathology of Judas, because the sad fact remains that he was Jesus's betrayer. Judas—who shared Christ's secrets, who had known his intimate friendship for several years—was guilty of betrayal, the foulest of crimes. And guess what. Judas was not alone in his treachery. There was Peter, in whom Jesus saw the lurking possibility of denial peeping out of his soul, especially as the disciple declared his fidelity to die with and for Jesus. And don't forget the other ten disciples who were silent but not free from the heinous crime of betrayal, because they didn't even go as far with Jesus into the zone of danger, as did Peter. At the critical hour, they either slept or slipped away under the cover of darkness.

Then there's us! My former boss and mayor of Hartford, Connecticut, used to say, "I have seen the enemy, and it is I." Back then, in my ignorance, I didn't understand the profundity of those words. But today, as we are gathered here at this table, I know the meaning. I am—we all are—guilty of betraying Jesus. We've also betrayed him with a kiss of empty sentiments on our lips while at the same time misrepresenting him in our lives. We betray him when we fail to follow his command to love one another in the same way he loves us. We betray him when we partake of this thanksgiving table, affirming our allegiance to his new covenant in his blood while nursing malice in our hearts toward others. So here's what we can do. Imagine that Jesus is sitting here, as he sat centuries ago with his disciples, knowing as only he does our hearts, souls, and minds—that we are capable of betraying him at any given moment. Look intently at him—the Lord Jesus who took bread, broke it, and gave it to his disciples, saying, "This is my body which is for you." What is it that shines out and evokes your gratitude, or mine, at this simple brunch?

The first thing that flashes out to me is his forgiveness of the unforgivable things we say and do. Is there anything more unforgivable than betrayal by a close friend? It takes years—and in a few cases, generations—to forgive friends who betray us. Yet, at some time or other, every one of us is that close friend who regularly sings, "What a friend we have in Jesus, all our sins and grief to bear," then goes from the table of remembrance to betray him with choices contrary to his will and Word. You see, sin blinds the eyes of our human spirit so that we cannot see God encouraging, supporting, urging us to choose him in the midst of temptation.

"This is my body given for you," said Jesus, all the time knowing that it was something in his disciples—that something called sin—that would cause his soul to be sorrowful unto death. In essence, he was saying, "Here is the darkest fruit of your treachery, and I have chosen to make it a gift of grace for your forgiveness now and for strengthening that will come into your life in the hour when sin rises up against you." It's as if he was saying, "This is my body given for you when life threatens to overwhelm you, especially when your worst trouble is that you cannot forgive yourself." And guess what, no matter how often we betray him—each time, he forgives us. Let us therefore make magnificent amends for our failure and faithlessness by thanking Jesus for forgiving our unforgivables in this gratitude brunch. As for me and my house, all we can say is "Thank you, Jesus!" Now I understand why we have and partake of this gratitude brunch.

The second thing that shines out from this sacred text like a bright beam in the darkness of our day is his gift of the bread that speaks of his deep trust in the untrustworthy—like us. You see, giving his disciples the bread, in his Eastern language of symbolism, meant, "I give you my confidence. I trust you with my friendship, even if and when you betray me. I put on your shoulders the greatest trust ever laid upon men and women—trust that you will discover the truth the dying world needs."

Just as Jesus trusted those fallible disciples, so he also trusts us, his fickle friends, today. He trusted them though their hearts were unstable as shifting sand. He trusted them to carry on his work and to hold in their minds and hearts the message of the kingdom of grace. Most of us would have given up on those faithless disciples. I know I would, because I'm brainwashed by the worldly-wise morality I often repeat in the maxim "once bitten twice shy." In fact, I'm embarrassed to admit that we, the members of the living body of Christ, practice this by giving up on others who fail us. But those disciples who betrayed Jesus were also his sole trustees. To them, as to us frail and faulty humans today, he has entrusted the whole future of his life and teachings. To us he has bequeathed the legacy of preaching and practicing his commandments. To us he has given the charge and challenge to hold on to the testimony of Jesus written in his Word. And all I can say at this gratitude brunch is "Thank you, Jesus!"

The third thing that shines out from Paul's inspired record of that which he received from the Lord is Christ's faithfulness in the face of our fickleness. How fleeting is our love to him; how easily checked our commitments; how often dried up like a river lost in the arid desert sands are our pledges of allegiance to his covenant of grace. But his love never fails. It flows on and on. John 13:1 tells us that "having loved His own which were in the world, He loved them to the end." To what end does Jesus love us? To the end of this life? Absolutely not! It's to the end of everything—to the end of the longest road of selfishness, to the end of sin from which we all must flee to him. To the end of disappointments, despair, and inconceivable disasters. Wherever or whatever lights go out in our fickle lives, the star of Christ's faithfulness shines on. So shine, Jesus, shine! Fill our hearts with the Father's glory!

In the powerful words of a song by Phillips, Craig, and Dean, I come to give thanks to God, saying, "How deep the Father's love for us, how vast beyond all measure, that He should give His only Son, to make a wretch His treasure. Behold the Man upon a cross, my sin upon His shoulders, ashamed, I hear my mocking voice, call out among the scoffers. It was my sin that held Him there, until it was accomplished. His dying breath has brought me life; I know that it is finished. I will not boast in anything, no gifts, no power, no wisdom; but I will boast in Jesus Christ, His death and resurrection."

Why should we gain from his reward? We cannot give an answer, but this we know with all our hearts: his wounds have paid our ransom.

Thank you, Jesus!

Type: A Topical Sermon

Title: "Preach the Word!"

Scripture: 2 Timothy 4:1–5

Theme: Revival through the power of preaching

Grace and her husband, Chuck, became youth leaders for the first time in their church, so they took the youth group for a "get acquainted" weekend retreat at a campground. On the long drive, they sang songs and listened intently as Grace regaled them with miracle stories to convince them that when you are saved, there are no problems, just opportunities.

As soon as they arrived, she noticed a sign on the bulletin board in the lobby. "See, young people," she said, pointing to the sign and bursting with excitement. She read loudly, "There are no problems, just opportunities!" Then she proceeded to hand out room assignments while Chuck and some of the youth unloaded the van.

A few minutes later, a boy rushed into the lobby, shouting breathlessly, "Grace, Grace, we have a problem. A serious problem."

Immediately she pointed to the sign on the bulletin board and chided the teenager, saying, "Jeff, there are no problems, just opportunities!"

"Well, if that's the way you want it," he said, turning to leave. "I thought you should know you assigned a girl to my room. But as you say, there are no problems, just opportunities."

The world to which you will return after this inspiring weekend of sacred music and worship is still reeling from the effects of such disasters as earthquakes, tsunamis, suicide bombers, mass murders, and numberless other random acts of violence. But they are not problems for the servants of God—they're opportunities to comfort with grace and truth those who mourn.

People everywhere struggle under the weight of severe emotional distress. Some are fainting under the pressure of poverty, while others are committing serious crimes in the name of the shrinking global economy. But these are not problems for worshippers of the Most High—they are opportunities to tell the world that Jesus is the answer to all our needs.

There's a spiritual drought in the pews of some churches out there whose members are thirsting for living water. The stale crumbs from the pulpit no longer satisfy their soul hunger for the real bread of life. But these will no longer be problems for participants in this music and worship conference. They will be opportunities to go tell it on the mountains, over the hills, and everywhere, that fresh manna has been found in the house of the Lord. So gather up all the fragments of inspiration after you've been filled so that you can fan the flames of revival and reformation in our church by observing the injunctions found in 2 Timothy 4:2 and 5.

In order to obey these commands, we must understand the context out of which they came. Paul, the aged apostle, wrote this short letter to encourage Timothy to live up to his name, which means "to honor God." It's also an appeal to all believers commissioned by Christ and committed to the cause of honoring God to abstain from wickedness. In chapter 1, Paul urged his beloved son in the Lord to let the Holy Spirit in him guard the treasure of sound words entrusted to him. Then in chapter 2, he exhorts Timothy to be strong in the grace that is in Christ Jesus and to minister as one not ashamed of the word of truth. And in chapter 3, Paul provides reasons why Timothy must be strong in the Lord (verses 1–7, 13–15; 4:1).

"Now that I have your attention," wrote the apostle, "here are some commands you must obey."

Preach the Word—proclaim, publish. Be a herald, an official spokesperson of the King. Back in those days, heralds blew a trumpet, and the people would drop everything and immediately gather in the town to hear the message.

We must be clear as to what is "the word" we are to preach. Some would say, and rightly so, that it's the everlasting gospel mentioned in the message of the first angel of Revelation 14:6.

This gospel is everlasting because its creator is God the Father, its promoter is Jesus Christ, and its instructor is the Holy Spirit.

This gospel is everlasting because of its unalterable nature, according to Galatians 1:9, in which Paul asserts that anyone who preaches anything contrary to it is to be accursed.

This gospel is everlasting because it will outlast the power of Satan and his evil minions, who know that they are running out of time to deceive the world.

If then it's the everlasting gospel, you may conclude that the command to preach the word is for the clergy, men and women who have accepted the high calling to ministry. But before you relax and pass the baton of responsibility to professional preachers, let's look a little deeper into what Paul wrote, especially the language he employed.

He could have used *graphe* (written word), but the apostle ignored that. He might have chosen *rhema* (spoken word), such as Jesus said to Satan in Matthew 4:4. But he didn't. Nor did he select *epos*, the articulated expression of a thought rendered in Hebrews 7:9 as "so to speak." Instead, he picked *logon*, the term for the living Word that became flesh in the person of Jesus Christ. He chose *logos*— the personal Word and title of the Son of God—to remind every believer who receives him as their Savior that they are commanded to preach the Word and sometimes use words, for they are to be the Word enfleshed. According to Ellen G. White, the best sermon ever preached is the one lived consistently for Christ. Whenever we preach the Word, we must include three important messages.

First, that God became human in the person of Jesus Christ, lived a sinless life, was crucified, and conquered the second death on the cross before he died the death of sleep from which he rose and said, "O death, where is your sting! O grave, where is your victory!"

Second, when Jesus suffered the second death on the cross during those three hours of silence reported in Matthew 27:45, he successfully met, answered, and eliminated every claim of sin so that we can be saved and set free from its power and penalty. Then, when Jesus comes, we'll be free from sin's presence.

Third, Jesus Christ is coming again to receive us to himself so that where he is, there we may be also—always (John 14:1–4). So when idolatry creeps into the church, preach the Word, and it will expose and exterminate it.

When selfishness seeps into our hearts like a nasty virus that distorts our desires, preach the Word, and this diabolic disease will be eliminated.

When prejudice—one of the many sperms of pride—impregnates the mind and breeds conceit in the heart of God's chosen people, preach the Word, and divine power will abort the offspring of the father of lies.

It's a grave mistake to restrict the preaching of the Word to pastors and preachers when it's a command to all members of the priesthood of believers. It's a grave mistake to hoard this Word for saints, while sinners outside our camp are dying without Jesus. And it's a grave mistake to stop preaching when the command says that we must be ready in season and out. The term Paul used for *season* is *Kairos* (the appointed time)—not *chronos* (the duration of time). This means to be always prepared to preach or live the Word as if every moment is the appointed time or season. It also demands that we take a stand in all sorts of circumstances—the dry ones, the difficult ones, the rainy ones, the stormy ones. So stand although the heavens fall. Stand although the floods of fear appear to wipe out your confidence. Stand although the contrary winds of worry threaten to blow down your house of faith.

We must preach the Word when we are in affliction or adversity, being praised or persecuted—for Jesus is the Man for all seasons, and now is the acceptable time for us to seek and save the lost. Now is the day of salvation, when the world is broken, beaten down, and too weak to deny or discredit the Word. We must publicize the Word made flesh beyond the borders of our safe, sanitized communities of faith. This means that some of us must move out of our comfortable cocoons into the real world that God loved so much that he gave his only begotten Son to save it (John 3:16).

But before we go into the world, judgment must begin in the house of the Lord, where we are to

* reprove—convict by reproving.
* rebuke—censure boldly, like Nathan to David. ("You are the one.") Not severe, cold condemnation, but with compassion.
* exhort (*parakaleos*)—up close and personal, with great patience and loving instruction, remembering that humanity is fallen and frail.

Here are some reasons Paul provided as to why we must take a stand and preach the Word continually:

The appointed time will come when, according to 2 Timothy 4:3–4, people will not endure the sound doctrines reported in 2 Timothy 3:16.

They will reject those who not only preach but practice the Word with the authority given by Christ (Luke 9:1, 2). They will long for watered-down words, fiction, fables, religious soap operas, and comedy over biblical truth. They will want their ears tickled, like the ancient Athenians who created a job for "ear ticklers" to entertain them in their bored state of excessive wretchedness. They will turn from a plain "Thus says the Lord" to ideas that inform and excite rather than transform. They will turn their ears from the truth, like Paul and his cohorts at the stoning of Stephen (Acts 7:51). They will hire their own teachers and preachers to fill them with bizarre concepts, implausible humanistic new age myths that they enforce as rules of faith.

But you—you observe these other injunctions. Be sober in all things at all times.

This means the preacher must avoid drinking the harlot's wine of immorality, which is, according to Revelation 17:2, false doctrines. Keep your head at all times, especially when others around you are losing theirs, by living for Jesus a life that is true. Endure hardship—do not despise adversity and affliction, because they are divine tools to shape us. Take your share of hardship and bear up under pressure as you press on and preach the Word! There's no mountain high enough, no river deep enough, no ocean wide enough to keep you from preaching the Word! Be an evangelist—point people to Christ.

And finally, fulfill the duties of ministry at all times.

To fulfill doesn't mean "to complete," but rather to fill up to the brim, with living for Jesus a life that is true and free. God didn't call us to sit and complain. He summoned us to stand firm and preach the Word!

BIBLIOGRAPHY

Books

Barna, George. (1998). *The Second Coming of the Church.* Nashville: Word Publishing.

Bartholomew, Craig C. (2015). *Introducing Biblical Hermeneutics: A Comprehensive Framework for Hearing God in Scripture.* Grand Rapids: Baker Academic.

Best, Harold M. (2003). *Unceasing Worship: Biblical Perspectives on Worship and the Arts.* Downers Grove, Ill.: InterVarsity Press.

Blomberg, Craig L. (2004). *Preaching the Parables: From Responsible Interpretation to Powerful Proclamation.* Grand Rapids: Baker Academic.

Brooks, Philip. (?). *Lectures on Preaching: Delivered Before the Divinity School of Yale College in January and February 1877.* London: Allenson.

Brueggemann, Walter. (2001). *The Prophetic Imagination.* Minneapolis: Fortress Press.

_____. (1989). *Finally Comes the Poet: Daring Speech for Proclamation.* Minneapolis: Fortress Press.

Campolo, Tony. (1990). *The Kingdom of God Is a Party: God's Radical Plan for His Family.* Dallas: Word Publishing.

Carter, Terry C., Duvall, J. Scott and Hays, Daniel J. (2005). *Preaching God's Word: A Hands-On Approach to Preparing, developing and Delivering the Sermon.* Grand Rapids: Zondervan.

Chambers, Oswald. (1931). *Baffled to Fight Better: Job and the Problem of Suffering.* Grand Rapids: Discovery House Publishers.

_____. (1934). *Not Knowing Where.* Grand Rapids: Discovery House Publishers.

_____. (1935). *The Place of Help: God's Provision for Our Daily Needs.* Grand Rapids: Discovery House Publishers.

_____. (1935). *My Utmost for His Highest.* Grand Rapids: Discovery House Publishers.

_____. (1936). *Approved unto God with Facing Reality: The Spiritual Life of the Christian Worker.* Grand Rapids: Discovery House Publishers.

_____. (1958). *If You Will Ask: Reflections on the Power of Prayer.* Grand Rapids: Discovery House Publishers.

Childers, Jana, and Schmit, Clayton J. (2008). *Performance in Preaching: Bringing the Sermon to Life.* Grand Rapids: Baker Academics.

Christ, Carol P., and Plaskow, Judith. (1979). *Womanspirit Rising: A Feminist Reader in Religion.* San Francisco: Harper & Row Publishers.

Clowney, Edmund P. (1979). *Preaching and Biblical Theology.* Phillipsburg: P&R Publishing.

Cooke, Phil. (2003). *Successful Christian Television: Make Your Media Ministry a Reality*. Santa Monica: Xulon Press.

_____. (2006). *Creative Christian Media: Secrets of Successful Media Ministry*. Santa Monica: Xulon Press.

_____. (2008). *Branding Faith: Why Some Churches and Nonprofits Impact Culture and Others Don't*. Ventura: Regal.

Craddock, Fred B. (2001). *As One Without Authority (Revised and with New Sermons)*. St. Louis: Chalice Press.

Craddock, Fred B., Hayes, John H., Holliday, Carl R., and Tucker, Gene M. (1994). *Preaching Through the Christian Year*. Harrisburg: Trinity Press International.

Collins, Jim. (2001). *Good to Great: Why Some Companies Make the Leap . . . and Others Don't*. New York: HarperCollins Publishers Inc.

Crittenden, Jeff. (2014). *Three Goals for Preaching in Our Context*. Canada: Touchstone 32.

Davidson, Richard M. (2007). *Flame of Yahweh: Sexuality in the Old Testament*. Peabody: Hendrickson Publishers.

Edersheim, Alfred. (1992). *The Life and Times of Jesus the Messiah*. New Updated Edition, vol. 1. Peabody: Hendrickson Publishers Inc.

Elliott. Mark Barger. (2000). *Creative Styles of Preaching*. Louisville: Westminster John Knox Press.

Eslinger, Richard L. (1995). *Narrative imagination: Preaching The Worlds That Shape Us*. Minneapolis: Fortress Press.

Fee, Gordon D., and Stuart, Douglas. (2014). *How to Read the Bible for All Its Worth.* 3rd edition. Grand Rapids: Zondervan.

Ferm, Dean William. (1981). *Contemporary American Theologies: A Critical Survey.* New York: The Seabury Press.

Foster, Richard J. (1992). *Prayer: Finding the Heart's True Home.* New York City: HarperCollins Publishers.

Gates, Rachel, Forrest, L. Arick, and Obert, Kerrie. (2013). *The Owner's Manual to the Voice: A Guide for Singers and Other Professional Voice Users.* New York: Oxford University Press.

Gladwell, Malcolm. (2000). *The Tipping Point: How Little Things Can Make a Big Difference.* New York: Little Brown & Company.

Gopinath, M. A. (1976). Colon Classification in A. Maltby (ed.) *Classification in the 1970s: A Second Look* (rev. ed.), London: Clive Bingly.

Hare, Eric B., and Spalding, Arthur W. (1948). *Christian Storytelling.* Nampa: Pacific Press Publishing Assn.

Hybels, Bill. (2002). *Courageous Leadership.* Grand Rapids: Zondervan.

Keller, Rosemary Skinner and Reuther, Rosemary Radford, eds. (2000). *In Our Own Voices: Four Centuries of American Women's Religious Writing.* Louisville: Westminster John Knox Press.

King, Michael A., and Greiser, David B., eds. (2003). *Anabaptist Preaching: A Conversation Between Pulpit, Pew & Bible.* Telford: Cascadia Publishing House.

Lischer, Richard. (2001). *A Theology of Preaching: The Dynamics of the Gospel.* Eugene, Ore.: Wipf and Stock Publishers.

Lischer, Richard. (2005). *The End of Words: The Language of Reconciliation in a Culture of Violence.* Grand Rapids: William B. Eerdmans Publishing Company.

Logan, Samuel T. Jr., ed. (2011). *The Preacher and Preaching: Reviving The Art.* Phillipsburg, N. J.: Presbyterian and Reformed Publishing Company.

Long, Thomas G. (1989). *Preaching and the Literary Forms of the Bible.* Philadelphia: Fortress Press.

_____., and Tisdale, Leonora Tubbs, eds. (2008). *Teaching Preaching as a Christian Practice: A New Approach to Homiletical Pedagogy.* Louisville: Westminster John Knox Press.

Manning, Brennan. (2009). *Souvenirs of Solitude: Finding Rest in Abba's Embrace.* Colorado Springs, Col.: NavPress.

McClure, John S. (1989). *Preaching Words: 144 Key Terms in Homiletics.* Louisville: Westminster John Knox Press.

McMickle, Marvin A. (2006). *Where Have All The Prophets Gone? Reclaiming Prophetic Preaching in America.* Cleveland: The Pilgrim Press.

Mitchell, Ella Pearson, ed. (1988). *Those Preaching Women: Sermons by Black Women Preachers.* 2 vols. Valley Forge: Judson Press.

Noren, Carol M. (1992). *The Woman in the Pulpit.* Nashville: Abingdon Press.

Parker, T. H. L. (1992). *Calvin's Preaching.* Louisville: Westminster John Knox Press.

Peterson, Eugene H. (1987). *Working the Angles: The Shape of Pastoral Integrity.* Grand Rapids: William B. Eerdmans Publishing Company.

Plaskow, Judith and Christ, Carol P., eds. (1989). *Weaving the Vision: New Patterns in Feminist Spirituality.* San Francisco: HarperCollins Publishers.

Platt, David. (2010). *Radical: Taking Back Your Faith from the American Dream.* Colorado Springs, Col.: Multnomah Books.

Proctor, Samuel D. (1994). *The Certain Sound of the Trumpet: Crafting A Sermon of Authority.* Valley Forge: Judson Press.

Quicke, Michael J. (2011). *Preaching as Worship: An Integrative Approach to Formation in Your Church.* Grand Rapids: BakerBooks.

Robinson, Haddon W. (2001). *Biblical Preaching: The Development and Delivery of Expository Messages.* Grand Rapids: Baker Book House.

_____ and Larson, Craig Brian, eds. (2005). *The Art and Craft of Biblical Preaching: A Comprehensive Resource for Today's Communicators.* Grand Rapids: Zondervan.

Scott, Susan. (2002). *Fierce Conversation: Achieving Success at Work and in Life, One Conversation at a Time.* New York: Berkley Books.

Smith, James Bryan. (2000). *Rich Mullins: A Devotional Biography: An Arrow Pointing to Heaven.* Nashville: Broadman & Holman Publishers.

Spalding, Arthur W. (1948). *Christian storytelling and stories for parents, teachers and students.* Nampa: Pacific Press Publishing Assn.

Spencer, Jon Michael. (1990). *Protest and Praise: Sacred Music of Black Religion.* Minneapolis: Fortress Press.

Stott, John R. W. (1961). *The Preacher's Portrait: Some New Testament Word Studies.* Grand Rapids: Wm. B. Eerdmans Publishing Company.

Straus, William and Howe, Neil. (1991). *Generations: The History of America's Future, 1584–2069.* New York: Broadway Books.

Swindoll, Charles R. (1987). *Living Above the Level of Mediocrity: A Commitment to Excellence.* Waco: Word Books.

Taylor, Barbara Brown. (1993). *The Preaching Life.* Cambridge: Cowley Publications.

Thomas, Bettye Collier. (1998). *Daughters of Thunder: Black Women Preachers and Their Sermons, 1850–1979.* San Francisco: Jossey-Bass.

Tickle, Phyllis. (2012). *Emergence Christianity: What It Is, Where It Is Going, and Why It Matters.* Grand Rapids: Baker Books.

Tisdale, Leonora Tubbs. (2010). *Prophetic Preaching: A Pastoral Approach.* Louisville: Westminster John Knox Press.

Tozer, A. W. (1976). *The Pursuit of God.* Bromley: STL Books.

_____. (2016). *God Still Speaks: Are We Listening?* CrossReach Publications.

Verploegh, Harry, ed. (1987). *Oswald Chambers: The Best from All His Books.* Nashville: Oliver Nelson.

Walker, Alice. (1983). *In Search of Our Mother's Gardens: Womanist Prose.* New York: Open Road Integrated Media.

Walsh, John D. (2003). *The Art of Storytelling: Easy Steps to Present an Unforgettable Story.* Chicago: Moody Publishers.

White, Ellen G. (1923). *Testimonies to Ministers and Gospel Workers.* Nampa: Pacific Press Publishing Assn.

_____. (1952). *Welfare Ministry: Instructions in Christian Neighborhood Service.* Washington, DC: Review and Herald Publishing Assn.

Williams, Delores S. (1993). *Sisters in the Wilderness: The Challenge of Womanist God-Talk.* Maryknoll: Orbis Books.

Williams, Hyveth. (1996). *Will I Ever Learn? One Woman's Life of Miracles and Ministry.* Hagerstown, MD: Review and Herald Publishing Association.

_____. (1998). *Theleia Theology: A Preaching Model for Women (dissertation).* Boston: Boston University School of Theology.

Wogaman, Philip J. (1998). *Speaking Truth in Love: Prophetic Preaching to a Broken World.* Louisville: Westminster John Knox Press.

Woods, Robert H. Jr., and Patton, Paul D. (2010). *Prophetically Incorrect: A Christian Introduction to Media Criticism.* Grand Rapids: Brazos Press.

Encyclopedias and Dictionaries

Buttrick, George Arthur, ed. (1962). *The Interpreter's Dictionary of the Bible: An Illustrated Encyclopedia.* Nashville: Abingdon Press.

Botterweck, Johannes G., Ringren, Fabray, eds. (1995). *Theological Dictionary of the Old Testament*. Grand Rapids: William B. Eerdmans Publishing Company.

Harris, Laird R., Archer, Jr, Gleason Z., Waltke, Bruce K., eds. (1980). *Theological Wordbook of the Old Testament*, vol. 2. Chicago: Moody Press.

McKim, Donald K. (1996). *Westminster Dictionary of Theological Terms*. Louisville: Westminster John Knox Press.

Tan, Paul Lee. (1998). *Encyclopedia of 15,000 Illustrations: Signs of the Times*. Dallas: Bible Commentators, Inc.

Vine, W. E. (1978). *Vine's Expository Dictionary of Old and New Testament Words*. Iowa Falls, Iowa: The Bible Publishers.

Wilson, Paul Scott, ed. (2008). *The New Interpreter's Handbook of Preaching*. Nashville: Abingdon Press.
Willimon, William H., and Lischer, Richard, eds. (1995). *Concise Encyclopedia of Preaching*. Louisville: Westminster John Knox Press.

Vine, W. E., Unger, Merri; F., and White, William, Jr., eds. (1996). *Vine's Complete Expository Dictionary of Old and New Testament Words*. Nashville: Thomas Nelson Publishers.

Commentaries

Barclay, William. (1975). *The Gospel of Matthew*, vol. 2. Edinburgh: Saint Andrew Press.

Kroeger, Catherine Clark, and Evans, Mary J., eds. (2002). *Women's Bible Commentary: An indispensable resource for all who want to view Scripture through different eyes*. Downers Grove, Ill.: The InterVarsity Press.

Nichol, Francis d., ed. (1978). *The Seventh-day Adventist Bible Commentary*. Washington, DC: Review and Herald Publishing Association.

Robertson, Archibald Thomas. *Word Picture of the New Testament*. Nashville: Broadman Press.

Periodical Articles

Morris, Derek, ed. (1995, 2000, 2016) *Ministry* (www.ministrymagazine.org). Nampa: Pacific Press Publishing Assn.

Williams, Hyveth, ed. (2015). *CURRENT: Faith Meets Life and Culture*. Berrien Springs, Mich.: Seventh-day Adventist Theological Seminary.

Websites

http://www.ccel.org/creeds/helvetic.htm

http://www.religionnews.com/2014/06/17/charitable-giving-religious-groups-philanthropy-improves-great-recession

http://pareonline.net/getvn.asp?v=11&n=10.

http://richardallenfarmer.com/product/making-the-mummies-dance

http://en.wikiquote.org/w/index.php?
https://www.barna.org/barna-update/article/5-barna-update/162-the-concept-of-holiness-baffles-most-americans

http://www.ehow.com/how_5424865_write-wedding-sermons.html.

http://en.wikipedia.org/wiki/Redemptive-historical_preaching.

(www.ministrymatters.com),

http://www.spurgeon.org/s_and_t/voice.htm

http://www.preachingtoday.com/skills/2014/august/6-problems-of-preaching-on-faith-and-work.html

http://www.adventistreview.org/church-news/ellen-g.-white-named-among-100-most-significant-americans

www.relevantBible

http://www.sermoncentral.com/illustrations/sermon-illustration-sermon-central-staff-stories-foundation-79625.asp.

http://www.biblicalarchaeology.org/daily/people-cultures-in-the-bible/people-in-the-bible/was-mary-magdalene-wife-of-jesus-was-mary-magdalene-a-prostitute/.

http://www.intrust.org/Portals/39/docs/IT413wheeler.pdf.

http://www.ats.edu/resources/publicationspresentations.

http://www.cnn.com/2013/01/31/world/africa/king-peggy-otuam-ghana/

http://www.nationalaffairs.com/doclib/20080709_19921096thepostcapitalistworldpeterfdrucker.pdf

http://www.boston.com/bostonglobe/ideas/brainiac/2007/12/the_socalled_si.html

http://www.cfnews.org/Mercier-Modernism.htm.

---

http://www.beatlesinterviews.org/db1966.0304-beatles-john-lennon-were-more-popular-than-jesus-now-maureen-cleave.html.

http://www.pewforum.org/2010/02/17/religion-among-the-millennials/

http://www.oldtestamentstudies.org/my-papers/other-papers/wisdom-literature/preaching-from-the-psalms/

www.sacred-texts.com/bib/cmt/vws/joh005.htm.

http://web.ovu.edu/missions/guidelines/chap8.htm#top

http://www.worldometers.info/world-population

https://www.csun.edu/science/health/docs/tv&health.html.

http://evangelism.intervarsity.org/how/conversation/how-not-speak-christianese.

https://books.google.com/books?id=pZJAAQAAMAAJ

http://www.albertmohler.com/2013/08/19/expository-preaching-the-antidote-to-anemic-worship/

http://secondnaturejournal.com/the-imminent-decline-of-contemporary-worship-music-eight-reasons

https://www.barna.org/barna-update/article/5-barna-update/85-focus-on-qworship-warsq-hides-the-real-issues-regarding-connection-to-god#.VWXfJ2RgYlw

https://www.thegospelcoalition.org/article/5-types-of-sermon-illustrations-and-how-to-use-them

COMMENTS FROM
OTHER AUTHORS

US Senate Chaplain Barry C. Black, PhD. Senate Chaplain's Office, S-332, The Capitol, Washington, DC, 20510. He wrote: "I look forward to devouring your final chapters, for I have been greatly blessed by what you had previously written. . . I believe this will be a significant contribution to the homiletical literature, combining scholarship and practicality as it is rarely seen, helping to fill a void."

Dr. Derek J. Morris. Director, Hope Channel, and former editor of *Ministry Magazine*, published by the Seventh-day Adventist Church and read by clergy of all faiths. He responded, "This is the best work I have read by an Adventist author on preaching. It's EXCELLENT!"

Pastor Adrian Craig. Australian church leader and internationally acclaimed preacher. He said, "Here are a few preliminary comments about your excellent book on preaching. In 321 pages, you have packed full a comprehensive and detailed volume on the art of preaching. One has to read and pause and absorb. Your terse verse, one-liners, and the illustrations are readily saleable. 'Mummies dancing,' the description of the horse as it relates to the pace of preaching, the Ravi illustration on page 99, and your repeated use of scripture to illustrate points shouts volumes of your commitment to the Word."

Made in the USA
Middletown, DE
31 July 2018